Finding God's
Will for Your Life

FUMC-Delmar

LIFE ON THE EDGE SERIES

Finding God's Will for Your Life

Money and Success

The Keys to a Lifelong Love

Love Must Be Tough

Getting Along with Your Parents

Emotions: Friend or Foe?

Trusting God When Life Goes Wrong

Finding God's Will for Your Life

Dr. James Dobson

WORD PUBLISHING

NASHVILLE

A Thomas Nelson Company

FINDING GOD'S WILL FOR YOUR LIFE

PUBLISHED BY WORD PUBLISHING, NASHVILLE, TENNESSEE.

Unless otherwise indicated, Scripture quotations used in this book are from The Holy Bible, New International Version (NIV). Copyright © 1973, 1978, 1984, International Bible Society. Used by permission of Zondervan Bible Publishers.

Other references are from the following source:
The King James Version of the Bible (KJV).

LIBRARY OF CONGRESS CATALOGING-IN-PUBLICATION DATA

Dobson, James C., 1936–
    Finding God's will for your life / by James Dobson.
        p. cm. — (Life on the edge series)
    Includes bibliographical references.
    ISBN 0-8499-4229-2
    1. Youth—Religious life. 2. Christian life. I. Title.
BV4531.3 .D63 2001
248.8'3—dc21

00-049970
CIP

Printed in the United States of America.

00 01 02 03 04 05 PHX 9 8 7 6 5 4 3 2 1

AMERICAN LIFE

DREAM AND REALITY

AMERICAN LIFE

DREAM AND REALITY

W. LLOYD WARNER

REVISED EDITION

Phoenix Books

THE UNIVERSITY OF CHICAGO PRESS

CHICAGO AND LONDON

This book is also available in a clothbound edition from

THE UNIVERSITY OF CHICAGO PRESS

THE UNIVERSITY OF CHICAGO PRESS, CHICAGO & LONDON
The University of Toronto Press, Toronto 5, Canada

*This
volume is dedicated*

to

ARTHUR COONS

and

ANNE MUMFORD

CONTENTS

LIST OF ILLUSTRATIONS

LIST OF TABLES

WHAT THE BOOK
IS ABOUT

This revised, new edition of *American Life* brings the past up to the present; moreover, aided by insights and understandings from ongoing research on the rapid advance and powerful thrust of the Great Society into the future, I discuss and attempt to relate the meanings of today with those of tomorrow; as such this book attempts to explain the American dream and its reality. It describes, analyzes, and interprets some of the important aspects of the social life of this nation. It is an effort to place this segment of human behavior in the scientific framework of social anthropology and comparative sociology.

All Americans know that what they are as men cannot ever be revealed by a cold account presented by a detached observer who is content to relate only what he has heard them say and watched them do in the daily round of their lives. Important and crucial as such evidence may be, it is insufficient and distorts the reality of their existence. The meaning of a man's life—in fact, the most significant part of it—must always include his dreams for tomorrow, since these are present guides for his daily conduct.

More often than not, the ideals by which we Americans judge our present inadequacies later become the realities on which we build our hopes for a realizable future. We are forever dedicating ourselves and our collectivity to new goals which our ideals cannot presently afford. We know that the "self-evident facts" about the nature of man and his existence proclaimed by our nation's founders were often no more than their dreams for a future they had resolved to make true. And we know that some of these hopes of the past are now part of social reality. Therefore, we, too, strive to make today's dreams become the "self-evident facts" of tomorrow.

The American story, both dream and reality, is essentially that of a great democracy trying to remain or become democratic and equalitarian while solving the problems of unifying vast populations and diverse enterprises. The story told here is, therefore, concerned with the values and ideals of a democracy and, less pleasantly, with the facts of social class and color caste. It examines the American "success story," the tale of rags-to-riches, in terms of the real facts of social mobility and social class. It analyzes the problems of social and ethnic minorities and reassesses the ideals of the melting-pot. It tells of the symbolic life of America in terms of such varied facts as radio programs and sacred ceremonies, all for the purpose of getting an inside view of Americans and their life.

For many years, in collaboration with social anthropologists and other social scientists, I have studied American communities in several regions of this country with the techniques used previously in the investigation of

Australian tribes and used by other anthropologists in Africa, Polynesia, and New Guinea. Numerous scientific monographs presenting detailed findings about our social life have been published.

Communities in most regions of this country have been examined. These now include metropolitan regions such as Chicago, the San Francisco Bay region, Kansas City, and others, as well as smaller cities, towns, and rural villages. The studies cover subjects and problems of great variety, among them the communities themselves, the family, factories, corporations, political behavior, personality development and symbolic phenomena such as religious behavior, advertising, newspapers, TV, motion pictures, and radio. Meanwhile, since the earlier edition, research interest has spread to the country-wide study of such occupations as managers of big business, military and civilian executives of the federal government, occupational mobility, and to the study of the symbolic facts and fancies of presidential elections.

Presently, research is continuing in most of these fields and is being extended to the problem of understanding the nature or the emergent change of the great American Society. All of these will be reported upon or utilized in this new edition of the present volume. The continuing research allows us to test the validity of the earlier hypotheses. This edition permits me to report upon these matters as *now* understood and with empirical research now in being on the nature and significance of this great emergent society.

By emergent, I mean that the nature of this society is such that change is an integral, pervasive, and "built-in" part of the system itself. For us to be what we are now as a people, we must be in a process of change in which the

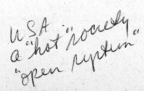

U.SA "hot "society" a "open system"

modified past moves into the present and, in so doing, itself merges with, and is incorporated into, the future. To be what we are as a society and as individuals, we must be in a continuing process of becoming something more and something less than we now are.

In popular belief modern man seems far removed from his Stone Age kinsmen of aboriginal Australia; but, despite obvious differences, the fundamental core of life of each is very much the same. Being a human being demands the same basic social and personal equipment in black Australia or in contemporary civilization. When he studies his own people, the social anthropologist who has had experience with primitive people soon loses his sense of strangeness, for he learns that they (and he) are very much like their primitive brothers. Perhaps at this present juncture in world affairs this is the most important thing we can learn about ourselves.

When I began my first research on the New England community we shall call "Yankee City," I had just spent three years studying some of the Stone Age people in the remote parts of North Australia. Much of their life was devoted to elaborate sacred rites celebrating their relations with their gods and symbolically expressing what they were as men in a sacred universe. From the beginning of the research on America I was struck with the basic similarities between the meanings and functions of American myth and ceremony and those of aboriginal Australia.

The first chapter describes the beliefs and rites of Memorial Day. It analyzes the meanings of this American sacred event, to learn why Americans have created such a ceremony to explain what they are to themselves and to say what they are as men. From it perhaps we shall learn what basic claims Americans make as members of the human family.

1

AN AMERICAN
SACRED CEREMONY

Memorial Day and Symbolic Behavior

Every year in the springtime when the flowers are in bloom and the trees and shrubs are most beautiful, citizens of the Union celebrate Memorial Day. Over most of the United States it is a legal holiday. Being both sacred and secular, it is a holy day as well as a holiday and is accordingly celebrated.

For some it is part of a long holiday of pleasure, extended outings, and great athletic events; for others it is a sacred day when the dead are mourned and sacred ceremonies are held to express their sorrow; but for most Americans, especially in the smaller cities, it is both sacred and secular. They feel the sacred importance of the day when they, or members of their family, participate in the ceremonies; but they also enjoy going for an automobile trip or seeing or reading about some important athletic event staged on Memorial Day. This chapter will be devoted to the analysis and interpretation of Memorial Day to learn its meanings as an American sacred ceremony, a rite that evolved in this country and is native to it.

Memorial Day originated in the North shortly after the end of the Civil War as a sacred day to show respect for the Union soldiers who were killed in the War between the States. Only since the last two wars has it become a day for all who died for their country. In the South only now are they beginning to use it to express southern respect and obligation to the nation's soldier dead.

Memorial Day is an important occasion in the American ceremonial calendar and as such is a unit of this larger ceremonial system of symbols. Close examination discloses that it, too, is a symbol system in its own right existing within the complexities of the larger one.

Symbols include such familiar things as written and spoken words, religious beliefs and practices, including creeds and ceremonies, the several arts, such familiar signs as the cross and the flag, and countless other objects and acts which stand for something more than that which they are. The red, white, and blue cloth and the crossed sticks in themselves and as objects mean very little, but the sacred meanings which they evoke are of such deep significance to some that millions of men have sacrificed their lives for the first as the Stars and Stripes and for the second as the Christian Cross.

Symbols are substitutes for all known real and imaginary actions, things, and the relations among them. They stand for and express feelings and beliefs about men and what they do, about the world and what happens in it. What they stand for may or may not exist. What they stand for may or may not be true, for what they express may be no more than a feeling, an illusion, a myth, or a vague sensation falsely interpreted. On the other hand, that for which they stand may be as real and objectively verifiable as the Rock of Gibraltar.

The ceremonial calendar of American society, this yearly round of holidays and holy days, partly sacred and partly secular, but more sacred than secular, is a symbol system used by all Americans. Christmas and Thanksgiving, Memorial Day and the Fourth of July, are days in our ceremonial calendar which allow Americans to express common sentiments about themselves and share their feelings with others on set days pre-established by the society for this very purpose. This calendar functions to draw all people together to emphasize their similarities and common heritage; to minimize their differences; and to contribute to their thinking, feeling, and acting alike. All societies, simple or complex, possess some form of ceremonial calendar, if it be no more than the seasonal alternation of secular and ceremonial periods, such as that used by the Australian aborigines in their yearly cycle.

The integration and smooth functioning of the social life of a modern community are very difficult because of its complexity. American communities are filled with churches, each claiming great authority and each with its separate sacred symbol system. Many of them are in conflict, and all of them in opposition to one another. Many associations, such as the Masons, the Odd Fellows, and the like, have sacred symbol systems which partly separate them from the whole community. The traditions of foreign-born groups contribute to the diversity of symbolic life. The evidence is clear for the conflict among these systems.

It is the thesis of this chapter that the Memorial Day ceremonies and subsidiary rites (such as those of Armistice or Veterans' Day) of today, yesterday, and tomorrow are rituals of a sacred symbol system which functions periodically to unify the whole community, with its conflicting symbols and its opposing, autonomous churches and associations. It is contended here that in the Memorial Day ceremonies the anxieties which man has about death are confronted with a system of sacred beliefs about death which gives the individuals involved and the collectivity of individuals a feeling of well-being. Further, the feeling of triumph over death by collective action in the Memorial Day parade is made possible by re-creating the feeling of well-being and the sense of group strength and individual strength in the group power, which is felt so intensely during the wars, when the veterans' associations are created and when the feeling so necessary for the Memorial Day's symbol system is originally experienced.

Memorial Day is a cult of the dead which organizes and integrates the various faiths and national and class groups into a sacred unity. It is a cult of the dead organized around the community cemeteries. Its principal themes are those of the sacrifice of the soldier dead for the living and the obligation of the living to sacrifice their individual purposes for the good of the group, so that they, too, can perform their spiritual obligations.

Memorial Day Ceremonies

We shall first examine the Memorial Day ceremony of an American town for evidence. The sacred symbolic behavior of Memorial Day, in which scores of the town's organizations are involved, is ordinarily divided into four periods. During the year separate rituals are held by many of the associations for their dead, and many of these activities are connected with later Memorial Day events. In the second phase, preparations are made during the last three or four weeks for the ceremony itself, and some of the associations perform public rituals. The third phase consists of the scores of rituals held in all the cemeteries, churches, and halls of the associations. These rituals consist of speeches and highly ceremonialized behavior. They last for two days and are climaxed by the fourth and last phase, in which all the separate celebrants gather in the center of the business district on the afternoon of Memorial Day. The separate organizations, with their members in uniform or with fitting insignia, march through the town, visit the shrines and monuments of the hero dead, and, finally, enter the cemetery. Here dozens of ceremonies are held, most of them highly symbolic and formalized. Let us examine the actual ritual behavior in these several phases of the ceremony.

The two or three weeks before the Memorial Day ceremonies are usually filled with elaborate preparations by each participating group. Meetings are held, and patriotic pronouncements are sent to the local paper by the various organizations which announce what part each organization is to play in the ceremony. Some of the associations have Memorial Day processions, memorial services are conducted, the schools have patriotic programs, and the cemeteries are cleaned and repaired. Graves are decorated by families and associations and new gravestones purchased and erected. The merchants put up flags before their establishments, and residents place flags above their houses.

All these events are recorded in the local paper, and

most of them are discussed by the town. The preparation of public opinion for an awareness of the importance of Memorial Day and the rehearsal of what is expected from each section of the community are done fully and in great detail. The latent sentiments of each individual, each family, each church, school, and association for its own dead are thereby stimulated and related to the sentiments for the dead of the nation.

One of the important events observed in the preparatory phase in the community studied occurred several days before Memorial Day, when the man who had been the war mayor wrote an open letter to the commander of the American Legion. It was published in the local paper. He had a city-wide reputation for patriotism. He was an honorary member of the American Legion. The letter read: "Dear Commander: The approaching Poppy Day [when Legion supporters sold poppies in the town] brings to my mind a visit to the war zone in France on Memorial Day, 1925, reaching Belleau Wood at about 11 o'clock. On this sacred spot we left floral tributes in memory of our town's boys—Jonathan Dexter and John Smith, who here had made the supreme sacrifice, that the principle that 'might makes right' should not prevail."

Three days later the paper in a front-page editorial told its readers: "Next Saturday is the annual Poppy Day of the American Legion. Everybody should wear a poppy on Poppy Day. Think back to those terrible days when the red poppy on Flanders Field symbolized the blood of our boys slaughtered for democracy." The editor here explicitly states the symbolism involved.

Through the early preparatory period of the ceremony, through all its phases and in every rite, the emphasis in all communities is always on sacrifice—the sacrifice of the lives of the soldiers of the city, willingly given for democracy and for their country. The theme is always that the gift of their lives was voluntary; that it was freely given and therefore above selfishness or thought of self-preservation; and, finally, that the "sacrifice on the altars of their country" was done for everyone. The red poppy became a separate symbol from McCrae's poem "In Flanders Fields." The poem expressed and symbolized the sentiments experienced by the soldiers and people of the country who went through the first war. The editor makes the poppy refer directly to the "blood of the boys slaughtered." In ritual language he then recites the names of some of the city's "sacrificed dead," and "the altars" (battles) where they were killed. "Remember Dexter and Smith killed at Belleau Wood," he says. "Remember O'Flaherty killed near Château-Thierry, Stulavitz killed in the Bois d'Ormont, Kelley killed at Côte de Châtillon, Jones near the bois de Montrebeaux, Kilnikap in the Saint-Mihiel offensive, and the other brave boys who died in camp or on stricken fields. Remember the living boys of the Legion on Saturday."

The names selected by the editor covered most of the ethnic and religious groups of the community. They included Polish, Russian, Irish, French-Canadian, and Yankee names. The use of such names in this context emphasized the fact that the voluntary sacrifice of a citizen's life was equalitarian. They covered the top, middle, and bottom of the several classes. The newspapers throughout the country each year print similar lists, and their editorials stress the equality of sacrifice by all classes and creeds.

The topic for the morning services of the churches on the Sunday before Memorial Day ordinarily is the meaning of Memorial Day to the town and to the people as

Christians. All the churches participate. Because of space limitations, we shall quote from only a few sermons from one Memorial Day to show the main themes; but observations of Memorial Day behavior since the Second World War show no difference in the principal themes expressed before and after the war started. Indeed, some of the words are almost interchangeable. The Rev. Hugh McKellar chose as his text, "Be thou faithful until death." He said:

"Memorial Day is a day of sentiment and when it loses that, it loses all its value. We are all conscious of the danger of losing that sentiment. What we need today is more sacrifice, for there can be no achievement without sacrifice. There are too many out today preaching selfishness. Sacrifice is necessary to a noble living. In the words of our Lord, 'Whosoever shall save his life shall lose it and whosoever shall lose his life in My name shall save it.' It is only those who sacrifice personal gain and will to power and personal ambition who ever accomplish anything for their nation. Those who expect to save the nation will not get wealth and power for themselves.

"Memorial Day is a religious day. It is a day when we get a vision of the unbreakable brotherhood and unity of spirit which exists and still exists, no matter what race or creed or color, in the country where all men have equal rights."

The minister of the Congregational Church spoke with the voice of the Unknown Soldier to emphasize his message of sacrifice:

"If the spirit of that Unknown Soldier should speak, what would be his message? What would be the message of a youth I knew myself who might be one of the unknown dead? I believe he would speak as follows: 'It is well to remember us today, who gave our lives that democracy might live, we know something of sacrifice.'"

The two ministers in different language expressed the same theme of the sacrifice of the individual for national and democratic principles. One introduces divine sanction for this sacrificial belief and thereby succeeds in emphasizing the theme that the loss of an individual's life rewards him with life eternal. The other uses one of our greatest and most sacred symbols of democracy and the only very powerful one that came out of the First World War—the Unknown Soldier. The American Unknown Soldier is Everyman; he is the perfect symbol of equalitarianism.

There were many more Memorial Day sermons, most of which had this same theme. Many of them added the point that the Christian God had given his life for all. That afternoon during the same ceremony the cemeteries, memorial squares named for the town's dead, the lodge halls, and the churches had a large number of rituals. Among them was the "vacant chair." A row of chairs decorated with flags and wreaths, each with the name of a veteran who had died in the last year, was the center of this ceremony held in a church. Most of the institutions were represented in the ritual. We shall give only a small selection from the principal speech:

"Now we come to pay tribute to these men whose chairs are vacant, not because they were eminent men, as many soldiers were not, but the tribute we pay is to their attachment to the great cause. We are living in the most magnificent country on the face of the globe, a country planted and fertilized by a Great Power, a power not political or economic but religious and educational, especially in the North. In the South they had settlers who were there in pursuit of gold, in search of El Dorado, but the North was settled by people seeking religious principles and education."

In a large city park, before a tablet filled with the names of war dead, one of our field workers shortly after the vacant-chair rite heard a speaker in the memorial ritual eulogize the two great symbols of American unity—Washington and Lincoln. The orator said:

"No character except the Carpenter of Nazareth has ever been honored the way Washington and Lincoln have been in New England. Virtue, freedom from sin, and righteousness were qualities possessed by Washington and Lincoln, and in possessing these characteristics both were true Americans, and we would do well to emulate them. Let us first be true Americans. From these our friends beneath the sod we receive their message, 'Carry on.' Though your speaker will die, the fire and spark will carry on. Thou are not conqueror, death, and thy pale flag is not advancing."

In all the other services the same themes were used in the speeches, most of which were in ritualized, oratorical language, or were expressed in the ceremonials themselves. Washington, the father of his country, first in war and peace, had devoted his life not to himself but to his country. Lincoln had given his own life, sacrificed on the altar of his country. Most of the speeches implied or explicitly stated that divine guidance was involved and that these mundane affairs had supernatural implications. They stated that the revered dead had given the last ounce of devotion in following the ideals of Washington and Lincoln and the Unknown Soldier and declared that these same principles must guide us, the living. The beliefs and values of which they spoke referred to a world beyond the natural. Their references were to the supernatural.

On Memorial Day morning the separate rituals, publicly performed, continued. The parade formed in the early afternoon in the business district. Hundreds of people, dressed in their best, gathered to watch the various uniformed groups march in the parade. Crowds collected along the entire route. The cemeteries, carefully prepared for the event, and the graves of kindred, covered with flowers and flags and wreaths, looked almost gay.

The parade marched through the town to the cemeteries. The various organizations spread throughout the several parts of the graveyards, and rites were performed. In the Greek quarter ceremonies were held; others were performed in the Polish and Russian sections; the Boy Scouts held a memorial rite for their departed; the Sons and Daughters of Union Veterans went through a ritual, as did the other men's and women's organizations. All this was part of the parade in which everyone from all parts of the community could and did participate.

Near the end of the day all the men's and women's organizations assembled about the roped-off grave of General Fredericks. The Legion band played. A minister uttered a prayer. The ceremonial speaker said:

"We meet to honor those who fought, but in so doing we honor ourselves. From them we learn a lesson of sacrifice and devotion and of accountability to God and honor. We have an inspiration for the future today—our character is strengthened—this day speaks of a better and greater devotion to our country and to all that our flag represents."

After the several ceremonies in the Elm Hill Cemetery, the parade re-formed and started the march back to town, where it broke up. The firing squad of the American Legion fired three salutes, and a bugler sounded the "Last

Post" at the cemetery entrance as they departed. This, they said, was a "general salute for all the dead in the cemetery."

Here we see people who are Protestant, Catholic, Jewish, and Greek Orthodox involved in a common ritual in a graveyard with their common dead. Their sense of separateness was present and expressed in the different ceremonies, but the parade and the unity gained by doing everything at one time emphasized the oneness of the total group. Each ritual also stressed the fact that the war was an experience where everyone sacrificed and some died, not as members of a separate group, but as citizens of a whole community.

The full significance of the unifying and integrative character of the Memorial Day ceremony—the increasing convergence of the multiple and diverse events through the several stages into a single unit in which the many become the one and all the living participants unite in the one community of the dead—is best seen in Figure 1. It will be noticed that the horizontal extension at the top of the figure represents space; and the vertical dimension, time. The four stages of the ceremony are listed on the left-hand side, the arrows at the bottom converging and ending in the cemetery. The longer and wider area at the top with the several well-spread rectangles represents the time and space diversities of stage 1; the interconnected circles in stage 3 show the closer integration that has been achieved by this time.

During stage 1 it will be recalled that there is no synchronization of rituals. They occur in each association without any reference to one another. All are separate and diverse in time and space. The symbolic references of the ceremonies emphasize their separateness. In general, this stage is characterized by high diversity, and there is little unity in purpose, time, or space.

Although the ceremonies of the organizations in stage 2 are still separate, they are felt to be within the bounds of the general community organization. There is still the symbolic expression of diversity, but now diversity in a larger unity (see Fig. 1). In stage 3 there are still separate ceremonies but the time during which they are held is the same. Inspection of the chart will show that time and space have been greatly limited since the period of stage 1.

The ceremonies in stage 4 become one in time and one in space. The representatives of all groups are unified into

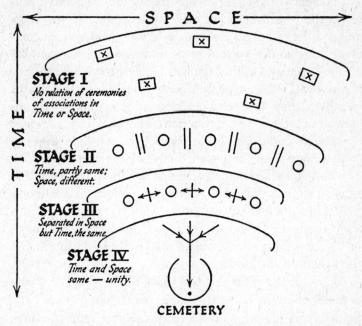

FIG. 1.—Progress of the Memorial Day ceremony

one procession. Thereby, organizational diversity is symbolically integrated into a unified whole. This is not necessarily known to those who participate, but certainly it is felt by them. The chart is designed to symbolize the progressive integration and symbolic unification of the group.

Moreover, at the conclusion of the ceremony, when the entire collectivity moves physically from diversity and extension, spread thinly throughout the city, into the inclosed, confined, consecrated unity of the receptacle (the cemetery as depicted in the chart), the celebrants themselves and their great ceremony symbolically incorporate the full spiritual power of the cemetery as a sacred symbol system.

Yankee City cemeteries are themselves collective representations which reflect and express many of the community's basic beliefs and values about what kind of society it is, what the persons of men are, and where each fits into the secular world of the living and the spiritual society of the dead. Whenever the living think about the deaths of others, they necessarily express some of their own concern about their own extinction. The cemetery provides them with enduring visible symbols which help them to contemplate man's fate and their own separate destinies. The cemetery and its gravestones are the hard, enduring signs which anchor each man's projections of his innermost fantasies and private fears about the certainty of his own death—and the uncertainty of his ultimate future— on an external symbolic object made safe by tradition and the sanctions of religion.

Although the cemetery is a place of the dead, it is also dependent on the living for its own existence. Yankee City, being a very old city, has many graveyards, some of which are ancient and no longer used. These were not part of the Memorial Day celebrations. As long as the cemetery is being filled with a fresh stream of the recently dead, it stays symbolically alive and a vital emblem, telling the living the meaning of life and death. But when the family, the kindred, and other members of the community gradually discontinue burying their loved ones there, the cemetery, in a manner of speaking, dies its own death as a meaningful symbol of life and death, for it ceases to exist as a living sacred emblem and, through time, becomes a historical monument. As a symbolic object it, too, is subject to the meaning of time. Its spirituality then resides in a different context, for it becomes an object of historical value in stable communities rather than a sacred collective representation effectively relating the dead to the living.

When cemeteries no longer receive fresh burials which continue to tie the emotions of the living to the recently dead and thereby connect the living in a chain of generations to early ancestry, the graveyards must lose their sacred quality and become objects of historical ritual. The lifetime of individuals and the living meanings of cemeteries are curiously independent, for both are dependent on an ascription of sacred meaning bestowed upon them by those who live. The symbols of death say what life is and those of life define what death must be. The meanings of man's fate are forever what he makes them.†

Lincoln—an American Collective Representation Made by and for the People

Throughout the Memorial Day ceremony there were continual references to Lincoln and his Gettysburg Ad-

† The reader should consult the Acknowledgments in the first edition of *American Life* for the use of the fifth volume of the "Yankee City" series for this particular section.

dress. The symbol of Lincoln obviously was of deep significance in the various rituals and to the participants. He loomed over the memorial rituals like some great demigod over the rites of classical antiquity. What is the meaning of the myth of Lincoln to Americans? Why does his life and death as conceived in the myth of Lincoln play such a prominent part in Memorial Day?

Some of the answers are obvious. He was a great war president. He was the President of the United States and was assassinated after the Civil War. Memorial Day grew out of this war. A number of other facts about his life might be added; but for our present purposes the meaning of Lincoln the myth is more important to understand than the objective facts of his life-career.

Lincoln, product of the American prairies, sacred symbol of idealism in the United States, myth more real than the man himself, symbol and fact, was formed in the flow of events which composed the changing cultures of the Middle West. He is the symbolic culmination of America. To understand him is to know much of what America means.

In 1858, when Lincoln ran against Stephen Douglas for the United States Senate, he was Abraham Lincoln, the successful lawyer, the railroad attorney, who was noted throughout the state of Illinois as a man above common ability and of more than common importance. He was a former congressman. He was earning a substantial income. He had married a daughter of the superior classes from Kentucky. His friends were W. D. Green, the president of a railway, a man of wealth; David Davis, a representative of wealthy eastern investors in western property, who was on his way to becoming a millionaire; Jesse Fell, railway promoter; and other men of prominence and prestige in the state. Lincoln dressed like them; he had unlearned many of the habits acquired in childhood from his lowly placed parents and had learned most of the ways of those highly placed men who were now his friends. After the Lincoln-Douglas debates his place as a man of prestige and power was as high as anyone's in the whole state.

Yet in 1860, when he was nominated on the Republican ticket for the presidency of the United States, he suddenly became "Abe Lincoln, the rail-splitter," "the rude man from the prairie and the river-bottoms." To this was soon added "Honest Abe," and finally, in death, "the martyred leader" who gave his life that "a nation dedicated to the proposition that all men are created equal" might long endure.

What can be the meaning of this strange transformation?

When Richard Oglesby arrived at the Republican convention in 1860, he cast about for a slogan that would bring his friend, Lincoln, favorable recognition from the shrewd politicians of New York, Pennsylvania, and Ohio. He heard from Jim Hanks, who had known Lincoln as a boy, that Lincoln had once split fence rails. Dick Oglesby, knowing what appeals are most potent in getting the support of the politicians and in bringing out a favorable vote, dubbed Lincoln "the rail-splitter." Fence rails were prominently displayed at the convention, to symbolize Lincoln's lowly beginnings. Politicians, remembering the great popular appeal of "Old Hickory," "Tippecanoe and Tyler too," and "The Log Cabin and Cider Jug" of former elections, realized that this slogan would be enormously effective in a national election. Lincoln, the rail-splitter, was reborn in Chicago in 1860; and the Lincoln who had become the successful lawyer, intimate of wealthy men, husband of a wellborn wife, and man of status was conveniently forgotten.

Three dominant symbolic themes compose the Lincoln image. The first—the theme of the common man—was fashioned in a form pre-established by the equalitarian ideals of a new democracy; to common men there could be no argument about what kind of man a rail-splitter is.

"From log cabin to the White House" succinctly symbolizes the second theme of the trilogy which composes Lincoln, the most powerful of American collective representations. This phrase epitomizes the American success story, the rags-to-riches *motif*, and the ideals of the ambitious. As the equal of all men, Lincoln was the representative of the Common Man, as both their spokesman and their kind; and, as the man who had gone "from the log cabin to the White House," he became the superior man, the one who had not inherited but had earned that superior status and thereby proved to everyone that all men could do as he had. Lincoln thereby symbolized the two great collective but opposed ideals of American democracy.

When Lincoln was assassinated, a third powerful theme of our Christian society was added to the symbol being created by Americans to strengthen and adorn the keystone of their national symbol structure. Lincoln's life lay sacrificed on the altar of unity, climaxing a deadly war which proved by its successful termination that the country was one and that all men are created equal. From the day of his death, thousands of sermons and speeches have demonstrated that Lincoln, like Christ, died that all men might live and be as one in the sight of God and man. Christ died that this might be true forever beyond the earth; Lincoln sacrificed his life that this might be true forever on this earth.

When Lincoln died, the imaginations of the people of the eastern seaboard cherished him as the man of the new West and translated him into their hopes for tomorrow, for to them the West was tomorrow. The defeated people of the South, during and after the Reconstruction period, fitted him into their dark reveries of what might have been, had this man lived who loved all men. In their bright fantasies, the people of the West, young and believing only in the tomorrow they meant to create, knew Lincoln for what they wanted themselves to be. Lincoln, symbol of equalitarianism, of the social striving of men who live in a social hierarchy, the human leader sacrificed for all men, expresses all the basic values and beliefs of the Middle West and of the United States of America.

Lincoln, the superior man, above all men, yet equal to each, is a mystery beyond the logic of individual calculators. He belongs to the culture and to the social logics of the people for whom contradiction is unimportant and for whom the ultimate tests of truth are in the social structure in which, and for which, they live. Through the passing generations of our Christian culture the Man of the Prairies, formed in the mold of the God-man of Galilee and apotheosized into the man-god of the American people, each year less profane and more sacred, moves securely toward identification with deity and ultimate godhead. In him Americans realize themselves.

The Effect of War on the Community

A problem of even greater difficulty confronts us on why war provides such an effective context for the creation of powerful national symbols, such as Lincoln, Washington, or Memorial Day. Durkheim gives us an important theoretical lead. He believed that the members of the group felt and became aware of their own group identity when they gathered periodically during times of plenty. For his test case, the Australian aborigines, a hunting and gathering tribe, this was the season when food was plentiful. It was then that social interaction was most intense and the feelings most stimulated.

In modern society interaction, social solidarity, and intensity of feelings ordinarily are greatest in times of war. It would seem likely that such periods might well produce new sacred forms, built, of course, on the foundations of old beliefs. Let us examine the life of American communities in wartime as a possible matrix for such developments.

The most casual survey supplies ample evidence that the effects of war are most varied and diverse as they are reflected in the life of American towns. The immediate effect of war is very great on some towns and very minor on others. During its existence it strengthens the social structure of some and greatly weakens the social systems of others. In some communities it appears to introduce very little that is new, while in others the citizens are compelled by force of circumstances to incorporate whole new experiences into their lives and into the social systems which control them.

In some communities during the Second World War there was no decided increase or decrease in the population, and war did not change the ordinary occupations of their people. Their citizens made but minor adjustments in their daily lives; no basic changes occurred in their institutions. For example, there were many small market towns servicing rural areas about them where the round of events substantially repeated what had occurred in all previous years from the time the towns grew to early maturity. A few of their boys were drafted, possibly the market crops were more remunerative, and it may be that the weekly paper had a few more war stories. Changes there were, but they were few and minor in their effect on the basic social system.

At the other extreme, most drastic and spectacular changes occurred in the Second World War. Small towns that had formerly existed disappeared entirely, and their former localities were occupied by industrial cities born during the war and fathered by it. Sleepy rural villages were supplanted by huge industrial populations recruited from every corner of America. Towns of a few hundred people, traditionally quiet and well composed, suddenly expanded into brawling young cities with no past and no future. Market towns became industrial areas. The wives and mothers in these towns left their homes and joined the newcomers on the assembly line. The old people went into industry to take jobs they had to learn like the youngest boy working beside them. This and that boy and some of their friends left high school because they received tacit encouragement from their elders and the school authorities to go to work to help in the war effort. In some communities the whole system of control that had formerly prevailed ceased to function or was superseded by outside authority. The influx of population was so great that the schools could teach but a small portion of the children. The police force was inadequate. The usual recreational life disappeared, to be supplanted by the "taxi dance hall," "juke joint," "beer hall," and "gambling dive." Institutions such as the church and lodge almost ceased to function. In some towns one could drive through miles of trailer camps and small houses pressed against one another, all recently assembled, where the inhabitants lived in squalid anonymity with, but not of, the thousands around them. They were an aggregate of individuals concentrated in one area, but they were not a community.

We have described only the two extremes of the immediate influence of war on the community. Soon, however, those communities which had been little affected by the war felt some of its effects, and those which had been disorganized developed habits of life which conformed to the ordinary pattern of American town life. The two extremes soon approached the average.

But wars influence the average town quite differently. Changes take place, the institutional life is modified, new experiences are felt by the people, and the townsmen repeatedly modify their behavior to adapt to new circumstances brought them by new events. These modifications do not cause social breakdown. The contrary is true. The war activities strengthen the integration of many small communities. The people are more systematically organized into groups where everyone is involved and in which there is an intense awareness of oneness. The town's unity and feeling of autonomy are strengthened by competition in war activities with neighboring communities.

It is in time of war that the average American living in small cities and towns gets his deepest satisfactions as a member of his society. Despite the pessimistic events of 1917, the year when the United States entered the First World War, the people derived deep satisfaction from it, just as they did from the last war. It is a mistake to believe that the American people, particularly the small-towners, hate war to the extent that they derive no satisfaction from it. Verbally and superficially they disapprove of war, but at best this is only partly revealed in their deeper feelings.

In simpler terms, their observed behavior reveals that most of them had more real satisfaction out of the Second World War, just as they did in the previous one, than they had had in any other period of their lives. The various men's and women's organizations, instead of inventing things to do to keep busy, could choose among activities which they knew were vital and significant to them and to others.

The small-towner then had a sense of significance about himself, about those around him, and about the events which occurred, in a way that he had never felt before. The young man who quit high school during the depression to lounge on the street corner and who was known to be of no consequence to himself or to anyone else in the community became a seasoned veteran, fighting somewhere in the South Pacific—a man obviously with the qualities of a hero (it was believed), willing to give up his life for his country, since he was in its military forces. He and everyone else were playing, and they knew they were playing, a vital and significant role in the present crisis. Everyone was in it. There was a feeling of unconscious well-being, because everyone was doing something to help in the common desperate enterprise in a co-operative rather than in a private spirit. This feeling is often the unconscious equivalent of what people mean when they gather to celebrate and sing "Hail, hail, the gang's all here." It also has something of the deep significance that enters into people's lives only in moments of tragedy.

The strong belief that everyone must sacrifice to win a war greatly strengthens people's sense of their importance. Everyone gives up something for the common good— money, food, tires, scrap, automobiles, or blood for blood banks. All of it is contributed under the basic ideology of common sacrifice for the good of the country. These simple acts of giving by all individuals in the town, by all families, associations, schools, churches, and factories, are given strong additional emotional support by the common knowledge that some of the local young men are representing the town in the military forces of the country. It is known that some of them may be killed while serving their country. They are sacrificing their lives, it is believed, that their country may live. Therefore, all acts of individual giving to help win the war, no matter how small, are made socially significant and add to the strength of the social structure by being treated as sacrifices. The collective effect of these small renunciations, it is believed, is to lessen the number of those who must die on the altars of their country.

Another very strong integrative factor contributed by a war that strengthens the social structure of the small town and city is that petty internal antagonisms are drained out of the group onto the common enemy. The local antagonisms which customarily divide and separate people are largely suppressed. The feelings and psychic energies involved, normally expended in local feuds, are vented on the hated symbols of the enemy. Local groups which may have been excluded from participation in community affairs are given an honored place in the war effort, and the symbols of unity are stressed rather than the separating differences. The religious groups and the churches tend to emphasize the oneness of the common war effort rather than allow their differing theologies and competitive financing to keep them in opposing groups. The strongest pressure to compose their differences is placed against management and labor. (The small number of strikes is eloquent proof of the effectiveness of such pressure.) A common hate of a common enemy, when organized in community activities to express this basic emotion, provides the most powerful mechanism to energize the lives of the towns and to strengthen their feelings of unity. Those who believe that a war's hatreds can bring only evil to psychic life might well ponder the therapeutic and satisfying effects on the minds of people who turn their once private hatreds into social ones and join their townsmen and countrymen in the feeling of sharing this basic emotion in common symbols. Enemies as well as friends should be well chosen, for they must serve as objects for the expression of two emotions basic to man and his social system—hatred and love.

The American Legion and other patriotic organizations give form to the effort to capture the feelings of well-being when the society was most integrated and feelings of unity were most intense. The membership comes from every class, creed, and nationality, for the soldiers came from all of them.

Only a very few associations are sufficiently large and democratic in action to include in their membership men or women from all class levels, all religious faiths, and most, if not all, ethnic groups. Their number could be easily counted on the fingers of one hand. Most prominent among them are the patriotic associations, all of them structural developments from wars which involved the United States. The American Legion is a typical example of the patriotic type. Less than 6 per cent of several hundred associations which have been studied include members from all social classes. Of the remaining 94 per cent, approximately half have representatives from only three classes, or less than three, out of the six discussed in Chapter 3. Although the associations which include members from all levels of the community are surprisingly few, those which stress in action as well as in words such other principles of democracy as the equality of races, nationalities, and religions are even fewer. Only 5 per cent of the associations are composed of members from the four principal religious faiths in America—Protestant, Catholic, Jewish, and Greek Orthodox—and most of their members come from the lower ranks of the society.

Lincoln and Washington and lesser ritual figures (and ceremonies such as Memorial Day) are the symbolic equivalent of such social institutions as the patriotic societies. They express the same values, satisfy the same social needs, and perform similar functions. All increase the social solidarity of a complex and heterogeneous society.

How Such Ceremonies Function in the Community

Memorial Day and similar ceremonies are one of the several forms of collective representations which Durkheim so brilliantly defined and interpreted in *The Elementary Forms of the Religious Life.* He said: "Religious representations are collective representations which express collective realities." Religious collective representations are symbol systems which are composed of beliefs and rites which relate men to sacred beings. Beliefs are "states of opinion and consist in representations"; rites are "determined modes of action" which are expressions of, and refer to, religious belief. They are *visible* signs (symbols) of the invisible belief. The visible rite of baptism, for example, may express invisible beliefs about cleansing the newborn infant of sin and relating him to the Christian community.

Ceremonies, periodically held, serve to impress on men their social nature and make them aware of something beyond themselves which they feel and believe to be sacred.

This intense feeling of belonging to something larger and more powerful than themselves and of having part of this within them as part of them is symbolized by the belief in sacred beings, which is given a visual symbol by use of designs which are the emblems of the sacred entities, e.g., the Cross of the Christian churches.

That which is beyond, yet part of, a person is no more than the awareness on the part of individuals and the collectivity of individuals of their participation in a social group. *The religious symbols, as well as the secular ones, must express the nature of the social structure of the group of which they are a part and which they represent.* The beliefs in the gods and the symbolic rites which celebrate their divinity are no more than men collectively worshiping their own images—their own, since they were made by themselves and fashioned from their experiences among themselves.

We said earlier that the Memorial Day rites of American towns are sacred collective representations and a modern cult of the dead. They are a cult because they consist of a system of sacred beliefs and dramatic rituals held by a group of people who, when they congregate, represent the whole community. They are sacred because they ritually relate the living to sacred things. They are a cult because the members have not been formally organized into an institutionalized church with a defined theology but depend on informal organization to bring into order their sacred activities. They are called a "cult" here, because this term most accurately places them in a class of social phenomena which can be clearly identified in the sacred behavior of non-European societies.

The cult system of sacred belief puts into the organized form of concepts those sentiments about death which are common to everyone in the community. These sentiments are composed of fears of death, which conflict with the social reassurances that our culture provides us to combat such anxieties. These assurances, usually acquired in childhood and thereby carrying some of the authority of the adults who provided them, are a composite of theology and folk belief. The deep anxieties to which we refer include anticipation of our deaths, of the deaths or possible deaths of loved one, and, less powerfully, of the deaths or possible deaths of those we know and of men in general.

Each man's church provides him and those of his faith with a set of beliefs and a way of acting to face these problems; but his church and those of other men do not equip him with a common set of social beliefs and rituals which permit him to unite with all his fellows to confront this common and most feared of all his enemies. The Memorial Day rite and other subsidiary rituals connected with it form a cult which partially satisfies this need for common action on a common problem. It dramatically expresses the sentiments of unity of all the living among themselves, of all the living to all the dead, and of all the living and dead as a group to the gods. The gods—Catholic, Protestant, and Jewish—lose their sectarian definitions, limitations, and foreignness among themselves and become objects of worship for the whole group and the protectors of everyone.

The unifying and integrating symbols of this cult are the dead. The graves of the dead are the most powerful of the visible emblems which unify all the activities of the separate groups of the community. The cemetery and its graves become the objects of sacred rituals which permit opposing organizations, often in conflict, to subordinate their ordinary opposition and to co-operate in expressing jointly the larger unity of the total community through the use of common rites for their collective dead. The rites show extraordinary respect for all the dead, but they pay particular honor to those who were killed in battle "fighting for their country." The death of a soldier in battle is believed to be a "voluntary sacrifice" by him on the altar of his country. To be understood, this belief in the sacrifice of a man's life for his country must be judged first with our general scientific knowledge of the nature of all forms of sacrifice. It must then be subjected to the principles which explain human sacrifice whenever and wherever found. More particularly, this belief must be examined with the realization that these sacrifices occur in a society whose deity was a man who sacrificed his life for all men.

The principle of the gift is involved. In simple terms, when something valuable is given, an equally valuable thing must be returned. The speaker who quoted Scripture in his Memorial Day speech, "Whosoever shall save his life shall lose it and whosoever shall lose his life in My name shall save it," almost explicitly stated the feelings and principles involved. Finally, as we interpret it, the belief in "the sacrifice of American citizens killed in battle" is a social logic which states in ultimate terms the subordinate relation of the citizen to his country and its collective moral principles.

This discussion has shown that the Memorial Day ceremony consists of a series of separate rituals performed by autonomous groups which culminate in a procession *of all of them as one group* to the consecrated area set aside by the living for their dead. In such a place the dead are classed as individuals, for their graves are separate; as members of separate social situations, for they are found in family plots and formal ritual respect is paid them by church and association; and as a collectivity, since they are thought of as "our dead" in most of the ceremonies. The fences surrounding the cemetery place all the dead together and separate all the living from them.

The Memorial Day rite is a cult of the dead, but not just of the dead as such, since by symbolically elaborating sacrifice of human life for the country through, or identifying it with, the Christian church's sacred sacrifice of their god, the deaths of such men also become powerful sacred symbols which organize, direct, and constantly revive the collective ideals of the community and the nation.

2

THE STUDY OF CONTEMPORARY SOCIETY

Social Anthropology and Modern Life

The last chapter, on Memorial Day in America, no doubt raised a number of questions in the reader's mind about the application of social anthropology to the study of contemporary man. Social anthropology until recently has been entirely concerned with gathering knowledge about the social life of savages. Before continuing with the remaining chapters on social structure and symbolic behavior in the United States, I shall take time to tell what a social anthropologist must do when he studies his own society. Simply put, the questions for which we will now seek answers are:

1. What must an anthropologist do as a social scientist

to study and understand his own culture and the individuals who occupy it?

2. Are the basic principles and problems of his investigations the same or different when he transfers his attention from the non-literate, simple, primitive societies to the literate, complex civilizations of contemporary man?

3. When he studies the latter, does the anthropologist find new and different situations which make changes in research procedure necessary?

4. If he must modify his theories, methods, and procedures, what is it that he must do, and how does he go about doing it?

The fundamental approach for research on modern society is not different from that used for the study of primitive groups; the basic body of theory and method remains the same. This is true because contemporary society does not differ in kind but only in degree from the other societies of the world. It is but one social form, admittedly an extreme one, among all the diverse groups of living men. As such, it is a system of interconnected, interdependent social statuses and social relations which governs the behavior of the individuals who occupy it and therefore can be studied by anthropologists, who examine the same phenomena in other societies.

Individuals are born into and "die out of" all social systems. During their brief lives, they are trained by those who precede them and learn how to train others who follow to behave in such a way that, as mortal men, they live in and become part of an "immortal" society. The "transient" individuals, whose births, lives, and deaths are momentary events in the eternal flow of the life of the species, must learn the morals, values, and beliefs of each society, or the society must perish. The facts and events of species life are re-formed and transposed by the values and beliefs of the moral order of each society. The feelings and experiences of men in nature and the experiences and feelings of individuals during their lives with others of their species are translated into the symbols, rules, and values of their culture. During the many millennia of man's existence the accumulating experiences of the members of the species with nature and with themselves have resulted in the formation of the most diverse tribes, groups, and nations, each different from, yet similar to, the others and capable of rewarding scientific study and comparison.

The behavior of all individuals in our society is subject to its order because of the continuing pressure exerted by members of the group on one another and because each individual, through continuous past and present learning experiences, has made the symbols, rules, and skills of the group part of himself and, by so doing, has become a person capable of conduct appropriate to participation in his group and in all or some of the statuses that are available to him. Consequently, the study of the individual in this society and of the society in him can be pursued by anthropologists with the same theoretical equipment that they have used elsewhere. This is so because the individual variations found here, although marked, are not different in kind but belong to the same types as those found elsewhere.

The Assumptions of Research on Contemporary Life

Two assumptions guiding research on contemporary life must be made explicit before we continue. Unfortunately, they are less obvious to more people than the research man ordinarily realizes. They are:

1. To make scientific sense, all statements about any

society and the individuals in it must be founded on full evidence or must be dependent on hypotheses based on partial evidence, and these hypotheses must always be designed for further testing by properly controlled research methods.

2. Since human societies range from the primitive horde to the metropolitan region and from the simple tribe to the great modern state, each, to be understood, must be studied as a separate entity. Thereafter, by use of the comparative method, each must be analyzed as a specimen within a series which includes societies of every kind and of all degrees of diversity and complexity.

Although, in the study of modern society, the anthropologist does not have to change his approach to the body of theory, he does have to change almost everything connected with method and technique. At the very beginning of his research on modern life, he is forced to modify his usual way of specifying, defining, and limiting the social object under investigation. Ordinarily, when he studies a primitive tribe, the anthropologist does research on the *whole* group. This concern about the whole group is almost the standard by which the adequacy of his work is judged, as well as being conventional for his profession. It is something generally taken for granted. To achieve this goal, he examines each institution, status, and social relation, to understand it and to learn how each fits into the structure of the whole society. He may study personality and its formation; before attempting this task, he knows that he must first make certain that he understands the culture of the group.

Usually the task of studying the whole group is not beyond the capacities of his professional equipment because most tribal units are small in population, territorially limited, and structurally simple. But the field situation in contemporary life is very different. Huge populations, vastly extended reaches of territory, complex and ever changing technologies, great specialization, complicated literate symbol systems, and labyrinthine social structures must be understood and accounted for in field studies, in the analysis of resulting evidence, the testing of hypotheses, and the formation of propositions derived from the research.

If the anthropologist doing research on contemporary society is to study it as a system of interconnected and interdependent relations, if he is to observe the acts and words of men as parts of a larger whole, and if he is to come out of his research with propositions scientifically tested about the whole of the society and the relations of its parts, he must construct a research design which will satisfy these requirements and, at the same time, be adapted to the practical necessities of the object of his study.

The Modern Community as a Laboratory

In an endeavor to fit the scientific criteria of anthropology to the requirements of the facts to be investigated and understood, the community was seized upon as a laboratory for research on contemporary American life.

Sociologists have studied the community not simply as a social system but as an aggregation of individuals or as a process in social time. At least one notable exception to this is the *Middletown* study of the Lynds. But studies of whole communities have been exceptions in the field of sociology.

In a previous generation the sociologists, in common with the anthropologists, when faced with the task of understanding society, took refuge in the formulation of broad, untested general theories which presumably accounted for everything about the nature of man, his society, and its institutions. Theoretical system-makers constructed their sociological empires and fought their rival empire-builders for survival and dominance. Illustrations, well-tailored for their purpose, served for evidence, the relaxed comfort of the armchair for the rigor of field study, and philosophical and broad general theories which could not be tested often took the place of sound method.

Those sociologists who were dissatisfied with the inability of untested theories to yield solid answers whose truth could be validated turned to research and field studies to look for their answers. Since it was impossible for them to study a whole contemporary state such as America, they bit off small pieces they could more easily manage and diligently chewed and digested them. Characteristically, they made studies of particular institutions, they specialized on parts of the whole and, accordingly, became authorities on certain aspects of social change or on institutions such as marriage and the family, racial and ethnic groups, or on social problems such as crime and delinquency, divorce, suicide, or antisocial adolescent gangs. Some of these studies have made solid and permanent contributions to our understanding of contemporary man. They have also fashioned new methods, many of which the social anthropologist should know for the study of primitive tribes.

Partly because of their desire to achieve a vision of the whole, another group of sociologists, foregoing the satisfactions of directly studying the intimate, eventful life of man, turned to broad statistical analyses where they used the resources of census data and vital statistics. They did achieve significant and meaningful generalizations about such things as trends in human affairs and the biological characteristics of the human aggregate; but their knowledge, important as it is, does not answer most of the questions the anthropologist asks. Knowledge about most of the rich and vital details of human living, believed necessary by all anthropologists, slipped through the rough mesh of their sociological statistics and left no meaningful trace.

The former aproach—the study of the part rather than the whole—cannot tell us much about the nature of our total society; the latter, the statistical and general one, gives us some understanding of the whole but provides insufficient knowledge about most of the vital human detail which anthropologists believe is the most important kind of evidence for understanding the social life of man. Awareness of these difficulties led me to seek different solutions, although I must emphasize that the results of both approaches are necessary parts of a science of man.

The Representative Microcosm

In my earlier research the local community was made to serve as a microcosmic whole, representing the total American community. When selected carefully to make sure that it is suitably located in economic, geographical, and social regions, it meets most, if not all, the necessary research specifications. Some twenty-two criteria were used to select the community we call "Jonesville." Questions of size, industrial life, agricultural background, marketing facilities and services, ethnic and racial composition, as well as the presence or absence of certain kinds of schools, churches, associations, civic enterprises, and governmental institutions were embodied in the criteria which served as a testing screen to eliminate hundreds of towns and cities in five large, middle-western states and to retain a very small number for further investigation. The few remaining communities could then be inspected by preliminary field investigations to validate the screening process and to select one of them for intensive study.

From what has been said, several questions immediately arise: In what sense are these communities representative? In what way are they typical? How adequately do they serve as trial laboratories for understanding American life? And does the microcosm of the community yield everything that a study of the whole society would yield?

Meaningful answers to these questions may take at least two forms: Are the cities and towns selected representative of the thousands of communities in the United States? And are they typical of the general culture of the United States?

To satisfy these questions, the criteria used were designed to identify communities which are expressions of some of the central tendencies of American society. Those which met the test possessed social and economic characteristics which most nearly approached the ideal-typical expression of these central tendencies. For example, we know America is a huge industrial nation, founded on a vast agricultural base; that it constantly assimilates and fails to assimilate large numbers of immigrants from different European cultures; that its religious life is largely Protestant but that it has a strong Catholic minority; that it has powerful political and economic hierarchies; that its associations and civic enterprises pervade the life of the whole society; and that there is a considerable distance from the bottom to the top levels of the socioeconomic heap. These and many other known facts supplied the materials for the selective criteria.

A community chosen by such criteria not only represents certain central tendencies of American culture but conforms to a basic type of American community. Although many other types do exist—for example, the isolated, poor-white mountain hamlet, the great metropolis, or the suburban industrial mill town—we believe that to start with they were less likely to give significant first answers about the core of American life than those chosen. Since then these and many other types of communities have been studied. With the enormous development of great metropolitan agglomerations, special studies have been made of some of them, others are now being pursued.

We should not continue without pointing out some of the difficulties. I have just indicated that the study of the central core of a society will not tell one what the varieties are, but such a study makes the varieties much more easily understood. However, there is still a need for a classification of communities composed of several types. Representative studies should be made for each type. It must be said, too, that community studies give only part of the evidence about the vast superstructure of American life. The greatly extended economic and political hierarchies, for example, whose centers of decision are in New York and Washington, can be only partly understood by these studies. However, careful examination of the evidence elicited from local studies, when related to what is known about our national economic life, gives great insight and sound knowledge about the processes at work throughout the system.

Let us conclude our discussion about the adequacy of the community study as a device used as a sample by saying that, although such studies do not provide all the answers, they do give us many of the most important ones and that, although they suffer from limitations, they open whole new areas for our understanding of modern man.

Problems of Community Study

A number of difficulties become immediately apparent as soon as the field researcher begins his work on contemporary communities. At first, these difficulties seem simple and obvious, but the implications of each become exceedingly subtle. One of the most important problems is the presence of written symbols to stand for oral words and statements.

The invention of written words to stand for oral communication and the more recent appearance of many inventions for the widespread distribution of such symbols have created a great variety of means of public communication. They interrelate millions of people in common reference to the same meaningful stimuli and present a very difficult and, at first, terrifying problem for the field researcher. The newspaper, the motion picture, radio, mass magazines, television, lithographs, and picture magazines present entirely new methodological problems; these mass media demand new field techniques and fresh analytical disciplines. The problems arising from the use of these mass symbol systems take several forms. The principal ones are as follows:

What are the meaning and significance of the symbols themselves, and what do they mean to their audience? What effect do they have on the individuals who see and listen to them? What effect do they have on various groups in the society? The latter question takes two forms: the first, what effect do mass media have on the thinking of the people; the second, what is the effect of such stimuli on the relations of the community, its several institutions, and on the larger American society?

How to deal with these problems is an exceedingly difficult question. To solve them, the anthropologist must depend on modifications of some of his old field procedures and borrow others from his colleagues in psychology, sociology, and the other social sciences. Although he must be primarily dependent upon the use of the interview, a whole series of psychological and sociological instruments must be added to his equipment. Some of them I might mention are techniques of analysis and measurement, schedules, tests, and numerous other devices which examine such things as the relation of the individual to the symbols, the relations of individuals to one another because of the presence of such symbols, and the functions of these symbols for the whole society.

From its earliest beginnings, anthropology has been concerned with social change; in fact, many anthropologists have defined their discipline as being no more than history or its reconstruction. Through use of the several subdisciplines—archeology, physical anthropology, linguistics, and ethnology—anthropologists have attempted to reconstruct the prehistory of our own and other societies. More recently, social anthropologists have dealt with history when they studied the processes of acculturation and assimilation following the impact of Western civilization on native cultures. Ordinarily, these studies, by their very nature, have to do with historical processes and forces emanating from *outside* the cultures, whereas the study of European and American social change, for the most part, necessarily searches for explanations of the changes emanating from *within* the culture.

When the social anthropologist turns his attention to modern society, he finds that the sociologists have developed a large body of valuable knowledge and a great variety of theories about social change in Western civilization. Social change has been studied in the form of social and business cycles, historical rhythms, the "social lag," and a great variety of other concepts which attempt to examine social behavior in terms of events that are in a time sequence.

Perhaps the most interesting thing about the study of social change is the fact that so much attention has been given to it and so little to social persistence. We largely take for granted that social groups persist. We rarely stop to ask why persistence occurs and try to determine its nature. The interdependence of personality development and the persistence of a social system as integral parts of the emergent process are now clearly demonstrable (see Chap. 8). They are but two aspects of the same ongoing process of socialization. The study of the effect of social class on personality can at the same time be an investigation of how social class persists in a free society.

Other problems harass the anthropologist who attempts to study contemporary social life. They are: the presence of complex number systems and their written forms, the existence of huge populations and multitudes of people and things to which the numbers are applied, and the fact that the number systems and their relations to the people and things have significance and meaning to the members of the society and are factors helping to control behavior. The problems thus created are exceedingly complex. I cannot claim very much for our efforts to solve them.

In the very simple societies, such as aboriginal Australia, mathematical systems are rudimentary and unimportant;

but in contemporary society problems of number continually appear, usually in the several forms just mentioned. Let me analyze the significance of this contrast between very primitive tribes and our own.

In a simple undifferentiated culture, one principal informant aided by assistants can tell the researcher what the ways of the society are for such things as marriage and divorce. Further interviewing with others will demonstrate that the evidence he cites is all that is necessary and available. He can do this because the universe for which he speaks is usually restricted in population, limited territorially, and simple socially.

In our own society the very opposite is true. Practices of marriage and divorce, for example, vary from group to group and within each group. How much and how often become questions of the utmost importance. The knowledge of the mere presence of divorce is insufficient. We need to know how frequent it is, in order to answer a whole variety of important questions having to do with everything from the family, child-rearing, and the status of woman to the meaning of contemporary mass media or the significance of certain fictional themes in our literature.

In primitive society, such as Australia, numerical concepts are simple, limited, and sufficient; "two or three people," "a whole lot of people," or "lots and lots of people" satisfy any intelligent aborigine. Not so the native of Yankee City. He wants to know what percentage of the total vote Jones received and how this percentage compared with those of Smith, Brown, and the others. He and his wife guide their behavior by numbers that stand for days of the year, by price indexes, and by huge columns of figures on the financial page. Out of all these calculations, diverse meanings and significances are reached which everyone uses to guide and direct his activities. In Yankee City, the Midwest, the Deep South, and the great emergent urban society of America, the meaning of numbers prevents and frustrates or sometimes positively stimulates the behavior of the members of these societies.

The use of statistics helps the scientist to solve the ordinary problem of how much and how many. Symbolic analysis gives some aid and a little comfort for the problem of the meaning and significance of numbers and their use by contemporary peoples. So far the understanding of the functions of numbers in modern life has not advanced much beyond the first step of asking some of the right questions.

I must briefly touch on another problem that besets the anthropologist foolish or hardy enough to tackle the study of his own society. I refer to ethnocentrism. Simply put, this means: Does he see and hear what he is looking at? And, equally simple and devastating: Will he look at, and give attention to, what there is to be seen and heard? Since he is a living product of his own culture and subject to its control and direction, can he look objectively at what he studies? It can be said that the processes of social science, with their constant testing and retesting, provide us with the same apparatus for identifying and analyzing social reality as physical science does for its subdisciplines. But, before accepting this persuasive argument, it must be remembered that science is one kind of symbol system recently invented by Western man. It, too, is an artifact of our culture, subject to the controls of our basic ideas and emotional systems. This argument holds true for the study not only of our society but of other societies as well. The same sets or ways of seeing and hearing things, products of our culture, will guide our thinking everywhere.

Fortunately, the comparative method of anthropology helps us out of this difficulty. The charge of ethnocentrism is difficult to combat when scientists of our society study only their own culture. Perhaps they do mirror only what is in the mirror; but, when other societies are studied and great diversities are recorded, they become capable of identifying social similarities and differences. Furthermore, when students from other cultures go to these same societies, including our own, and report the same cultural occurrences and events as we do, a large measure of assurance is given us that, insofar as man is capable of dealing with reality beyond himself, it seems likely that he can study himself, including investigations not only of his culture but of the private world of those who live in it.

I have mentioned some of the important difficulties that need overcoming; I have not told of the many advantages. I will do no more than list a few. Problems of language and meaning are partly reduced by the field worker's control of the language and the many scientific devices to check and control semantic problems. Mass media and other literate symbols are difficult to comprehend, but, as permanent documents, they provide evidence about our past and present that is used to first advantage by the scientific analyst. Numbers are often a curse to the researcher, but, when they accumulate, a certain amount of sense can be made from them. The intimate inner knowledge one has about himself and his own world often permits the sympathetic field worker to enter the private worlds of those he studies with greater ease and assurance than when he studies an alien group. Finally, the accumulated results, techniques, and skills of other social and psychological sciences are more available to the anthropologist who studies our society than to the students who do research on New Guinea, Australia, or the Amazon. The latter, too often, must be jacks-of-all-trades and masters of none.

The Concepts of Social Anthropology

Since the community is central to our discussion, we must now take time to say what it is as a social object, what we mean by "community" and similar terms, and show how this concept is related to the key concepts of social anthropology.

Sociology and anthropology employ a large number of terms referring to a great variety of human territorial groups. Some of those commonly used by anthropologists are hordes, bands, villages, as well as towns and cities; those more familiar to the sociologist are metropolitan areas, rural and urban neighborhoods, as well as cities, towns, villages, and hamlets. The term "community," although largely used by the sociologist to take general account of the variety of territorial groups of contemporary civilization, necessarily includes and defines all similar groupings among non-literate peoples. It can therefore be used safely as a term and concept that is meaningful for research which is done on the local groups of any society. Its customary usage is here extended to fit the needs of a science of man which refuses to separate contemporary society from its kind, namely, all societies of human beings.

A community so defined may be autonomous to the point that it is a separate group exercising complete sovereignty, possessing a complete economy and social system, and worshiping its own unique and ethnocentric deities; or it may be, as it often is in contemporary life, a smaller segment of a larger whole, a very tiny part of it, such as a small neighborhood in a larger metropolitan center, functioning only to provide living space for a group of families who earn their bread elsewhere, who have no political autonomy, belong to other social groups which meet beyond the territory of the community, and pray to gods whose churches are elsewhere and whose secular chiefs may be thousands of miles distant.

Or a community so defined may be coterminous with that of a national society. The society of the United States is rapidly becoming a primary community where daily social interaction, aided by rapid transportation and modern communication, takes place in a complex social structure extending across a continent where the multiple local communities have been and are moving toward integration into a single great society. (It must be added that other national communities also grow; and, vaguely, yet in fact, a world society, despite rivalrous ideologies, is forming and, with or not with leagues or united nations, making its demands and responding to the increasing human needs for that kind of society.

So viewed, the several varieties of communities and local groups studied by sociologists and anthropologists— although they vary widely among themselves, socially from the very simple to the very complex, technically from the low hunters and gatherers to the technology of the machine, and, in population, from a score or so to the millions of metropolises—are essentially the same in kind. They all are located in a given territory which they partly transform for purposes of maintaining the life of the group. All the individual members have social relations directly or indirectly with one another. The social relations are ordered, and together they form the social structure of the local group. Although social change continually occurs, rapidly or not, the organization of a group continues through the changing generations of individuals who are born into it. There may or may not be great variation in the autonomy exercised by the different groups and their differentiation from other communities; yet all differ sufficiently everywhere for the individuals in them to be conscious of belonging to one group and not to another, even though the other may be but little different from their own.

All societies are essentially adaptive orders where accumulated human learning experience is organized, contained, and directed in symbol systems which adjust human biological groups with varying degrees of success to their several environments. Although human adaptation *seems* largely social, there can be little doubt that its core continues to be species behavior.

Social organization should not be understood simply as a method which man invented to integrate otherwise isolated (non-social) individuals. There are no isolated human individuals. Since all are members of the species, they interact at a species level as well as at a social level. The rules and symbols of the social structure only modify the species system of relations and give it social form.

We must take time to examine what it means to be an individual in society, particularly our society, and what it means for the society to be in individuals, particularly those of our own society. The human individual is an organism which is interconnected with other members of his kind by interrelated acts of species behavior. Such factors as the hunger and sex drives, growth patterns, and the solid core of persisting social life are integral parts of what I call "species behavior." These interrelated acts are both inborn in, and learned by, the individual. As research on the social life of monkeys and apes demonstrates, species behavior is largely controlled and organized by the inborn nature of the species.

Such behavior, found in varying forms in all primates, includes a well-ordered social life having little or no dependence on symbols, tools, or their products. Individuals born into primate groups other than man must learn without the use of symbols how to behave within the group and are trained accordingly by their experiences to fit into the social system of the group. Research on the social life of monkeys and apes demonstrates that these creatures have a well-ordered social life, that there are social groups such as family and territorial groups, that they communicate among themselves with gestures and cries, and that the newly born and the young are taught by the old how to behave as members of the group. Whether the gestures and sounds can be called rudimentary symbols is a matter of dispute; but, whatever they are, they communicate accumulated experience so that the learning individual can act adaptively in the world around them and with the members of their own group. Learned behavior without the use of verbal mechanisms is passed on by the members of one generation to those of the next. It seems highly probable that the same kind of accumulated experience was possessed by man before he developed a language and that it forms the solid framework of our social life. The generations are held together by this chain of inborn and learned species behavior; culture as ordinarily defined is not necessary to explain the basic facts of persistence.

The problem of the social scientist is not the false one usually posed of how humans become social beings, but rather how they learn to become autonomous individuals. Later I shall consider certain aspects of this problem when

I discuss the meaning of the role and status of individuals.

From the larger point of view, all human society which is not species behavior is symbolic. A symbol thus conceived is anything which has meaning and significance for the human mind. Human society is composed of symbolic processes, in the sense that what we are to ourselves, what others are to us, what we are to them and they to themselves, consist outwardly of wards and acts which inwardly are beliefs to which we attach values. In other words, the social relations and entire social organization of any human society consist of evaluated beliefs and their expression in human conduct. They exist in the interaction of individuals within particular sets of relationships. Such are the rules and the conditions in which they operate. The sanctions enforcing them are socially defined, but the testimony from ape societies teaches us that we almost certainly inherited the rudiments of our methods for enforcing the rules from our animal forebears, for punishment and reward are the foundation stones not only of human learning but of animal learning.

The very technology that adjusts us to the natural environment, usually not considered a symbolic system, consists partly of knowledge, which directs, organizes, and adjusts our control over the natural environment. But here the symbolic analysis of all human conduct can be pushed too far. The tools, weapons, and instruments which man invents and uses for adjusting himself to his natural environment are things in themselves. Their form and function need no more meaning and no more interpretation by those who use them than knowing what it is they are and what it is they can and cannot do. They are facts in themselves. They do not necessarily stand for other things. In this sense, they are not symbols. But, in another sense, they are, for each artifact and each of its functions is a meaningful symbol of direct reference in the same way that the concepts and instruments of science are. The concepts of science represent reality; their instruments constantly test it. As such, they consist of a language and its related behavior. They directly refer to, and are tested by, the realities of natural experience. The science of today's technology is no more than a development of the simpler technologies of yesterday. Just as the meaningful and evaluated acts and words composing the social organization adjust human beings to one another, so the meaningful acts and tools of the technology adjust us to nature. A nature without meaning, that is to say, without symbolic representation in man's technology, would be a nature to which there was no technological adjustment.

Finally, our society and all others adjust man to the unknown and to all those forces which his technology and social organization cannot control sufficiently to give him the safety he feels necessary. Religion and magic, composed of myth and rite, are the evaluated beliefs, the meaningful words and acts, which all societies use to accomplish this fearful task. There can be no doubt about their symbolic nature. The sacred symbol systems are symbols of symbols. They relate man to sacred beings whose nature for science can be comprehended only by understanding to what they refer in human existence and what they mean for the inner world of man's emotions and his public world of social experience.

These three adaptations—technologies, the skills and tools which adjust man to nature; the rules, composed of meaningful words and acts; and religion, the symbols that relate man to the sacred—provide a basic framework not only for studying contemporary communities of our society but for comparing similar studies of other societies with our own.

These adaptations and their several environments are depicted in Figure 2.

The three adaptive subsystems—the technology, moral organization, and the rituals and beliefs of the sacred order—are represented by the circles in the left column. The first two environments (see the circles on the right) are that part of the natural environment which, for purposes of survival, is satisfactorily controlled by the skills and tools of the technology and the species, including its innate capacities, limitations, and the animal group life regulated by the rules, values, and sanctions of the moral organization. The third environment—imaginary or not—consists of the threatening, fearful, uncontrolled, and rationally unknowable world of nature and man which lies beyond the power of the technical and moral orders, where death and disaster are forever present—these being assigned by men to the ritual control of religion and its sacred symbols.

The double-headed arrows connecting the circles in the left-hand column, *a* and *b*, indicate that the several subsystems are in relations of mutual influence and make up one unified system. At the right, the single-headed arrows pointing toward the central circle indicate the influence of the other two environments on the species and show how their influence is felt in the adaptive system.

The two arrows which show the relations and influences between each type of adaptation and its environment need to be carefully noted, for they provide the foundations for understanding the symbolic forms and meanings of this and other societies. The empirical and pragmatic knowledge governing the skilled manipulation of tools

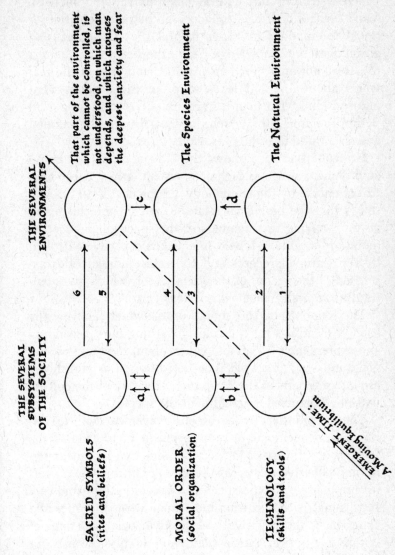

THE SEVERAL
ENVIRONMENTS

That part of the environment
which cannot be controlled, is
not understood, on which man
depends, and which arouses
the deepest anxiety and fear

The Species Environment

The Natural Environment

THE SEVERAL
SUBSYSTEMS
OF THE SOCIETY

SACRED SYMBOLS
(rites and beliefs)

MORAL ORDER
(social organization)

TECHNOLOGY
(skills and tools)

EMERGENT TIME:
A Moving Equilibrium

FIG. 2.—The emergent American Society

which transform the natural environment and increase man's control of it also broadens and strengthens the rational foundations of man's mental life. The increasing accumulation of knowledge from experience with the rest of nature not only broadens his understanding of the real world about him but leads to propositions about what nature is and what man is in his relations to it. This is all part of the process by which the ego subsystem is founded and structured into the personality of each individual.

Horizontal arrow 1 shows the influences of the natural environment in man's technical system; arrow 2, the control of nature by the technology. At the next level arrow 3 shows that the biological relations and their feelings and gestures among the members of the species influence the moral order, although held in check and partly controlled by the learned precepts and the rules and sanctions expressed in the usages of the social order, which gives cultural form to all biological relations (arrow 4).

The symbols of the moral order—which convey the group's meanings for the rules governing human conduct and express their beliefs and values about right and wrong, good and bad, and what is to be rewarded or punished—are integral parts of the basic moral relation of the culture with the organized animal life of the species.

The moral order, by its direct involvement with the interaction of members of the species, helps to channel the feelings of individuals in species interaction into meaningful and cohesive relations—thereby permitting the powerful life energies of the species to be culturally expressed. In this matrix the growing individual learns the rules and experiences the negative and positive social sanctions of criticism, physical punishment, and bodily rewards for acting or failing to act according to the precepts of the moral order. The moral order aids the technological in helping the individual to learn, use, and invent symbols which refer to and express outer reality. The environmental forces of animal life are felt by the moral order, and the knowledge of the technology presses heavily upon it and forces it to adjust itself to the natural environment. Social control of the species and the natural environment must be constantly synchronized, the consequence being a constant adjustment between them.

Changes in the skills of the technology, in man's moral relations, or in his sacred symbols influence all other parts of the sacred system. It is not until attention is turned to the sacred symbol system that the purest form of symbol system is found, combining species and social symbols. This system of supernatural adjustment reduces and helps to control the anxieties and fears felt by the species because of insecurity in the natural and moral environments. Man's inability to control parts of the environment on which he depends for his individual and group survival is the source of his deepest anxiety and accordingly a prepotent influence on sacred rituals and beliefs. It need only be mentioned that his anxieties come from his experience with the real threats of his natural environment and the equally real ones of his species existence, as well as from the fearful fantasies of his moral and social life.

The supernatural level combines and re-expresses the values and beliefs of the moral and technical orders; here they are charged and powerfully motivated by the animal life of the species. Here the wishes, hopes, fears, and pent-up longings of species life, combined and molded by the conventions of the mental, moral, and technical orders, hold sway. Here the deeply buried fantasies, the covert symbolic life of man, driving for a mastery over nature and his species which the social system does not provide, and a well-being which man rarely experiences in fact and can only find for the most part in imagination—here these hidden elements find not only expression but confident encouragement. Here man's wishes to conquer death—to provide food, shelter, and creature comforts in abundance —can be completely satisfied. Here the haunting fear and growing anxieties about his health, moral worth, and personal persistence can be assuaged. The oral and action rites publicly and privately performed by his group fill him with confident hope, which their supercontrol over the supernatural environment makes possible. His faith in these reified symbols expresses the "eternal" and infinite power of species and cultural life as they are felt within himself as part of his existence in the group.

These considerations place Durkheim's collective representations in a somewhat different setting. So viewed, the sacred world is not just a reified symbolic expression of the realities of the society but is also an expression of the ongoing group life of the human animal. Men can fully realize all they are as members of a species and a society at the supernatural level. Here they can love and hate themselves as gods and be loved and hated by the deities they have created.

The faith of the group in supernatural symbols, the sense of "integration," of "oneness," and the sacrifice of self for the survival of these sacred symbols now become meaningful. Whenever an individual can identify sacred symbols in which he believes with the integrated sociospecies symbols of his ordinary life he can have enough faith to believe in their supernatural efficacy and power. The source of their power is in and beyond him; these symbols unquestionably express for him a feeling of belonging to a vital eternal world which is all-powerful and—although beyond human understanding—knowable and true because of what he feels the symbols have "within them" and express for him.

Structural Complexity and Symbolic Diversity

The great complexity and diversity of American symbol systems are related to the high division of labor and the extreme complexity of its social structure. Two contrary tendencies operate in the symbolic behavior of contemporary America.

The first leads to increasing diversity of symbols almost to the point where a specific symbol can be fully understood only by a specific individual. For example, very small groups take a proud delight in being the only ones who understand certain kinds of poetry. The groups in which certain scientific languages are known and understood are necessarily small, for knowledge of the language requires a long period of time and the interest of particular kinds of personalities.

The small groups characteristic of a high division of social labor in complex societies are not only "interest" groups, held together by sharing common values, but also symbol-sharing groups. They can communicate with one another as they cannot with any other group. The reciprocal exchange of symbols which have a common significance for each member involved in the exchange holds the groups together; but the fact that they share the symbols only among themselves and cannot do so with others creates an exclusiveness and inclusiveness that strengthen the solidarity of the group. Since these characteristics are present in each symbol-sharing group, they clearly contribute both to each group's solidarity and to the maintenance of the society's heterogeneity. Such diversity demands the successful tying-in of the separate symbol systems to one another and to the common language of the whole group—otherwise they cannot be used and be an effective part of the division of labor.

As the society grows more complex and the symbol systems more diverse, a second tendency—an opposing but necessary one—also operates. There is increasing generalization and standardization of public symbols understood by all levels of the society and by every kind of person. Some of these public symbols, such as the communications of certain newspapers, are highly stereotyped and have common acceptance among the diverse groups within the masses of the people. The first symbolic process is related to the diverse structural units, social differentiation, and the increasing tendency of American society to form each individual into a semiautonomous unit and a private social system of his own; the second (symbolic) tendency is directly related to the social necessity of maintaining at least a minimum of cohesion and a larger solidarity. Over-all symbol systems which everyone understands and which evoke common sentiments and common values and beliefs in all members of the society are expressions of this second tendency. They provide the symbols which are exchanged by everyone in the group and are the materials most fitted for the daily newspaper, the radio, and the motion picture. Although there may be variation in the form in which they are expressed (print in newspapers and magazines as compared with pictures in television and the movies), they have a common unity in the beliefs they represent and the emotions they arouse.

Status and Role

Until this point in our discussion I have used the conventional definition of social organization normally used by most anthropologists, saying that it consists of social relations that are interconnected and interdependent. It is true that all social organizations are sets of recognizable social relations, but, whether they be families or great industrial hierarchies, they have another fundamental component that I shall refer to as "status."

The members of a family do not interact just as individual persons but as brothers and sisters, as daughters and sons, or as husbands and wives. These positions, or statuses, help to determine how an individual will act in any given family situation. Although she is the same person in the two statuses, Jane Doe in the position *wife* acts quite differently from the way she does when she is in the status *mother*. Her behavior with other members of the family is determined by the statuses she and they occupy.

All social institutions, formal and informal, as subsystems of the larger society, automatically create memberships and positions which are forms of status in every society. The status *wife* formally consists of rights and privileges, including economic support, fidelity, and rights to sexual relations. This status directly implicates the status *husband* and sets up a series of direct counterclaims and obligations by him. The rest of the society is indirectly related to this by what the members of the group define as the wife's obligations to the husband and to the society. The acts and words from which the scientist learns what the status *wife* is, being socially defined, are expressions of the evaluated beliefs of the group. Within these evaluated beliefs lie the rules which define certain behavior as that of a wife and exclude other behavior as beyond the limits of this status. These same rules declare that certain behavior for females is proper and permissible only within the confines of the limiting walls of this status.

In a factory, the subordinate status *worker* implies the superordinate status *manager*. Each has a set of obligations, rights, duties, and privileges in the plant hierarchy where he works and, through the plant, in the society. Each status in a factory helps to limit and define the other.

Another economic status, *owner,* implies other social factors. Although the owner's relation to the object of his ownership is a symbolic one in which each is involved, it is not as such a complete social relation. It becomes one because ownership implies recognition by others of the owner's rights, duties, and obligations to objects that are socially defined as property. His and the relations of others to the property put them in relations of interdependence and interconnection through their socially defined relations to the property. This is one of the basic ways in which material objects are implicated and become part of our social system.

It is my belief that our society, with its extreme division of social labor and its many diverse and autonomous individuals, cannot be comprehended unless there is clear understanding of the meaning of status—status as a social reality and status as a concept used by the social scientist who tries to understand it. Although status should be a key term for comprehending our complex society, there is the utmost confusion about what it is. Many writers confuse it with the role of the individual.

Status is the most general term referring to the location of the behavior of individuals or the social positions of individuals themselves in the structure of any group. It is a defined social position located in a social universe. The term is synonymous with social position, social place, or social location. Statuses may or may not be ranked as superior or inferior. Therefore, they fall into two general types—the ranked and the non-ranked.

Status, or social place, must be defined by reference to its form, what it is, and to its functions, what it does, within a social structure. Its form is identified and demonstrated to be what it is by observing the behavior of individuals to find out what they do and say.

The *functions* of a status may be determined operationally by reference to:

1. What it does for all or part of any given *society*.
2. What it may do for species and the *biological* functioning of the group.
3. What it does for some or all of the *individuals* who live in the group.

The *form* of a particular status is defined operationally by asking and answering the following questions: What are the rights and privileges enjoyed by those who occupy it? What are the rights and privileges of members of *other* statuses that are directly or indirectly related to it? What are the duties and obligations of those who occupy a given status, and what are the duties and obligations of others who are in statuses which are related to it? To restate this in somewhat different terms, we need to know the rules of conduct and the appropriate symbols used by those who are in, or in relationship to, a given status.

Status always implies and is related to the larger social universe in which it has its place. It is definable in large part explicitly or implicitly by reference to its relations with other parts of the social system.

Each social position (or status) is understandable by

reference to the other positions with which it is in direct or indirect interaction. Ultimately, full understanding of a particular status can be gained not only by knowing what it is as a social object and how it is interrelated with other statuses but by understanding its relation to, and place in, the whole society.

A status includes and at the same time excludes certain individuals or behavior and thereby limits and gives form to at least two social universes: there is an inner world and an outer one, there are those who are in and those who are outside it.

The limits of one status provide the boundaries of one or more statuses with which its members interact. By its very nature, a status cannot exist alone; it is always dependent on other statuses for its existence. It is only by knowing what they are that a given position can be defined.

Statuses possess varying degrees of inclusiveness and exclusiveness. For example, the highly inclusive status, *citizen of Yankee City,* in these respects is quite different from the highly exclusive one, *mayor of Yankee City.* There are also varying forms of inclusion and exclusion, depending on the presence or absence of various social characteristics and functions; consequently, such forms are as diverse as the societies in which they exist.

The concept of role is often confused with status. It should not be, for the role concept should place primary emphasis on the person rather than on the society. It should be a reference to the individual as a personal being occupying one or more social statuses. Role tends to accent how an individual stylizes his behavior. The role an individual plays is the way he defines himself as a person, the way as a person he is defined by others, the way he acts toward himself and others act toward him as a person. The social evaluation and conception of a role tends to become a stereotype composed of one or more public symbols which refer to the way, it is believed, certain individuals stylize their behavior. Such symbols always have personal rather than structural reference.

Essentially, role is a product of personality traits, real or attributed, whereas social status is a product of the interconnection of social relations. In America such terms as "big sister," for the woman who solves everyone's troubles, "little mother," for the young girl who protects other children, and "clubwoman," for an individual active in civic life, are terms for female roles. They designate a particular kind of personality. Essentially, they are terms which recognize and give a label to the conceptions which people have of several kinds of feminine personalities.

Generally speaking, status emphasizes membership and place in a social universe and can be defined by reference to a relational context, whereas role emphasizes personality and is definable by reference to how individuals act or are believed to act by those around them.

In the next several chapters I shall describe and analyze certain types of status and show how they function in contemporary America. Later, I shall discuss the problem of roles when I deal with certain kinds of symbolic behavior.

3

SOCIAL CLASS AND COLOR CASTE IN AMERICA

Social Class in a Democracy

It is impossible to study with intelligence and insight the basic problems of contemporary American society and the psychic life of its members without giving full consideration to the several hierarchies which sort people, their behavior, and the objects of our culture into higher and lower social statuses. They permeate every aspect of the social life of this country. In America, as elsewhere in a world of large populations, complex social structures, and advanced civilization, there are at least four polar types and other intermediate varieties of rank. One form includes those systems, such as factories and governmental organizations, which segment the society—hierarchies which place their members in relations of superiority and inferiority within their own limits but not in the whole community. Another form cross-cuts the community, placing all people in superordinate and subordinate ranks.

Modern social systems are developing increasingly the segmentary, large-scale type of rank order to solve certain social and economic problems and to maintain cohesion and order in a rapidly changing world. Such institutions as cartels, huge factories, great service enterprises, chain stores, producers' and farmers' co-operatives, and vast mail-order houses, such as Sears, Roebuck, are examples of elaborate economic hierarchies which regulate part of the lives of some of the individuals in American society but not the entire life of any individual within their ranks. Nor do they directly control any of the lives of those who do not belong to them. In the sense that these hierarchies directly affect only their members and part, but not all, of the behavior of these members, they are hierarchies that segment society.

Before examining more concretely the results of the field studies of social class and color caste in America, we must give brief attention to their place in the comparative taxonomy of all the forms of rank from all societies and thus achieve one of our original objectives of moving the study of specific status systems from the particular to the general and from this process abstract empirically founded statements and principles of rank not bound to any one body of data.

The criteria for the comparative study of rank in which American caste, social class, and other forms of rank can be categorized are founded on such basic considerations as human adaptations, the effect on the life chances of the individual and the biological persistence of the species.

Two kinds of basic questions about access to each other of the members of the species of any given group help us meet the demands of the several tests; first, are the statuses (or a status) within a system of rank open to movement to and from them so that those who might seek access or seek to leave them may do so? Is the system of assignment of status such that each individual's position is free so that he can move vertically or horizontally toward others and they to him? Can he and they compete for higher status or strive to maintain their own? Or is the status system closed so that men cannot move from status to status, their own individual positions thus being so fixed that their careers are confined to one status (or level of rank) and competition for any other status not possible?

The second kind of basic question may be stated: To what extent are the life of a society and the activities of each individual controlled by any order of rank? Is the order's province limited to certain activities and not others? Is it limited to particular periods and times? Is it limited to certain individuals and not others? Does it regulate part of the lives of some people for part of the time but not all of it? What and how much does it control? In brief, and to apply terms, is it a limited hierarchy segmenting the membership and activities of the group, or is it inclusive, generally comprising everyone and all or most of the activities that make up the round of life of the group and each individual?

When the two polar types of status control, the closed form (not accessible to free competition) and the open (accessible to movement into it and allowing movement out) are combined with the two polar types of hierarchy (the general and all-inclusive one, which covers most or all of the activities of the individual and the society, and the segmentary or limited one whose controls are confined to a limited part of the society and its behavior) four basic forms of rank are logically recognizable. Each of the four logical types is now satisfied by empirical reality.

The four extreme types are:

1. The inclusive (or general) system with open statuses where free competition prevails among individuals (and families) for position. Social class in the United States is but one variety. Successful competition is expressed in social mobility.

2. The limited (segmentary) system within which the ranked statuses are open to free competition and there is movement in and out of the available statuses.

3. The inclusive (general) system whose statuses are closed and not open to competition. The position of the individual is fixed in a caste system.

4. The limited (segmentary) system closed to free competition where, for the purposes of the hierarchy, the position of the individual is fixed and there is no movement from status to status.

It will be noted that social class, which allows competition for the more prestigeful and powerful positions, is at one extreme and that color caste, which prohibits movement and competition, is at the other extreme of status closure. The position of the individual and his family is not fixed in social class, for his life chances and those of his family can be (by the nature of the system) improved by competing freely for higher position. The position of the individual and his family in a (classical) caste system is fixed and determined by birth. He is not free to compete for all or some of the prestige and power of the higher caste. His life chances (so far as caste is involved) are limited. The two forms of rank, however, are alike inasmuch as each covers the whole or most of the activities of those who are members of either system.

The values and the spirit of the rules of social class, color caste, and subordinate minority groups encompass the lives of individuals within their confines. Although this is particularly true of caste, it holds sufficiently true for the others to make the statement accurate. They divide the whole population and determine behavior very much as age and sex classes do. There may be indeterminate social areas, in which it is not clear whether the people or the behavior is clearly in one status or another, or something that is a mixture of both. But, when class or caste is present, it divides the society and those to whom the terms apply into distinct levels.

Social class in America is not the same as economic class. Social class refers to levels which are recognizable in the general behavior and social attitudes of the people of the whole community where the levels exist. Although economic factors are of prime importance and are some of the principal determinants of social class, they are insufficient to account for all social-class behavior or for its presence in contemporary America.

The levels of social class are ranked into superior and inferior levels according to the values of the community. The things wanted and actively pursued and the things disliked and, where possible, actively avoided are distributed unevenly among the members of the whole society, the distribution being controlled by the order of rank of the classes present. In such a system, the old precept, "to him that hath shall be given," is often a powerful determinant of how the available rewards are given to those who compete for them.

The rules and norms of marriage in a social-class system have two modes. The values of social class about marriage

72 AMERICAN LIFE

are such that it is felt to be proper and correct for a man or woman to marry at his or her own level (endogamy); yet it is also believed to be correct and proper for an individual to marry above or below his social position (exogamy). In all truth it must be admitted that a person who "marries up" is said to have made a "good marriage"; and the fortunes of the other spouse in this marital venture are often recognized by such invidious gestures as raised eyebrows and knowing smiles or by the elaborate explanations of friends and family which point out the great moral, aesthetic, or even monetary worth of the marital partner. Unwittingly and unwillingly, they indicate that the marriage is not an exchange of equal status, that it needs the weight of added material or spiritual properties to balance it satisfactorily; thus the ideals of romantic love are not outraged, and the spirit of justice on which all freely chosen permanent contracts must rest is strengthened and maintained.

In a social-class system, the child inherits the status of its parents. It is the family that socially orients him to, and trains him for, the community. It is the family that establishes his social location; within it he has his early experiences and learns to be a human being and a person.

Although social classes are rank orders placing people and their families in higher and lower orders, they do not permanently fix the status of either the individual or his family in America. Despite the fact that a man inherits the class position of his family, his inherited position is not necessarily the one he will always occupy. From the point of view of the total social system of a community, each class is open to properly qualified people below it. Vertical social mobility, the rise and fall of individuals and families, is characteristic of our class system.

Social Class in New England, the Middle West, and the South

The class systems of the communities in the several regions of the United States are basically similar. A good test of this statement is that people who move from one region to another recognize their own and other levels in the new community and know how to adjust themselves. But variations are present, for example, in number of class levels, size of the population of each level, and differences in the culture and social composition of the various strata. Furthermore, the amount and kind of social mobility permitted between two or more levels and the strength of the class system itself differ regionally. In general, the older and more stable regions of the East and South have more highly organized class systems than the West.

On the eastern seaboard of New England there are six recognizable class levels. The upper class is divided into a new and old aristocracy (see Fig. 3). The so-called "old-family" level at the top provides the keystone to the status arch. Immediately beneath it are the people called the "new families," who are new to the status rather than to the community. They are the fortunate mobile people who have climbed to a level where they participate with the top group in their clubs and cliques. These lower-upper-class people recognize that they are below those born to high position with lineages of several generations. The old families hold their position by virtue of inheritance, validated by the possession of a recognized social lineage; the new families, by competition with others and by translating their material successes into acceptance by their social betters. On the average, the new families, socially inferior to the old ones, have more money, better houses, more expensive automobiles, and other material goods that are superior in dollars and cents to those of their social superiors. But if the success of the new families is due to wealth, their money is felt to be too new; if due to occupational triumph, their achievement is too recent; if the source of their new social power is educational attainment, what they have learned, while highly valued, is too newly learned and insufficient. The inherited culture of an upper class, firmly supplemented by higher education in the proper preparatory schools and superior universities and colleges, is more highly regarded.

The hard core of the upper-middle class, the level below the top two, consists of the solid citizens who are the active civic leaders of the community. They are thought of as the "joiners," for they belong to the associations which are better known to the public and are given more respectful attention by the public press. The upper-middle class feels itself to be, and in fact is, above the Level of the Common Man just beneath it. Its members are acutely aware of being socially inferior to the upper classes. To the upper-middle families that are not anxious to move up socially, this problem is not particularly distressing; but, to those that are socially mobile, the presence of an upper class sufficiently open to make it possible for some of their level to climb into it is a source of continuing frustration or anxious anticipation. Combined, the two upper levels and the upper-middle, comprising about 15–25 per cent of the people of most communities in America, are what might be called the "Level above the Common Man." The upper two classes alone rarely comprise more than 5 per cent of the total population of a city.

The lower-middle class, the top of the Common Man Level, is composed economically of small businessmen, a few highly skilled workmen, and a large number of clerks and other workers in similar categories. Members of this class tend to be extremely proper and conservative. They are joiners, belonging to patriotic organizations, fraternal orders, secret societies and auxiliaries, or other associations based on family membership. They live in the regions of the little houses, with the well-kept but cramped gardens and lawns, on the side streets rather than the better residential ones. The upper-middle class tends to live on the broad residential streets, in the better houses with the larger gardens. Upper-middle-class dwelling areas in the smaller communities are sometimes indistinguishable from those of the class above them.

The men and women of the lower-middle class tend to approach the ideal typical of the Protestant ethic, being careful with their money, saving, farsighted, forever anxious about what their neighbors think, and continually concerned about respectability.

The people in the upper-lower class are the semiskilled workers, the small tradesmen, and often the less-skilled employees of service enterprises. They, too, are highly respectable, limited in their outlook on the world around them, and are thought of as "honest workmen."

The people of the lowest level, the lower-lower class, by social reputation are not respectable or are the pitied unfortunates. Sometimes they are the new "greenhorns," the recently arrived "ethnic" peoples. These new people throughout American history, with their diverse cultural, linguistic, and religious backgrounds, have migrated here and settled. Starting at the bottom, they begin their slow ascent in our status system. They differ culturally rather than racially from the dominant group in America. Lower-lower-class people live on the river-banks, in the foggy bottoms, in the regions back of the tanneries or near the stockyards, and generally in those places that are not desired by anyone else. Their reputation is such that they are believed to lack the cardinal virtues in which Americans pride themselves. Although in standards of sexual behavior many differ from the classes above, others are different only because they are less ambitious and have

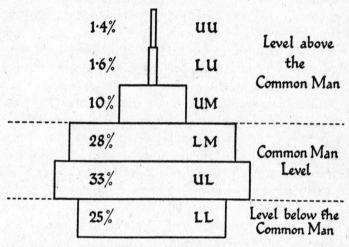

1·4%	uu	Level above
1·6%	LU	the
10%	UM	Common Man
28%	LM	Common Man
33%	UL	Level
25%	LL	Level below the Common Man

Fig. 3.—The class levels of Yankee City. The exact social-class placement of a small number (less than 1 per cent) was unknown; they are distributed somewhere from *LM* down through *LL*.

little desire to fulfil the middle-class goal of "getting ahead." Their reputation for immorality often is no more than the projected fantasy of those above them; as such they become a collective symbol of the community's unconscious!

The lower-lower level is not the largest in the community, having but 25 per cent as compared with the upper-lower, the largest class, with 33 per cent, and the lower-middle, with 28 per cent. The profile chart (Fig. 3) shows the proportions of Yankee City's people in the several classes. Other communities and cities throughout America show similar distributions. The study of Jonesville in the Middle West reveals that 3 per cent are upper class, 11 per cent upper-middle, 31 per cent lower-middle, 41 per cent upper-lower, and 14 per cent lower-lower.

A study in the state of Georgia in the Deep South gave a somewhat different distribution of the populations of the several classes. Here the two upper classes had 4.2 per cent of the total, the upper-middle 22 per cent, the lower-middle 35 per cent, the upper-lower 28 per cent, and the lower-lower 10 per cent.

Studies of Kansas City brought out the following composition of the class levels: the upper and upper-middle 9.4 per cent, the lower-middle 36.1 per cent, the upper-lower 40.0 per cent, and the lower-lower 14.5 per cent. The statistical study of metropolitan Chicago's class levels showed that 8 per cent were upper and upper-middle, that 27 per cent were lower-middle, 43 per cent upper-lower, and 20 per cent lower-lower (2 per cent, unknown).

The class differences among the communities of the several regions are significant and need comment. The newer regions of America, because of rapid social change and their comparative recency, tend not to develop a superior old-family class. This is true of many of the communities throughout the prairie states of the Middle West. An old-family group may be present in the community and feel some claim to superior recognition, but ordinarily communities in new regions look upon them as no more than the equals of the new-family group. It will take several more generations to validate their claims to a rank above the more recently arrived.

The lower-lower group is smaller in the middle-western

towns and Far West because there are fewer recently arrived ethnic peoples and the towns are too new to produce a so-called "worthless" class; furthermore, they are market centers for large agricultural areas, making it less likely that economic forces will help to produce an industrial proletariat.

The lowest white group in parts of the South is smaller and the higher classes larger than elsewhere in America because there is a large rural Negro peasant group on which much of the market economy of the town is founded.

For purposes of clarity, the lines on the chart (Fig. 3) depicting the place of each class indicate sharp divisions. Actually, each class merges into the class above and the one below it. A class system where there is movement up and down by individuals and families in an open social system where there is territorial as well as social movement necessarily makes no sharp distinctions between one class and contiguous ones. The reader should not suppose that all individuals are alike in a particular class, any more than he should assume that all men in our society who occupy the status *father* are alike either as men or as fathers. They do share common characteristics, but clearly diversity and heterogeneity must exist in a society when social change is rapid and individualism is stressed. But, in our recognition of the differences among men, we should not overlook the many similarities which permit the scientist to establish modal types. Despite the variations, the core of the status structure of America, as it has been studied in various communities throughout the United States, remains remarkably the same. Although there are regional and cultural differences, the basic arrangement of the social classes and the kinds of people in them show far greater similarities than differences.

The question arises about how we know what and how many classes are present. It must be answered by describing the research operations which identify and measure the several classes.

Methods for Observing Class Behavior

We are presently using two fundamental methods for the study of status. We call them Evaluated Participation and the Index of Status Characteristics, or I.S.C. It will be necessary to describe each method briefly.

The I.S.C. is a rating system based on four easily obtained and comparatively objective social characteristics. They are occupation, source of income, house type, and dwelling area. All families in the community are rated for each of the four characteristics. The sum of the combined scores for the four characteristics becomes an index of a family's class position. The Index of Status Characteristics as a measurement of social class is based on two propositions: (1) that economic and other prestige factors are highly important and closely related to social class; and (2) that these social and economic factors, such as talent, income, and money, if their potentialities for rank are to be realized, must be translated into social-class behavior acceptable to the members of any given social level of the community. This method is designed to provide an objective method for establishing the social level of everyone in the community and to do so by simple, inexpensive means.

The techniques of Evaluated Participation are based on observation of behavior and the use of interviews in the field studies. They are based on the propositions that the people in the social system of a community judge the participation in that community; that they similarly judge the place in the system where each individual participates;

and that they are consciously or unconsciously aware of such ratings of social class and can communicate them to an investigator. Thus, they are analytical techniques which identify the status values and rating systems used by the members of a community to class one another. What an informant says in an interview or what a group does when its members are together provides the basic evidence for this analysis. The principal technique of Evaluated Participation is called "Matched Agreement," which will be briefly described to indicate what we do when we use this method.

The technique of Matched Agreement consists of interviewing people by use of a free-association method and without prompting as to what is expected of them. This elicits their values and beliefs (among other things) about the social-class configuration of the community in which they live. Each interview of this type contains at least four kinds of information about social stratification. They are: (1) the class levels believed to exist and the informant's names for them, (2) some of the characteristics of the several levels, (3) the names of some of the people who belong to each level, and, of course, (4) some of the relations of the several social classes. The several informants' class patterns are later examined to determine the amount of correspondence for class levels recognized and to match their responses to learn how closely different kinds of informants' ratings of their townsmen correspond. If there is high correspondence among the various informants' placements of individuals and families, then it is obvious that what is being talked about is a social reality rather than an individual one, a rank order that exists in the minds of people as a social map which directs and organizes the activities and lives of the people of the town. From one matching of ten informants there were 810 agreements and only 42 disagreements; none of the latter represented a discrepancy of more than one class.

To make the class system of Jonesville, a middle-western prairie city, more real and meaningful, approaching, I hope, the meaning it has for the informants, and to show how the technique of Matched Agreement works, I will briefly quote from some of the interviews. The sets of attitudes that show how Americans consciously or unconsciously rate themselves will also be revealed. I will include the ratings from a number of informants.

For the upper class of Jonesville (it does not distinguish between old and new families), informants used the following designations or symbols and stereotypes: "the 400," "the 398's who think they're 400's," "landed gentry," "the people with family and money," "people so high up they are social history around here," "the aristocrats," "a group founded on wealth and ancient family," "people who look down on everyone else in town," "the fancy crowd," "the silk stockings," and "snobs." These same informants, in the same interviews, referred to the upper-middle class with the following symbols: "people a notch or two below the fancy crowd," "people not in the top group but good, substantial people," "people who are in everything," "above average but not tops," "the strivers who are working hard to get into the 400," and "upper-middle class."

They listed the lower-middle-class people as "the top of the common people," "people just below the country-club crowd," "nobodies but nice," "people with nice families but they don't rate socially," "good common people," "people who are more religious than intelligent," and "good plain people like most of the Baptists."

The upper-lower class were designated as "the real poor people but honest and fine," "people at the bottom of the pile," "the poor but hardworking people," "poor people with nothing the matter with them," and "the little people."

The expressions used for the upper-lower must be compared with those for the lower-lower class to see the social discriminations that are being made. Many are not easily spoken in polite discourse. I will mention only a few of them: "the poor but not respectable," "people who scrape the bottom," "river rats," "poor whites," "the chronic reliefers," "the lowest class," "the lulus," "people who live just like animals and are not worth a damn," and "all those people who live back of the tannery."

The interviews of the informants giving the rank and names of the several classes, when accompanied by lists of those who belong to each class, permit the analyst to match the class placements of the several informants to learn the amount of agreement among them.

Although social-class categories are not sharply defined and, by the very nature of social class, there can be no high wall separating one level from another, nevertheless there is in American communities a clear understanding of the social differences, values, and behavior which compose a class system. This is revealed by the use of the method of Evaluated Participation.

Another method of study, the I.S.C., rates four social characteristics, normally possessed by everyone, on a seven-point scale. Let me briefly indicate how this was first done to show how the method was validated and to indicate why this simpler method can be used for special studies without being combined with Evaluated Participation. After several hundred individuals had been placed by

Evaluated Participation, several so-called "objective" social characteristics were chosen, among which were the four that were ultimately used, and by trial-and-error a first group of families was rated. From this procedure, we learned how to rate each of the four characteristics and what weight to assign to each.

For example, occupation ranges from high professionals and proprietors of large businesses, rating a top 1, down through several other levels to unskilled workers, who rate a 7; source of income, from inherited wealth with a perfect 1, to public relief and non-respectable income; house type, from large houses in excellent condition to houses in very bad condition; dwelling area, from the superior region to the lowest slum.

We learned to give the proper weight to the four characteristics: occupation received a 4; source of income and house type, each a 3, and dwelling area, a 2. This means that if a man scored a 1 for each characteristic and each was multiplied by its proper weight, he would receive a perfect 12, placing him at the top of the upper class. On the other hand, if an individual scored an unfortunate 7 for all four, he would rank at the very bottom of the class system with an 84.

The upper class extended from 12 to 22; the lower-lower, at the other extreme, from 67 to 84. Between them the upper-middle ran from 23 to 37, the lower-middle from 38 to 53, and the upper-lower from 54 to 66.

Once we understood how to do this, the rating of any family by the I.S.C. was easy. For example, let us assign a class status to Mr. Henry Jones. He is a clerk. He gets a salary, lives in an average-sized house in average condition, in a neighborhood that is residential but is beginning to deteriorate, which people rate by saying that "it is O.K.

but it's beginning to slip." Let us rate Mr. Jones for each status characteristic, as in the accompanying tabulation.

	Rating	Weight	Score
Occupation (clerk)	3 × 4		12
Source of income (salary)	4 × 3		12
House type (average)	4 × 3		12
Dwelling area (below average)	5 × 2		10
Mr. Jones's score			46

By this method, we can predict with a high degree of certainty that Mr. Jones and his family are very likely to be lower-middle class. This prediction we base on the fact that the I.S.C. has been validated by tests showing that there is a high correlation between given ranges of the I.S.C. and the several social-class levels measured in other ways.

Properly understood, the I.S.C. is something more than a yardstick. The authors of *Social Class in America* state:

The most important fact to remember about using the I.S.C. as a measurement of social class is that, in order for it to be a reliable instrument and an accurate index of social class, each of the four characteristics and the points in their scales must reflect how Americans feel and think about the relative worth of each job, the sources of income which support them, and the evaluation of their houses and the neighborhoods in which they live. For it is not the house, or the job, or the income, or the neighborhood that is being measured so much as the evaluations that are in the backs of all of our heads—evaluations placed there by our cultural tradition and our society. From one point of view, the four characteristics—house, occupation, income, and neighborhood—are no more than evaluated symbols which are signs of status telling us the class levels of those who possess the symbols. By measuring the symbols, we measure the relative worth of each; and by adding up their several "worths," reflecting diverse and complex economic and social values, we get a score which tells us what we think and feel about the worth of a man's social participation, meaning essentially that we are measuring his Evaluated Participation or social class.

Color Caste and Social Class

The scientific term "caste" ("class," too), as employed here, is used at varying levels of abstractness of ideas. At the most general one, the cross-cultural level, societies of diverse types are compared for purposes similar to those of the zoologist comparing various bone structures, and generalizations of a very abstract nature are made. The latter scientist compares the structures of different animals for purposes of classification and broad generalization. Terms used in his classificatory scheme refer only to a few of the essential characteristics of an order, a family, or a species. Members of the Primate order of men, monkeys, and apes share a number of common anatomical characteristics which, for certain scientific purposes, make them alike among themselves and different from other animals. Despite the anxious beliefs of certain people, no biologist asserts that men are the *same* as monkeys. He merely states that they are alike and similar in certain respects and adds that they are likely to be near-relatives in the biological tree. At the common-sense level and in popular speech when we say that a Pomeranian, a St. Bernard, and a Siberian wolf are canines, we thereby say they belong to the same biological family; we are not implying that they are exactly alike but that they share common anatomical characteristics.

We must move down to lower and more detailed levels of abstraction before the systems of reference we use denote different kinds of monkeys and different kinds of men. We need to go to still less abstract and less general levels and still more specific and detailed ones if we are to refer to a particular monkey or man. The same, of course, is true for the comparative study of any kind of social institution or system of ranking.

Caste belongs to an order of human relations which places people in superordinate and subordinate relations. Social class systems and other forms of ranking belong to this same order. But in many respects the several kinds of rank differ. The caste societies of the world, including those of India, Africa, and contemporary America, share certain characteristics, notably the fixing of the permanent rank of an individual and a family and the regulation of marriage within each level. Indian, African, and American castes vary in many respects, and it should be added that in India itself there is a large variety of caste systems and there is no one variety throughout that country. Simpler, less generalized, and less abstract concepts are needed to denote what it is they are and are not. In America the uniformities are greater, but anyone who knows the "color situation" in Charleston, New Orleans, rural Mississippi, and Chicago knows there is diversity. Yet the diversity is within a common mode of conduct. "Caste" (or "class") is a term that can be used at all these levels of similarity, from the broad comparative and cross-cultural level to the detailed study whose description points out some of the "unique" characteristics of a particular group.

On first examination, color caste appears to be the same as, or very similar to, social class. The values of the members of the society rank people in superior and inferior statuses; the symbols of status which are given positive or negative values are also unequally distributed, and all individuals are born to and inherit the status of their parents; the family in color caste establishes an individual's rank at birth. These are the attributes of color caste and social class that have persuaded some writers to view them as the same phenomena. The characteristics listed are important but insufficient to prove that caste and class in America are the same thing; there are others of crucial importance which make the two systems quite different. Moreover, these additional factors have a powerful effect on the lives of individuals who are controlled by them and on the society where they are found.

Whereas marriage above or below the social level of an individual is possible and within the spirit of a class system, such a union is impossible and violates the spirit of color caste. In many states in America the laws are explicit on intermarriage, and, in all of them, custom, social usage, and sanction make marriage between two people defined as Negro and white exceedingly difficult, painful for those involved, and, more often than not, impossible. Caste endogamy in America, consisting of rules, strong feelings, values, and sanctions permitting marriage only *within* the caste, is more strict, severe, and controlling than in many parts of India. There are very few legally sanctioned marriages between American Negroes and whites; where they, or common-law marriages, or casual unions result in offspring, the children are placed in the socially deprived lower caste. This supplies a powerful sanction to hold the socially responsible to marriages that are endogamous.

Color caste, an example of status in which the position of the individual is fixed, when combined with social class, where movement and freedom of the individual are stressed, creates a most extraordinary structural and status configuration. Color caste declares that people bearing the stigmata of color and certain other physical characteristics that have become status symbols can have only one status throughout their lives and must not change it. Social class and the precepts of American democracy insist that each man be rewarded according to his worth and be advanced according to the moral and technical rules of social mobility. It would be supposed by the logical that, because the rules of the two systems are contradictory, the two systems could not exist together in the same society; but those who are logical reckon on rationality and individual logic. The more permissive social logics used by all human groups act as principles which allow for contradiction and adjust social behavior so as to avoid open conflict. Meanwhile, the conflict expresses itself in a variety of customs and very often in social change which may establish a trend toward the elimination of one of the conflicting systems.

Rationality and logic, if applied arbitrarily, could easily force the issue and result in conflict and possible bloodshed. Throughout America, accommodations have been made, so that class and caste systems are intricately interconnected and mutually influence each other as parts of the larger American social structure. Furthermore, social change has also been related to this interconnection of the two rank orders. I wish to examine the relations of the three variables: color caste, social class, and the emergent society.

Our attention was brought to this complex problem in the state of Mississippi in the Deep South, where in some respects certain Negroes outranked many whites or, to state the obverse, certain whites were, for given purposes, inferior to many Negroes, despite the fact that color caste operates strongly and is backed by very severe sanctions. Further inspection and analysis of this problem led us to the conclusion that, while all Negroes are considered socially inferior and are categorically subordinate to all whites in color caste, many of them are superior and superordinate by social-class position to many, if not most, whites. To be more specific, a small but rapidly increasing percentage of Negroes who are upper and upper-middle class have a superior position in class status to well over 50 per cent of the white people who belong to the lower-middle and lower classes of the various communities of the South. Because social class in America tends to operate by oblique and indirect reference, it has not been difficult for such Negroes to occupy positions of class superiority, despite the fact that the category of color caste clearly subordinates them in their social relations with whites.

Perhaps the many variables and the relations involved in this pattern of contradiction can most effectively be studied by examining Figure 4. It will be noted that the heavy double line running diagonally across the rectangle from near the top on one side to near the bottom on the other separates the upper white caste from the subordinate Negro one. (Perhaps some have seen an adaptation of this chart borrowed from us by Gunnar Myrdal in his study, *The American Dilemma*.)

The horizontal broken lines represent the separate class systems within the two castes; the double-headed arrow indicates that upward and downward mobility takes place within each color caste, but not between them. The Negro who acquires the highest education and the impeccable name of a southern gentleman, follows the highest of professions, and becomes a wealthy man—all characteristics

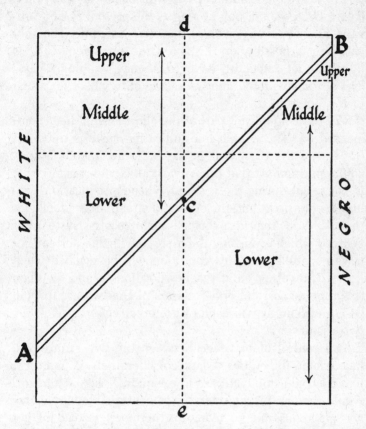

FIG. 4.—Relation between the caste system and the class system in the Deep South. This diagram is not intended to portray the exact numbers of people in each group. Rather, it indicates relative positions in vertical social space and permits a quick analysis of superordinate and subordinate relationships between the strata of the society.

which would lift a lower-class white man to one of the levels Above the Common Man—will rise to the top of the Negro class system; but, as long as the present system prevails, he will never rise above his own caste line. The only way he can possibly do this is to beat the system. If he is light and not detectably a Negro, he may be able to "pass" and become white in another community where his social past is not known.

The most significant part of the chart has not been commented on. The double line indicating caste is tilted. At the end of the Civil War it was in approximately a horizontal position. At that time almost all Negroes were equal in class. But during the years, by virtue of education, economic enterprise, and the class and equalitarian ideologies that pervade American society, a Negro class system has evolved which is pushing the caste line farther and farther toward parallelism. This condition will be reached when line *AB*, pivoting on *c*, reaches positions *d* and *e*. When this time comes, the upper classes of the two groups will be equivalent, as will each of the other class levels in the two castes.

The control of marriage between the two groups will face major difficulties. Class considerations in marriage may become dominant. A lower-middle-class white girl would then find it considerably to her advantage to marry an upper-class Negro man. Furthermore, instead of her children being in an inferior caste, they would be at the top of the class system. Once the caste rules on marriage no longer control sex relations between the two groups, the whole system is likely to change rapidly.

Since it is impossible to study the social life of all Americans, we selected a community that greatly contrasted with Mississippi to learn about the variations of color caste and social class and the trends and direction of social change. We picked Chicago in the urban North. Before comparing the differences in color caste, a brief review of the social differences between the two communities will be presented.

Color Caste in the Urban North and Rural South

Chicago has changed rapidly; Mississippi, slowly. Chicago is an industrial metropolis; Natchez, the community we studied in Mississippi, is a small market town for an agricultural area. Mississippi has few immigrants and has found it unnecessary to accommodate its social system constantly to intruding peoples. Chicago, on the other hand, has been constantly faced with the problem of modifying itself to adjust to a great variety of ethnic cultures and a large number of people who have come from all parts of the world. In the North the rules and sanctions of color caste are less well developed than in the South, and in the great cities such rules are likely to be even more lax than they are in the smaller communities and rural areas.

Finally, it should be pointed out that in Chicago, a great metropolis, the Negro population has had an opportunity to develop many institutions favorable to the increase of their status, institutions which would not have the opportunity to grow in a rural region or, for that matter, in most parts of the South. In other words, Natchez and Chicago represent the polar extremes and crucial cases for studying some of the directions of social change and for testing whether color caste as a *type* of superordination and subordination exists all over America or whether the claims of many northerners are true—that the position of the Negro is sufficiently different there to say that the relations of Negroes and whites in this region cannot be classified under the same category of race relations as those in the South.

Some of the most significant characteristics of color caste in the Deep South and in the urban North will be analyzed and compared. We have said earlier that the family and the rules of marriage and descent are at the very core of the maintenance of color caste. In the Deep South, interracial marriage is legally impossible, and there is an increasingly smaller number of common-law marriages between white men and Negro women. In Chicago, marriage is legally possible but socially disapproved; there are strong informal sanctions applied to those people who are willing to oppose the informal rules of society. A large number of such marriages were systematically studied; more often than not they were between colored men and white women, and an outstanding number of them were unhappy because of the social pressures applied to those who had entered them.

We also examined the question of sexual relations outside marriage between Negroes and whites. In the Deep South the relations between Negro men and white women are highly disapproved of; violent sanctions are applied to the point that in some cases the Negro man might be killed and the white woman forced to leave the community. Such relations are exceedingly infrequent. In most Chicago social groups they are disapproved and those involved ostracized. Although generally infrequent, they do exist and are more frequent than in the South. There are indications that interracial sexual relations in Chicago are becoming more frequent as time passes. The relations of white men and Negro women outside marriage are disapproved of in the South. Although they do occur, they are less frequent than formerly. Today the so-called "patriarchal family"—

a name used to refer to a family where a white man is the admitted father of Negro children and acts in his father role—is rare in the Deep South.

One of the most crucial questions concerns descent. The descent of children of mixed matings, both in the North and in the South, is the same, for they are always defined as Negroes if their parentage is known by the community. However, in larger urban centers where the Negro parent is light, it is quite possible for the children of a mixed marriage to pass as white at least for part of their social activity. It is not an uncommon occurrence in Chicago for many light Negroes to pass as white on a job but live their more intimate lives as Negroes. This would be an exceedingly difficult undertaking in most parts of the South.

In southern communities the only associations in which both Negroes and whites may be members are those very unusual ones that have to do with reform, where left-wing southerners join associations that include Negroes for the purpose of trying to change the caste order. In Chicago, Negroes are often excluded from associations that organize professional men and women, although there is an increasing tendency for certain liberal groups of professional men, such as some of the lawyers, to include Negroes in their membership. The characteristically American lodges and secret societies in Chicago and elsewhere in the North very rarely, if ever, include Negroes. This is also true of most social clubs, particularly and obviously those that have to do with helping to maintain the status of the white elite.

Because of recent Supreme Court decisions, the number of Negroes voting in the South is rapidly increasing, but in Mississippi and in many states of the South voting is very different for the Negro. In some communities it is not permitted except for a very few who are often considered by the other Negroes to be "Uncle Toms," overly compliant and obsequious to the white man's will. In the urban North, the vote of the Negro is sought and encouraged. It has become an increasing force in the politics of the large cities. A case might be made for the proposition that the vote of the Negro in the urban centers of the region north of the Mason-Dixon Line largely determined the outcome of the presidential election in 1948, and contributed significantly to the outcome in 1960.

Office-holding of any kind in most of the South is not permitted to Negroes. In the urban North, Negroes have been appointed to high and low levels, but not in proportion to their place in the population. A number of Negroes now hold quite prominent positions in the federal government primarily because of the voting strength of their group in the big cities. Most of these people have been appointed. In such cities as New York, Negroes have been elected to high and low positions, but only a very few have been elected to high political place. Furthermore, most of those who are elected come from Negro election districts. There seems to be a tendency at the present time for this system of discrimination to break down. Negroes are now running in the districts that are composed of Negroes and whites and receiving substantial voting support from white voters.

Several powerful leaders of political machines that organize the larger Negro vote, now concentrated in the corporate limits of huge northern metropolitan aggregates, are highly influential in municipal, state, and national politics. Since these great cities are located in states with large electoral votes such as New York, Michigan, Illinois, and California, these Negro leaders and their voters are courted and exercise great influence at all levels of the American government.

To compare the caste relations of two regions, it is also necessary to examine the educational institutions. In the Deep South, segregation of the children and the teachers into separate schools is "legal," despite federal juridical and military intervention. The children there are ordinarily separated from one another. In the North, despite the fact that there are few laws against segregation, informal segregation is often present. There is a kind of informal arrangement in many cities by which Negroes tend to be placed in schools that are thought of as Negro schools and whites in schools that are considered to be white schools. However, there is increasing mixing, and in those regions where the Negro population is small, Negroes attend white schools as a matter of course.

One of the most crucial tests of caste subordination is the length of time children of the two races stay in school. In much of the South, the period for Negroes tends to be very short; many rural Negroes are almost illiterate because the system operates in such a way that Negro parents, usually because of lack of motivation and opportunity, do not keep their children in school. In Chicago, the period in school for Negroes compares favorably with whites of the same socioeconomic and social-class level.

The term "Jim Crow" is a vivid expression for the prevalence of strict rules about the spatial separation of the two groups in communities throughout the South and in many parts of the North. Despite the comparative rigidity of the system in the South, there are certain contradictions that do not fit the common pattern. There is less segregation of dwelling areas in Natchez, Mississippi, for example, than there is in Chicago. In Chicago, despite Supreme

Court rulings and the consequent movement of Negroes into the larger community, the Black Belt still is a definite part of the city and is clearly discernible. As a matter of fact, despite the improvement and greater flexibility of race relations now as compared with previous periods in Chicago, there is more segregation in dwelling areas than two generations ago, probably because of the great influx of rural Negroes that has been occurring since the First World War. In public recreational areas there is little or no mixing through most of the South; in the urban centers of the North there is some mixing, but most white people disapprove of it.

From this analysis it can be seen that, when one compares these two extremes, the position of the Negro in Chicago is more agreeable and more like that of a white than it is in the Deep South; but color lines still exist, and the relation is still one of superordination and subordination, despite the many changes that are now occurring. In type, the Negro-white relations in Chicago still conform to the color-caste pattern.

Throughout the United States, at the present time, wherever there are large populations of Negroes there is developing a prosperous and increasingly powerful upper-middle class which is beginning to function for the Negro group in a manner similar to the way this same social class has operated in white society. These people tend to be civic leaders, to take strong moral positions, to have influence and power, and to support civic institutions such as the school and the church which bring self-respect and credit to the whole Negro group. They also tend to be the source from which many improvements of Negro life are being introduced into the whole Negro group. This same group is increasingly drawing closer to the upper-middle-class people of the white group, not so much from ethical motives as because of similar interests and political and economic forces. In my opinion, one of the most important developments in race relations in the last generation has been the appearance of an upper-middle-class Negro group. If American society continues to develop in its present form, it seems likely that the leadership of the upper-middle-class Negro will be a potent force in gaining for the Negro all the rights and privileges that are enjoyed by the presently dominant white group.

Fixed status for the individual and color caste in the society are not likely to continue in America. There are many indications that color caste is yielding rapidly to the stronger influence of class mobility and that many Americans socially classed as Negroes are gaining many of the rewards for their efforts and their accomplishments enjoyed by those classed as whites. Throughout the South, there is strong evidence that many changes are occurring which are perceptibly modifying the caste line. With these changes, color caste approaches more and more what has been called parallelism.

Whether the changes will continue, of course, is an open question. It is possible that too strong pressure from the liberal urban North on the rural conservative South may ultimately react on southern liberals in such a way that the latter can no longer act as initiators of social change in an equalitarian direction. There is also the danger that southern as well as northern white people, with the reforms they have accomplished, may become too complacent and not continue to push for betterment in race relations until Negroes and whites share not only equal economic opportunity but equal social opportunity. It is possible that some new development will slow down present progress, now more rapid than at any time since the Emancipation Proclamation. But the realities of the present bi-racial situation indicate a continuing change in the race relations of America toward equalitarianism and democracy. Perhaps it would be better to say they indicate a new democracy which permits everyone to be judged on the basis of his mobility achievements and his social class rather than on the fixed status of caste and social inheritance. Fixed status violates all the basic values of social class and contradicts the most elementary conceptions that Americans have about what they are as a democratic people and what they believe is right and wrong. The processes of change now going on are reacting to this basic contradiction and moving away from fixed status toward that of changing or free status. Above all, the symbol "Negro" means something quite different today from what it did only yesterday, and by yesterday is meant no earlier than the period of the First World War.

The caste stereotype of all Negroes as lazy, ignorant, incapable of learning, and morally low is being supplanted by new ones which recognize them as having the same diverse intellectual and moral virtues and vices as white men. These new class concepts are being used increasingly by whites when they think about Negroes. Such conceptions make it difficult to reinforce the system of prejudice which has previously been successful in allowing white men to feel moral in their subordination of Negroes simply because Negroes were believed to be inherently low.

The Negro is rapidly moving into the main current of American life. The changes which America has been undergoing apply more and more directly to the Negro than they have ever before in his history. His struggle for equal recognition and for equal opportunity is increasingly a part of the fortunes and misfortunes of all other Americans; what happens to the routes of social mobility in the American class system is beginning to affect the Negro much as it does the whites. Furthermore, his future and the future of all America, black and white, will be integrally and primarily involved with the fortunes of all mankind. All men everywhere must be brothers, either in the deadly sibling rivalry and bloodshed of Cain and Abel or in a comradeship of mutual aid and mutual respect. Color customs in America (and elsewhere) inevitably will yield to the larger realities of today and tomorrow.

The tradition of an old and well-integrated social system such as color caste, even when part of the larger emergent American society, dies slowly and often with conflict. Their values lie deeply in the collective unconscious and their significances are firmly and toughly in the power structure controlled by the dominant group. But the increasingly rapid development of the Negro middle classes, particularly the upper-middle, the rapid spread of Negroes throughout the northern metropolises, and the changing symbolic significance of Negroes to themselves and others are rapidly bringing a new kind of social world into being. The last and most powerful barrier of color caste, mixed marriage, holds firm and seemingly remains unassailable, yet the highly publicized mixed marriages of notables, celebrities, and occasionally upper-status people are not now condemned in the public press.

The meanings of such marriages and the public response may be symbolically predictive of the collective mass facts of tomorrow. The demands of an emergent society for an ever increasing fluidity of movement and flexibility to utilize its personnel will necessarily destroy fixed status in our economic and social systems. Whether or not this movement will extend to full acceptance of "racial" intermarriage is not presently predictable.

4

THE FAMILY IN A CLASS SYSTEM

The Families of Orientation and Procreation

The lives of all human beings are deeply imbedded in the structure of their own families. What each man is to himself and to other men is, in large part, an expression of his past and present experiences within its creative and controlling matrix. Born into his family of orientation a weak and unprotected animal, he is transformed by its influences into a thinking being, a moral agent capable of knowing and distinguishing right from wrong. Within our society, at least, he achieves a high degree of antonomy, and, as an emergent person, he acquires the moral and intellectual ability to make his own decisions.

When he marries and has children, he establishes his family of procreation. In this family he assumes a status which transmits the social behavior he has learned to those he helps to procreate. Out of the nuclear structure of these two families the larger kinship structure is formed, and, on it, much of the larger society is founded. Within it most of the animal behavior of the species is confined and the life continuity of human beings maintained.

The family of birth, of social orientation, takes charge of all the little human animals, with the basic demands of their species and all the needs of growing organisms, and, by following the precepts and principles laid down by the society, directs their learning until they have established their own inner controls sufficiently to permit them to live with other members of their society. Since each individual, through birth into a family, is given his first social-class placement by virtue of his family's position, the way he learns what his society is, what he is, and what he has to do to become a functioning member of the society is largely class-controlled. His social class, through his family, gets the first opportunity to teach him and thereby establishes most of the basic structure of his personality.

Since the core of the family structure is largely the same in all classes, what each person learns through his early experience in a family is basically similar. Nevertheless, the social-class bias of each family has full opportunity to exert its influence on the child. The weak ego of the young child feels, and yields to, the press of social reality and becomes a person in a social-class environment. Furthermore, the moral principles embodied in the parental models inevitably are class-structured so that the child learns in a class-defined system what the real social world is, at the same time that he learns what he is as a moral being. To say it in Freudian terms, he acquires a superego that he internalizes through his experiences with his class-defined parents.

For anyone to know himself and understand what he is as a person—unique, yet very much like everyone else; autonomous, yet a product of, and strongly controlled by, his society—he must seek within his family for most of the more important answers. To know himself, he must know his family. To achieve scientific understanding of what he is, not only must he know the family life of his own society, but, in American society, he must know the differences among the families of the several classes and understand how they function.

Generally, the family performs three kinds of necessary functions for man, and, in so doing, influences all levels of his existence. It organizes and controls the species behavior having to do with procreation and the care and protection of the young at the biological level. On the social level it trains the young in the use of symbols, skills, and rules and teaches them to evaluate what they and others think and do with the basic values and beliefs of the society. At the psychological level it helps evoke a way of life within each individual organism which is a private world of emotions, beliefs, and conscience that is unique and different from all other personalities. These processes, once begun in the early life of all individuals, do not stop but continue to exercise control over all individuals throughout their lives.

All people everywhere must solve certain fundamental problems in training the newborn child to allow it to take its place in the larger group and in the various subgroups which exist in the society. But the methods used in solving these problems vary greatly by society and, within stratified societies such as America, by class. The basic problems connected with weaning and food habits, toilet and sex training, independence training, and the control of aggression are largely solved by the family for the individual. The general standards of child training throughout the American social structure are similar, because all Americans belong to the same society, but the methods vary according to social class. The early training experiences of the child during the first five years and the subsequent training during the following ten years are decisive in forming his personality and his pattern of social participation which will determine the place he takes in society.

As Dr. Allison Davis and Professor Robert Havighurst say:

To students of learning, and especially to those who wish to study the processes of socialization, a detailed understanding of American social class cultures and motivational patterns is now an absolute necessity of both research and therapy; for the social class of the child's family determines not only the neighborhood in which he lives and the play groups which he will have but also the basic cultural acts and gratifications towards which he will be trained.

The social-class system maintains cultural, economic, and social barriers which prevent intimate social intermixture between the slums, the upper class, and the middle class. We know that human beings can learn their culture only from other human beings who already know and exhibit that culture. Therefore, by setting up barriers to social participation, the American social-class system often prevents the vast majority of children of the working class or the slums from learning any way of life except that of their own group. Thus the pivotal meaning of social class to students of human development is that it defines and systematizes different learning environments for children of different classes.

In the numerous studies that have been made on child development and social class since the Yankee City studies on social class in America, the interaction between parents and children has been given particular attention; decided differences have been reliably demonstrated in the relations of parents and children in the several classes and, of course, in many cases great differences in adult personality structures have appeared. The research methods and techniques which combine social and psychological procedures are well described in the original monographs which served as sources for this chapter.

The Child in the Class Structure

In the lower class, it has been found that the mother is physically closer to her baby. Her breasts are sources of food and emotional satisfactions to the child more frequently and for a longer period than in the other classes. Weaning is delayed, as compared with the middle class, and the process of weaning is far less abrupt than in the upper-middle class. Bowel and bladder control also is delayed, and the attitude about this matter is that it is a normal physical function rather than unclean or filthy (the latter being an emotional attitude very common among the God-fearing, puritanically clean, middle-class mothers).

The year-old lower-class child is more dependent upon his mother than the child of other classes. His relations to his outside world, mediated through the mother, are likely to be more passive because his demands tend to be immediately satisfied. His demands and his impressions are less inhibited and more easily and freely expressed. He enjoys greater freedom from adult constraint and generally lives in an environment which permits him to do more and in which his bodily satisfactions, at least at this time, are far greater than those experienced by the middle-class child. Furthermore, he is not inhibited in experimental genital play and his sexual and genital knowledge is greater.

Children learn the intimate details of sexual relations at an early age; often, too, they know of sexual affairs of their brothers and sisters, of extra-marital relations of their parents, and see illegitimate children brought into their family. Their attitude toward these experiences is usually adapted to their environment; sex is a normal and natural part of their lives.

A study of white and Negro lower- and middle-class mothers and children in Chicago reported the following class differences in child rearing:

1. That more lower-class than middle-class babies are breast-fed only.
2. That more lower-class babies are fed at will.
3. That more lower-class babies have the breast or bottle longer than twelve months.
4. That lower-class children are weaned later.
5. That bowel training is begun earlier (on the average) with middle-class children.
6. That bladder training of middle-class children (on the average) is begun earlier.
7. That middle-class children are expected to help at home earlier.
8. That middle-class children are expected to assume responsibility earlier.
9. That lower-class children stay up later, stay in the streets later, and go to the movies more often—in other words, have fewer restrictions placed upon them in time and space.

Despite greater permissiveness in infant and child training now expressed by upper-middle-class parents, the culture of the lower levels is much less demanding and requires less mental and moral discipline.

In general, one can say that the environment in which lower-class children receive their training gives them more gratification and easier outlet for their organically based drives. The discipline of their culture controlling their eating, eliminating, and the exploration of their immediate environment is far more lenient and much more gradual than that found in the restrictive world in which the middle-class child develops.

Careful research demonstrates that the personality of the middle-class individual during its development is greatly influenced by the strong middle-class taboos on freer sex expression and on permitting more direct outlets for aggression. The middle-class child learns from earliest childhood that physical aggression must be controlled or he will suffer social ostracism and physical punishment. He also learns that any overt sexual expression is felt to be improper and indecent. As a consequence of this, the chief problem areas of the middle-class personality tend to be focused around aggression and sex. They ordinarily are highly masked, and it is very difficult even for the psychoanalyst, by his refined techniques, to relate the feelings of frustration in these areas to the core of demand for their expression.

Quite the opposite is true for the lower-class child. Living as he does in a world of anxiety about the immediate provisions for his basic needs of food, clothing, and shelter, he learns to seek immediate gratification in whatever he does. He is closer to his mother than is the middle-class child, partly because of the fact that she is less "adult" (and more "childlike") in age, less autonomous, and, in general, more subordinated than the middle-class mother. Whereas the middle-class child is expected to assume responsibility for himself and take responsibility for his judgments at an early age and is thereby prepared for the goal of moral autonomy and self-reliance, the lower-class child continues in physical and social dependence on his mother.

In the lower class, both children and adolescents are permitted more gratification for their sexual and emotional responses. Rage is freely expressed, and fights are seen between children and their fathers and between husband and wife. Children are taught to fight with their fists or with knives and to hit first. Lower-class behavior, which may be regarded as delinquent or shiftless and unmotivated by other groups, is usually realistic and responsive to the cultural situation. Their anxieties and taboos are different from those of higher groups. Disapproval and ridicule are greatly feared, and rejection by the family or the group can arouse terror.

Anxieties in this group are based more often on physical than social causes. Hunger and cold and lack of adequate clothing are always present or just around the corner. When there is plenty of food and fuel, these people overeat and keep their houses too warm.

When the middle class judges the lower class and its apparent lack of responsibility and social conformity, it expresses ignorance of the motivations and goals of this class. A family cannot learn to save and budget when there is no prospect of regular income which would give the relative security which must underlie these habits. The cultural goals in the slums mean subsistence.

Restraint, foresight, and moderation are characteristic of the goals and performance of the middle class. Sexual responses and physical aggression must be inhibited or controlled. Where the lower-class adolescent boy is expressing his aggression through fist fights, the middle-class boy is expressing his through initiative, ambition, verbal dexterity, and learned economic skills. Meanwhile, he is learning to fear early sexual relations. Anxiety and guilt about physical aggression and sexual intercourse on the part of the adolescent of the middle class are strong proof of his adjustment to his class culture.

The upper- and middle-class children are expected to do well in school, to be intelligent, and to make friends among children acceptable to their parents. They are trained to appreciate their own status and to evaluate it in relation to others. Upward mobility in the middle class is always encouraged and strongly rewarded, not only in the training of the child by the parent and his schoolteachers, but in the later rewarding experiences he has when he strives for success as a mature person in an adult world.

Children of the middle and upper classes are raised with their eyes on a goal of achievement for which they must, if necessary, make present sacrifices. They are expected to go to college and to strive for high occupational status. Restraint is put on present activities for the sake of future gain.

Upper-class child training varies from middle-class in that there is an increasing emphasis placed on taste, manners, and good form, on the proper way to do things; although the child is trained to be superior, little emphasis is placed on the crass facts of lifting one's self by one's bootstraps to a higher place in the status system of the society. The middle-class child constantly faces the conflicting forces within the Protestant ethic of obeying the moral rules and precepts of brotherhood characteristic of Christianity and, at the same time, adjusting himself to the forces of social mobility that drive him to do everything possible to compete successfully against these same brothers. (Perhaps it is not too much to say that sibling rivalry, so well studied and publicized in the field of brother and sister relations in the family, is found to be most acute in the great arena of the social world of all middle-class adults.) Other conflicting factors bother the upper-class child. He is concerned about embodying within himself the spiritual values of his own level. Much of this is symbolized in his concern never to do anything that would bring disrepute to the family name. Questions of honor, etiquette, and discretion are far more emphasized in the lives of the people of this class than they are in the middle-class groups.

The very fact that the status placement of members of the upper-upper class is based essentially on "old-family" membership indicates that, while individualism is important, it cannot be carried to an extreme and that the family relations cannot be easily severed from the life of any individual. The mobile middle-class person very often must be able to sever all emotional, and sometimes all social, ties from the family into which he was born if he is to succeed in consolidating his social achievements in a higher class. This emphasis on separateness is exactly reversed in the upper-upper class.

There is considerable evidence, but none of it systematically organized as yet, to show that the daughters of "old families" tend to cling more closely to their parents, particularly their fathers, and that the sons of these same families are socially more closely related to them than are those in the middle class. From fragmentary evidence, not yet properly tested by psychological and social research, it seems possible that the upper-class man may gain psychological independence from his mother because, in this particular class, emphasis is placed on early masculine training and separation from females. It is also possible, however, that the very emphasis upon early definition of masculinity and the separation of the two sexes to the social advantage of the male may operate in exactly the opposite way and produce greater psychological dependence of the male upon his mother. Further study is needed on this problem.

Sexuality and Class Training

So far we have dealt with research evidence from children and adolescents; we have not given attention to what we know about the sexuality of adults in the several classes. In beginning a discussion of this subject we need no more than remind ourselves that the pattern of sexual behavior of the adult is begun in early childhood through family training and social-class conditioning. The lower-class individual, reared in a permissive environment which allows him freer genital play and freer adolescent sexual activities, ordinarily accepts sex as a normal and pleasurable satisfaction. He gives much less thought about whether it occurs before, in, or outside of a marriage relationship.

The middle class injects a moral issue into sexual activity from the time the infant seeks satisfaction in genital play. For this class, morality and sexual morality are very often synonymous.

Although there is a wide divergence of standards of sexual behavior acceptable to the lower and middle and upper classes, the standards within each class appear to follow a set code. The middle class looks upon lower-class sex behavior as unmoral and "just like animals." These middle-class people do not realize that this behavior is as rigidly standardized as their own. If they did, many of the golden fantasies of middle-class people about not giving a damn and living as they please, "the way those people do down in the shanties," would have to find another locale. Fortunately for the self-respect and ego satisfaction of the middle class, there is little communication between the two levels on such subjects. For the middle class would probably be shocked to see that people of the lower class consider much of middle-class sexual behavior and many of their attitudes as "dirty" and "unnatural."

In an intensive study of a lower-class slum of an American city on the eastern seaboard, Professor William Whyte of Cornell University reports that these people have an elaborate and highly developed sex code. Sex play among young boys was comparatively unregulated, but a code of sex behavior began to crystallize as these children approached maturity. Relations between the adolescent boy and girl varied according to the girl's known sexual experience and "accessibility."

Elaborate precautions were taken by the boy against becoming too attached to a "one-man girl" for fear he would become too involved emotionally and marry her at too early an age. The most desirable girl for non-marital sexual relations for these young men, who were born American, but largely of Italian extraction, were girls of old-American stock, blonde, with fair skin, and of a higher social status than the slum boy. The possession of such a girl was always the subject about which the young man could brag before an interested and willing audience. The most desirable girl for a wife, on the other hand, was a virgin of Italian extraction but born American and with some family connections with relatives or friends of the boy.

The sexual code of these boys also comprises categories of social relations within which it is proper or improper to have sexual contact. Females of certain specified familial ties, blood relations, and certain relatives by marriage and relatives of friends are tabooed, and all others accessible. Since it is important to the boy's prestige to be able to boast of his sexual conquest, little happens in the community that is not known unless the girl goes outside the local area. All the boys know with whom she has had relations and how often. After marriage, the wife is expected to be completely faithful, but the husband may indulge in extra-marital ventures as long as he is a good provider, affectionate with his family, and does not make his extra-marital life an open scandal. The wife may protest, but the husband continues to look upon the feminine world just as he did before marriage.

A mother tries to keep her daughter a virgin because this is highly prized in a prospective wife, but a lower-class girl —like the lower-class boy—is trained by her clique and age mates to be openly aggressive in her behavior, and this includes sex behavior. The girls who are distrusted are the ones who are "feminine," meaning passive and non-aggressive, and have soft ways. They are suspected of being troublemakers, men-stealers, and home-breakers. Aggression, contrariwise, is regarded as open and honest.

Our studies of the influence of social class on the maturing individual help confirm the results of the study done by Dr. Alfred Kinsey and his associates on the sexuality of American males. In the earlier phases of his research, Kinsey gave little attention to the social groups of the individuals he studied. He told us that he finally came to the conclusion that it was necessary to use some method of placing his subjects by status because it had become clear to him and to his research group that it was necessary to have at least an approximate knowledge of the status level of the individuals if they were to obtain meaningful results about the factors involved in their subjects' sexual behavior.

Kinsey used educational and occupational criteria to make status distinctions among his subjects. While education and occupation correlate highly with social class, they do not give the fine distinctions provided by a combination of criteria. I am quite sure that, if Kinsey's sample were grouped according to the necessary class criteria, even greater differences in sexual behavior would appear among his various levels. Nevertheless, the criteria used clearly indicate the class levels of the individuals studied.

Dr. Kinsey and his associates show that the sexual behavior of males at lower educational and occupational levels has a consistent pattern of frequent, simple, heterosexual contact. The college group, with the great importance it places on virginity, shows the greatest incidence of eroticism of various sorts in its sexual contact and the highest incidence of petting, including a number of techniques which are tabooed by the lower level and looked upon as perversions. There is a definite limitation upon the heterosexual contacts of this group and a higher frequency of solitary behavior.

Sexual maladjustments of these superior educational levels were found in about three-fourths of the marriages that ended in separation and divorce. Failure of the male in sexual skill and failure of the female to show deep emotion in sexual relations were strong factors.

Despite the fact that the Kinsey results have been criticized, primarily because of the sampling methods used, the general picture they present of the sexuality of America and of its relation to the American status order conforms very closely to the more intensive studies that our own group has made. Our interests, however, were not so much in the problem of sexuality as in the differences of moral principles found among the social classes and the way these differences were transferred by the older to the younger generation of each class.

The Upper-Class Family

In contrast to the caste system which prohibits movement across the caste line, the American social-class system allows mobility up and down the social hierarchy. American society positively sanctions the bettering of one's social position by "marrying up" and frowns on anyone who "marries beneath himself." Ordinarily, because of the emphasis on the name and lineage of the father, the position of the male spouse tends to be the socially dominant one. There are, however, exceptions, when the family of the female may be sufficiently strong and sufficiently imbedded in the upper-status levels of the society to make it possible for a male marrying her to enjoy a position similar to hers. More often than not, however, such marriages are likely to end in divorce or continue in difficulty.

In those communities of the United States, particularly the older regions, where there is a strongly developed upper-upper class, the families maintain the greatest social distance from the other classes. Their official ideology is always heavily democratic and equalitarian, but their behavior and their values tend to separate them out as being superior to, and different from, the classes below them. This social distance is achieved in such ways as the use of geographic distance and institutions partly based upon spatial factors. Among them are private schools, spacious grounds, large houses, and the use of private rather than public conveyances. A family often is considered to be in the top level of the upper-class group only if it has participated in this upper-class behavior for several generations. The members of the lower-upper group, having moved up socially very often through money and its "correct" use in imitation of upper-class behavior, achieve final acceptance as solid members of the top level only through the passage of time, often three or more generations.

Another factor in the expression of social distance of the upper-upper class is the identification of the relations of families within the group. Kinship terms (such as "Uncle," "Cousin," etc.) are often used in referring to members of other families within this social position. They are used as a kind of expression of the extension of the family to indicate the strong mark of common identity of the group, even where there is no immediate or extended kinship relationship.

The upper-upper class is highly endogamous—most of its members marry within the group—so that the use of these terms of kinship is more often realistic than symbolic. So strong is the system of endogamy within this group that, when many of the young men leave the smaller cities to go to the larger metropolises in pursuing their careers, the young females who remain in the community very often do not marry at all.

Members of the lower-upper class are usually lacking in the upper-upper characteristic of extended kinship identifications. Many of these people come to a community as married couples with children. The older generation as well as brothers and sisters are left in the home town. Those who have arrived in this social class from within the community are segregated not geographically but by lack of "correct" kinship connections. They often feel and express a sense of isolation and lack of identification with the old-family group.

This lack of extended kinship ties, especially when the authority of the superordinate generation is not present to back up the claim for status, is one of the factors contributing to the instability sometimes found within the families of the lower-upper group. Another powerful factor is the disruptive effect of the repudiation of the standards which were taught in youth and the substitution of the standards of the class into which the family has moved. Social modes and acceptable behavior, learned in the earlier period through the gradual processes of child training of the people who are born to the position, have to be acquired swiftly and self-consciously by the mobile lower-upper people from a group which is resistant to the newly arrived family and very often hostile to it.

Unless the mobile individuals have acquired the ability to change their behavior and to adapt easily to each new situation, very often serious personality difficulties appear. Feelings of uneasiness and lack of personal worth, sometimes coupled with deep hostility, may develop. The adopted behavior, which in the upper class is highly ritualized and gradually learned, frequently remains strange and external to the mobile family. The hostile class environment in which they have to learn the new modes often makes it quite impossible for them ever to behave freely and easily. Moreover, they are made more uncomfortable by the characteristic security of the established upper class, which makes it possible for this group to repudiate much of the moralistic behavior of the middle class and to act with complete disregard of the severe criticism of the middle class about their private morals. The lower-upper person, being between the two groups, is doubly anxious. On the one hand, he understands and feels the moral criticism of the level from which he has just risen, and, on the other, he is not sufficiently secure to feel the inner ease and satisfaction necessary to reduce his anxieties to manageable proportions.

Mobile lower-upper parents are in an anomalous position with respect to their children. The parents as individuals are in a subordinate position to the upper-upper parents and, in social place, to the children of these parents. Yet their own children associate with upper-upper children in school and, through friendship and clique ties with the upper-upper class, tend to assume a social place higher than that of the parents. Such relationships help the lower-upper children to rise in the social scale, but they widen the social distance between them and their parents. Conflict and unhappiness often result from the relations of parents and children in this class level.

Family life within the homes of the old-family, upper class is highly formalized. Their homes are spacious; many of them have been in the family for generations and have well-known lineages of their own. The house itself, as well as many of the rooms and some of the furnishings, takes on a spiritual quality from long association with personages belonging to the family lineage. In such houses, each member of the family has his own room to which he can retire and be a separate, autonomous person in an environment which reinforces such feelings about himself. When he takes his place with other members of the family in the formal living-room or dining-room, the circumstances are often ritualized. There is a close relationship between the position of the family in the social structure and the degree of ritual which surrounds it, especially in the eating of meals. The etiquette involved in the preparation of the table and the serving and eating of meals becomes a ritual expressing the relations among members of the family and between them and their servants. Objects having aesthetic and traditional value for the family are used in these rituals.

They give objective expression to the inner feeling of the persons involved about themselves, help to reinforce the person's opinion of himself, and increase his sense of security.

On the other hand, the lower-upper-class family, more recently arrived, must imitate such household rituals and acquire the ritual objects by purchase. This buying of antiques and period furniture may be an effort to buy something more valuable as a social than as a material object. And, through this very necessity of payment, the objects themselves lose some of their psychological value for the maintenance of the status of such people.

Some of the members of the lower-upper class learn so well what they must do and what they must have that they surround themselves with more objects of ritual value and perform secular rituals more perfectly and with more elaboration than do the members of the old families themselves. They acquire beautiful houses with long lineages, furniture which is perfect as examples of the finest periods, and cultivate gardens that are showplaces famous everywhere, particularly in the magazines that circulate out of New York which celebrate the way of life of the upper class. Since this lower-upper group, more often than not, has a higher income than the class just above—in fact, the highest income of the entire community—it has the financial resources to buy the material objects which symbolize their position. Resistance of the upper class to the acquisition of such objects by purchase is strong and is often expressed in their ridicule and satire. The novels of W. D. Howells (*The Rise of Silas Lapham* is a good example) or those of J. P. Marquand, for instance, *Wickford Point* and *Point of No Return*, are filled with observations about the inadequacies of the recently arrived.

Child Training: Fact or Ideal

In most of the studies that we have done on the relation of class values to the development of the child, the emphasis has been on child training at the behavioral level. It is believed that it is important to know what actually happens and continues to happen in the family in the process of training the maturing, growing organism for his adult role in society. It is clear that, while study of behavior is of primary importance, it is insufficient; for, after all, the values and concepts lying behind the training, the purposes expressed and implied in the methods used in child training, are also significant and important. Furthermore, an important question arises as to whether there are significant discrepancies between what people think of this training behavior and the behavior itself.

Dr. Evelyn Duvall at the University of Chicago studied 433 mothers and their children from four class levels. The attitudes, values, and concepts of these mothers were examined. The research took the form of trying to find out what these women considered to be a good or bad mother and a good or bad child.

An analysis of the responses indicated that for certain people a good or bad relationship between mother and child conformed to the earlier and more traditional and customary usages of the mother-child relationship in American society. On the other hand, the responses of a large number could be referred to as new and developmental. To be more specific, the traditional mother said that a good mother kept house, washed and cooked and cleaned and mended; she took care of the child physically by trying to keep it healthy. She fed and bathed and clothed it, she established regular habits, provided a regular schedule, and sought to keep regular hours for the child. She disciplined it by reprimands, by scolding, by punishing, by making demands of obedience, and by rewarding good behavior. She believed she had to make the child good by teaching it obedience and instructing it in morals, building character, praying for it, and seeing to its religious education. What was called the "modern" or developmental type of mother was one who stressed training for self-reliance and citizenship by encouraging the child to be independent, teaching it how to be a good citizen, and training it for self-help and encouraging it in independence. This same type of mother stressed doing all she could to develop the emotional well-being of the child by doing such things as making a happy home, making the child feel welcome and a part of things, and helping the child to overcome needless fears. She was also concerned with helping the child to develop socially, by supervision of the child's play, by providing toys that helped in his development, and by taking time to play with the child herself. She stressed development of the child's mental growth by creating educational opportunities, by providing stimulation to learn, by reading to the child, and by giving careful attention to what the child was doing in school.

This same woman felt that a good mother was someone who was calm and what she called a "growing" person, someone who had outside interests in the community and who attempted to help herself. She further believed that the mother should learn to be sufficiently flexible to give the child freedom to grow on its own. Above all, she believed that she should be a loving and affectionate mother who enjoys her child and is interested in what the child does.

I will not attempt to describe what each type of mother considered a good child to be. What I have said indicates what she would want the child to be. It cannot be too strongly stressed that what was learned from this study was the ideal or official ideology of such women; but it cannot be demonstrated that there is any necessary correlation between what a woman said should be done and what she did or how she actually behaved with her children. The responses to these categories and their frequency were analyzed by racial, religious, and social-class groupings. The mothers were divided into two racial categories of Negro and Caucasian, and the latter was redivided into Christians and Jews. All were redivided into four social classes, beginning with the upper-middle and ending with the lower class.

An analysis of the responses on a class basis showed that the mothers at the top level tended to think of their children as developing persons with rights and privileges of their own which should be respected. A good mother should discipline her child, help him develop socially, and guide him with understanding and love.

Moving down the class scale from the upper-middle to the upper-lower, it was found that the official ideology was less progressive and developmental and more traditional and conservative. The good mother in the upper-middle class tried to act correctly according to the dictates of science, depending for guidance on her pediatrician. The mothers of the lower levels were more likely to depend upon the authority of tradition; especially the lower-class woman was guided by what she had learned from her mother and older women. Although there were slight differences according to religion and race, the same fundamental patterning of the beliefs and values about the good mother and the good child prevailed in all three groups.

This official ideology, particularly that of the upper-middle class, differs from much of the actual behavior reported in these studies; in actuality, upper-middle-class mothers are not so progressive and developmental as they say they are. In fact, most of them tell the interviewer what is often no more than the reigning ideology of the pediatricians of this particular time. The upper-middle-class mother's behavior and ambivalent feelings demonstrate that she trains her children to rigid standards of eating, cleanliness, self-reliance, and independence.

The conflict between the developmental ideal and the traditional behavior that she exhibits is possibly due to a period of transition in her life between the older traditional behavior and the new developmental ideology. Or, it may be no more than a temporary submission to some of the new rules which pediatricians have recently developed which may soon drop out of her system of beliefs and be accorded a place in history as nothing more than a fad. The lower-lower class, unfortunately not included in this study, is the most permissive with its children, allowing them to achieve early independence as individuals through the least inhibited behavior among the children and the adults who surround them.

The values of the developmental type of child training still need to be tested against the hard facts of social reality. We know from our own studies that the upper-middle class tries to maintain and reinforce the basic virtues of the society, emphasizing pragmatic goals. The continued development of American society and its technological progress are highly dependent upon people who have been trained by the traditional values of this group. The emphasis upon restraint and restriction on the individual's free movement and the emphasis upon putting off today's pleasures for tomorrow's gain are the very essence of the middle-class ethic and have been principally responsible for maintaining the continuing drive of individuals to advance themselves.

Whether these middle-class values are good or bad, they are deeply ingrained in the culture; despite the present popularity of the new ideology of the pediatrician, it seems unlikely that the new faith in how to rear a child is likely to survive the opposing social necessities of the middle class and the larger American society.

5

INDIVIDUAL OPPORTUNITY AND SOCIAL MOBILITY IN AMERICA

The Function of Rank in a Democracy

For the last generation there has been an increasing feeling of disquiet and concern in the minds of many Americans about the well-being of the social and economic system in which they live—a system that maintains them as a people, provides them with a life that is satisfying, and gives meaning to their lives. Most Americans believe that their free-enterprise system is a productive mechanism that is second to none and capable of producing abundance for all their people, and most believe that their free society provides men with spiritual values which help to maintain individual self-respect and individual freedom. But none of them can fail to read the evidence that the masses of their people have lost much of the great faith they had in the 1920's for free enterprise and the leadership of businessmen.

Evidence of their dissatisfaction can be seen in the workers' separation from management; in millions of workers' turning to unions and union leadership; in worker hostility to, and conflict with, management; and in the common people's turning to the state rather than to free enterprise to solve an increasing number of their economic and social problems.

When conservative Americans remember that Britain, once a citadel of free enterprise, has become a socialist state and that Britain's economic developments often anticipate their own, they know that their anxieties about maintaining their present economic and social world are real.

There is consensus among most Americans that it is time to understand the factors which are causing some of these developments. It is the belief of many, myself included, that social science can and does provide accurate diagnoses of the underlying factors which seem to be responsible for these changes in American beliefs and values.

It is clear to those of us who have made studies in many parts of the United States that the primary and most important fact about the American social system is that it is composed of two basic, but antithetical, principles: the first, the principle of equality; the second, the principle of unequal status and of superior and inferior rank.

The first declares that all men are equal and that all men must have equal opportunity to get the good things of life. The second, seldom openly stated but nevertheless potent and powerful, makes it evident that Americans are not always regarded as equal and that many of the values they treasure, that provide them with a will to do and to achieve, can continue to exist only as long as they have a status system. I wish to affirm that, paradoxical as it may seem, both these antithetical principles, when properly balanced, are necessary for the proper functioning of contemporary American democracy.

The principle of equality is necessary to provide all men with a sense of self-respect and to establish the secular essentials of the Christian belief in brotherhood. It is also necessary to give each citizen the right to participate in making the decisions about the destinies of all.

The principle of rank and status is necessary to provide men with the motives to excel by striving for positions of higher prestige and power for themselves and for their families. It is also essential to equip the nation, communities, and their institutions with responsible leadership hierarchies which co-ordinate and regulate the lives of their inhabitants and help maintain an orderly way of life, in which their citizens can cultivate the morals and manners of a high civilization.

The life of the greatest of all Americans, Abraham Lincoln, clearly exemplifies both principles, for he was born "a man of the people" and gave his life "to make all of us free and equal." But he was also the man who, aspiring to greatness, rose from a log cabin to the White House, leaving the lower reaches of American society and climbing to the highest levels of power and prestige. In the story of Lincoln and other similar success stories, all Americans find themselves, for such life-stories are symbols which combine the antithetical American virtues of equality and status.

I do not believe that the American system could operate,

that the present method of carrying on human affairs could continue, if Americans did not possess the kind of status system which it has been their good fortune to develop. It is necessary in any society to co-ordinate the efforts of men who work; those who perform this task are inevitably put into positions of power and prestige. Status systems must always exist, for people to accomplish the work necessary for their survival as a group. The only possible choice for Americans is not between their status system and a perfect system of equality but between their kind of hierarchy and some other—more likely, one that could not work satisfactorily in a democracy. (In passing, it might be said that the Russians went through an "equalitarian" revolution in the hope of establishing a pure democracy and succeeded in exchanging the status system of czarist Russia for the more rigid soviet system of status and castelike inequality.)

The most significant characteristic of the American class system—and the reason Americans think of it as being democratic—is the firm belief that there must be equality of opportunity for all and a chance for everyone to have his turn at bat. Such a belief means that the system must provide for the rise of men and their families from lower to higher levels, or, to say it in the jargon of the social scientist, vertical social mobility must continually function in the lives of men if their system is to be democratic and successful. To say it in everyday speech, they believe that a man, by applying himself, by using the talents he has, by acquiring the necessary skills, can rise from lower to higher status and that his family can rise with him. The opportunity for social mobility for everyone is the very fabric of the "American Dream." The American Dream is not a mere fantasy that can be dismissed as unimportant to those who think realistically, for it does provide the motive power for much of what Americans do in their daily lives. It is the basic, powerful, motivating force that drives most of them and makes all Americans partners in the well-being of each, since each feels that, although he is competing with the rest, he has a stake in the common good. When the principles of social mobility in the United States are not operating, there are troubles ahead not only for those who do not experience mobility but for every American.

Where we studied social behavior in the various regions of the United States, the forces and values of social mobility were always found to be basic and powerful for the free-enterprise system and a free society. Social mobility is a basic motivation for the worker as well as for the manager. It gives not only the worker and manager their chance to get ahead but their sons and families their chance to advance and improve themselves. It is the driving force in the United States that really makes the man on the job do the extra things that are beyond the ordinary requirements, and very often it is what makes him function beyond himself to become a first-rate man and a candidate for promotion.

As long as Americans know that the opportunity for advancement is available for anyone who wants to try, the American Dream is real and true for them. When they do not feel that the traditional channels of mobility are clear, their satisfaction yields to frustration and hostility. There is strong proof now that without educational preparation the American worker, as well as others, can no longer expect to advance and achieve success with anything like the same probability as did his father and grandfather.

The American system, in order to survive and develop

its full potentialities for human living, must be as meaningful and significant in the lives of the workers and their families as it is felt to be by those who own and manage business and individual enterprises. It cannot be a way of life that satisfies the needs and aspirations of merely the managerial levels. It must also fill the material wants of the workers generally and, beyond this, provide the necessary rewards for those ambitious workers who strive to advance themselves on the job and better their families' positions in the community.

The Routes of Mobility

Before developing this statement further, let us briefly examine the routes of mobility. Although American social classes are a rank order, placing people and their families in higher and lower levels, they do not permanently fix the status of either the individual or his family. Despite the fact that a man inherits the class position of his family, his inherited position is not necessarily the one he will always occupy. From the point of view of the total social system of a community, each social class is open to properly qualified people below it.

Since the individual's social position is not necessarily fixed, he can move up or down by his own efforts or the efforts of others, or he can be born to a family moving up or down, or marry into one that is climbing from another class level. Social-class systems permit vertical movement of the individual or his family; but there are always exact rules and social sanctions which regulate how this can and cannot be done, such rules applying not only to upward but also to downward mobility. Knowledge of them arouses anxiety in mobile individuals and families but also often provides security for them, since, when they know what the rules are, they can depend on them as guides for safe conduct to prevent loss of position and to achieve higher status. (Downward mobility, by the way, is something more feared than anything else in a class system.)

Vertical mobility in the United States is accomplished by most people through the proper use of certain recognized sources of social power, the principal ones being occupation, education, talent, sexual attractiveness and marriage, and the exercise of skill in a variety of social and technical activities, such as the successful manipulation of highly prized symbols. A young man of lower status may win a fellowship to a liberal arts college, or earn his way through school, spend a year or two in a professional school, then enter a large industry and work his way to the top. Meanwhile, he has changed his behavior and unlearned much of what he was taught in the family of his birth. Later he may marry a girl from a social level far superior to the one in which he began his career. Or, as an alternative, a young man or woman may develop a talent, become an author or an artist, and use these highly valued artistic symbols to acquire the necessary prestige for higher social acceptance.

Any activity or characteristic which can be ascribed to an individual's personal power, when properly understood, can be used for increasing the prestige of the person and his social place in the class system. Ordinarily, if the proper adjustments are made, his advance means that the members of his immediate family will move up with him. Should they not, it is likely either that the family will break or that the individual himself will not be able to maintain his new position. In the majority of cases the family is the ultimate unit which determines whether or not social mobility, once begun, is successfully completed.

In the United States it is commonly assumed that it is necessary only to accumulate money for an individual to increase his own and his family's status. This is only a partial truth. Those who acquire more money, superior occupation, or education, or achieve control over any other source of social power, must transform it into other highly valued symbols and behavior acceptable to the superior levels, in order to achieve the approval and social acceptance necessary for social advancement. In the ordinary mobile career, one finds five stages (the order of the intermediate stages may vary) that are recognizable to the social analyst. There is the early preparatory one, during which the individual equips himself with some of the skills necessary to acquire the prestige of money or a superior occupation; this phase is followed by the consolidation of the acquired prestige and power into a set of limited immediate relations with higher people, set up by the new position. Once this has been done, the third stage occurs, when there is a translation of power and prestige into suitable behavior, accompanied by the acquisition of approved symbols; then movement into institutional statuses that increase his interaction and identification with the superior class. This is often a period of social learning for the mobile person and his family, accompanied by attitudes of watchful probation by those whom he seeks to join—they observe the furnishings of his new house as well as his behavior when he joins their country club.

The final stage is reached when there is consolidation of the individual's status within his new social class so that he is conceived to be not only *with* those in it but *of* them. None of this is necessarily too pointed or explicitly stated in what he or his family says or does. There is every reason to explain mobile behavior by other motivations. The manners and morals of social mobility demand that those who are involved in it always give good economic, moral, and strong democratic reasons for what they are doing. If they are too open and direct in their efforts to increase their status, they are likely to be branded as "social climbers," and, if the term is made to stick, it is often sufficient to block advancement.

Social mobility in the United States acts as an incentive system, driving the man who climbs occupationally and his whole family, who share the rewards. Its prizes are largely responsible for the extra effort made by the ambitious to do more than the job demands in the hope that such behavior will be rewarded by economic and social advancement. The directives of social class demand that mobile individuals be highly flexible in their behavior. They must learn new behavior, which is never easy, and also do something more difficult—unlearn old behavior which is no longer appropriate for their advanced position. This means that they must be highly adaptable emotionally and intellectually and be able to tolerate continuing uncertainties and to live in insecure situations. Anxiety and fear, always present, must be kept under constant control and directed, or the competitive race and its prizes are likely to be lost.

At one time apprenticeship to an occupation, not educational preparation, was the principal route used for the upward climb of those who were ambitious. For young men preparing for life, apprenticeship and job training outranked all others as the route to advancement, success, and higher status. The ambitious needed only to start at the bottom of the ladder, learn what they had to do in each job, apprentice themselves for the job above, and be assured that, with the necessary talent, it was likely that they would continue to advance toward their goals.

Our studies at the present time indicate that something has happened to this route to success, for occupation as a means of mobility is diminishing in importance. In fact, it no longer is the principal form of mobility. The studies that we have made in the several regions, as well as certain national studies of various industries, show that the occupational routes are not so directly open as they once were and that in certain industries the chances for the uneducated worker to move out of his status into management have almost ceased to exist.

The studies of Taussig, Joslyn, and others on American business leaders, which in 1928 examined the lives of several thousand representative top-level businessmen from the principal industries of the United States, showed, it was believed, that there had been a definite trend toward tightening and decreasing upward mobility through occupation. They concluded:

The present generation of business leaders has been recruited in greater part from the sons of businessmen, and only to a minor extent from the sons of farmers and manual laborers. . . . The slack created by the decreasing proportion of farmers' sons among business leaders is being taken up, not at all by the sons of manual laborers, but almost entirely by the sons of businessmen and, among them, by the sons of major executives in particular. . . . It is entirely possible that, by the middle of the century [meaning 1950], more than two-thirds of the successful businessmen in the United States will be recruited from the sons of business owners (large or small) and business executives (major or minor).

Higher Education: A Hurdle Race

Young people enter the public schools available for everyone, eager for an opportunity to acquire the skills necessary to train their varying talents for purposes of achievement. The Committee on Human Development at the University of Chicago and other research groups have made exhaustive studies of what the school system does to the aspirations of children coming from the different socio-economic levels of the status system. The findings do not provide categorical encouragement to those of us who would like to believe that, since the occupational route no longer is as free as it once was, education is providing an adequate substitute.

We have learned that too often the children of parents belonging to the lower socioeconomic levels—even though they do have opportunities to choose the course that will put them on the social escalator—are not taking courses that prepare them for college or for better positions. The parents of these children represent from 50 to 60 per cent of our total population. Since the people in the lower socio-economic levels have more children per family, it is prob-able that their children represent an even higher percent-age of the total. Certain investigations show that a sizable per cent of the children of the lower group do not finish grammar school and that an even larger per cent of these children do not finish high school, most of them dropping out by the second year.

When these figures are quoted to the intelligent layman, he often asks why young people fail to get an education where the schools are free and it is possible for everyone to attend the first twelve grades (grammar school and high school) without cost. The two most frequent replies to this question are that the families of the children do not have money and that the children who quit do not have suffi-cient intelligence to continue in school and compete with other children. It is true that each factor operates to some extent; but, in my opinion, our studies indicate that, while money is important, other factors are more crucial.

Exact studies of the I.Q.'s of students who dropped out of school have been made; there seems to be no necessary difference between those who drop out and those who stay in. As a matter of fact, it can be demonstrated that the child who has a very high I.Q. and who comes from the lower-lower class may drop out earlier than the one with a lower intelligence. He is likely to be the very person who uses his intelligence in solving problems that do not have anything to do with good academic records but with "bucking" the school system and finding ways and means of successfully avoiding going on to higher grades.

The answer to our question—Why does such a large percentage of lower-class children drop out of school before they are sufficiently prepared?—is in the total social system and its operations in training children of different classes to assume their roles in American social life.

Educators and personnel men know that a grammar-school education is insufficient to provide these young men and women with the skills necessary to qualify for positions in much of the industrial life of modern America. Certainly, they are not sufficiently trained for supervisory jobs; certainly, they are not sufficiently equipped with the ordinary general skills necessary to get to the places where many of them want to go in the job hierarchy of the factories where they work.

I am not trying to say that the American public school system is set up formally to prevent future workers and potential managers from achieving their goals. The public school system is fitted into the American status system in such a way that this is what happens. Many children, even when they have the economic wherewithal and the brains, do not have the necessary motivations within them and the pressures from without to keep them in school long enough to give them the training which they need for advancement—or, for that matter, for adequately doing many of the jobs necessary for the proper functioning of business and industry.

An open class system, providing for the rise and fall of families according to social rules, is the most important factor in helping maintain the equalitarian principles of the social-class society. When functioning to maintain these principles, it also contributes to the maintenance and strengthening of the belief in the free individual. Given the Christian belief in the soul and the equality of all in the spiritual brotherhood of men through the Fatherhood of God, given the philosophical belief firmly imbedded in American society that each individual is autonomous and capable of good and evil, then the presence of social mobility makes it possible for each person to free himself from some of the strong status controls which tend to fix an individual's social position. With freedom to act independently available to all, and exploited by a considerable proportion of the population, American belief in individualism is reinforced and strengthened. The improvement in the positions of various people indicates that they are free, that there is something within the individual which makes him more than a helpless particle in an omnipotent social universe.

Americans—devout advocates of individualism—believe that individualism means that each man has within himself the right to make his own choices and to make or break his life-career on the basis of his own judgments. If a man makes a decision and it does not turn out right in the American system of social logics, we, more often than not, believe that it is his own fault. We may feel sorry for him, but still we feel that it is likely to be his own fault. On the other hand, if he makes good decisions and does well, we think he should be rewarded. The rewards most sought are advancement to positions of higher prestige. Whenever the American system of equal opportunity and individualism operates successfully and a man can make his choices and be rewarded when he does well, then Americans believe the system is fair, and their way of life is understandable to all because they can live and act as individuals and be rewarded accordingly.

When American workers equip themselves with the skills necessary and play the game according to all the traditional rules of learning on the job, and almost no one wins, then the individuals playing no longer blame themselves. Rather, they blame the system. Consequently, they tend not to act as individuals with separate decisions and separate consciences but feel themselves to be a group which has a common grievance against "those who run things." They act as they think. The consequences of this change are significant and important for the proper functioning of a free society.

We must now return to the problem of blocked mobility on those workers with little education and see the meaning of our analysis of American individualism and its relation to social mobility in our contemporary life.

The Effects of Blocked Mobility on the Workers

The consequences of blocked mobility on insufficiently educated men become clear as soon as one recognizes it as a scientific problem and part of the larger one of understanding status structure and social mobility in the United States. The effects on the society are numerous. Obviously, blocked mobility reduces the competition between them and the educated young men who are pushing their way to the top and the sons of families who are already advantageously placed in the economic and social order. It can be argued that, when this happens, the competitive system (which acts as a screen through which those with higher talents are more often selected for higher positions) does not function so well as when the routes of mobility are open and permit those who are on the way up to compete with people who are already there.

Furthermore, those who occupy these positions, if their competition is reduced, are likely to be far less alert, much less active, and less anxious to exercise their skills in doing a good job. On the other hand, it must be said that, if the system of mobility operated so that the man at the top possessed no method of giving his child some of the advantages of his own position, it would reduce his incentives to do his very best. Clearly, a balance of some kind must be reached by which those who have possession are assured not only that they can compete successfully but that their children can. Still, if democracy is to function successfully, the routes of mobility must be present and open for the young men of talent who come from the lower socioeconomic levels.

Whenever a society with social classes moves toward a fixed status and away from an open and changing one, there is the likelihood that the increased fixity of status will immobilize the energy that might have been projected into social action. An open system provides incentive for the greatest output of individual energy for the society itself. For, in such a system, each individual, in his efforts to succeed, gives all he can to achieve his goals and to reap the rewards of success.

Moreover, in a society in which the technology is changing rather rapidly and, for most purposes, is improving man's adjustment to the natural environment, there is a need for a flexible social structure to accommodate the social life of the society to the changes that occur in the technical system. Fixed status, or an approximation of it, produces ways of acting and attitudes for the members of the society which discourage and impede social change. It can be argued that the slowing-down of our technological change might be a good thing. I am not arguing for or against this proposition. But the processes of technological change are likely to continue, and, even though there might be a period of slowing down if social mobility is lessened, the ultimate consequences would be a dislocation between the technology and the social organization which would produce conflict and disorganization.

The political implications of blocked mobility are exceedingly important. The present ideologies of mobile lower-class people in the United States tend to approximate the beliefs and value systems of the mobile people in the higher classes. On the other hand, fixed status tends to produce an ideology fitted to the needs of a particular class level of an immobile status system. Where the political ideologies of classes tend to be purely on the basis of socioeconomic levels, there is greater opportunity for conflict and less for accommodation between the several classes of the society. It is my opinion that the class conflict which Marx describes is essentially one that does not take account of social mobility, of a system in which families move up and down, where mobile people in the lower-middle class have many of the same values, hopes and fears, and political and economic beliefs that one finds among mobile individuals in the upper-middle class. When mobility is not operating, there is a greater likelihood of the development of a totalitarian state with a political elite such as the Communist party playing the role of a dedicated priesthood, which explains, interprets, and administers what is believed to be the sacred ideology of one class. This does not mean that there will be one class within such a society. Quite the contrary; there must be several. But the class order of such a society is likely to be closed, with status fixed for the individual and mobility available only for that small fraction that learns how to enter the priestly elite.

The effect of blocked mobility on the inner world of the individual can be observed in many situations among a variety of people. Frustrated workers who find opportunity unavailable often cut down on work output. Some become "troublemakers," who are constantly on the alert to find situations that they can exploit to prevent satisfactory adjustments for the other men on the job. Others may take a more positive stand, join a union, and become union leaders who use the union hierarchy to satisfy their aspirations.

Social anthropologists and psychologists, under the leadership of certain doctors at the University of California, have been conducting studies of the relation of status and mobility to the presence of diseases, such as those of the heart, ulcers, etc. Their work gives strong indications that there is a definite relationship between status anxiety and the presence of certain kinds of illness that heretofore have been attributed to purely organic factors or to internal psychological problems rather than to the social situation in which the individual finds himself. The ulcer has become such a common phenomenon in the United States that it is often accepted as the physical symbol of an upper-middle-class American. It is not altogether clear yet how the social and psychological conditions operate that result in an ulcer, but we know from the case histories of many individuals that blocked mobility is definitely a factor in some of them.

I had the opportunity of studying the development of a strike in a community in New England where there had not been strikes before and where there had been no union organization (see Chap. 6). During the course of our study two things happened. The strike was won by the workers, and, during this period, all the factories in the town in this particular industry were completely unionized.

When we examined why these events happened, a number of things soon became apparent. Among the variety of reasons given to explain these two results, one essential factor stood out far above all others: the old skill hierarchy for the advancement of workers was gone. The routes of mobility were closed. The route for "getting places" on the job was no longer there for those who worked in the factories. It was not difficult to organize the workers' discontent and focus it against management, for the aspirations of these men were no longer entirely invested in the open system of equal opportunity, once provided by the factory hierarchy, but now more in the world of union organization.

When those who compete for the prizes of life find that the rules of the game have been changed and social mobility no longer permits the rise of those who strive to advance, then the systems of free enterprise and equal opportunity are doubted, and the common people seek other ways to get what they want. To be more concrete, when large numbers of talented men and women who have committed their careers to industry without first obtaining a higher education try to acquire the skills and knowledge thought necessary for advancement and, through no fault of their own, either fail to get them or fail to be rewarded when they do, they necessarily lose faith. Since many people in our civilization pay lip service to the creed of success and make little effort to advance themselves, these people, too, blame the system rather than their own lack of initiative.

Solutions for the Problem of Blocked Mobility among Workers

To strengthen the American people's belief in their way of life and to continue their faith in a traditionally free society, it is necessary that the two basic routes of mobility —occupation and education—be open, so that the aspirations of workers for themselves and for their children can be realized, at least for those who are ambitious and have a will to succeed.

Can equality of opportunity in the United States for those who are minded to use it be increased, thereby giving all Americans a greater stake and a greater belief in our free society? The answer is certainly "Yes."

There are a number of efforts now being made to widen and improve the success channels, the routes of social mobility, in the United States. There are programs to increase public educational opportunities for the youth, by early discovery of real talent and of the urge for success among young people, and by making special efforts to keep outstanding lower-status young people in school through better guidance and counseling. This will prevent many young people from going to work before they have prepared themselves with the necessary educational skills to compete for advancement. A number of plans to keep the routes of mobility open in business concerns have been put into effect. Since blocked mobility is a major cause for some of the decline in a worker's faith in the capitalistic system (or any other hierarchical order), where such a blocking exists it is believed by many to be the duty of management to do all that it can to free this system and make the worker realize that opportunity does exist for him and that management is alert to help him. Mobility channels can be kept open much better by a corporation's making careful inventories of job specifications and the skills of workers already existing in the company. Job requirements should be specific, and every effort should be made to let everyone know about them; they should be fair and considered so by everyone. Information about a worker's background should be obtained for every employee in the plant, with special emphasis on learning aptitudes, social skills, specialized experience, and abilities that might help workers to qualify for better jobs.

The knowledge that management has such an interest and is trying to do something about helping the worker to help himself encourages all ambitious workers to believe that free enterprise provides a way up for them. Each company should have a policy of promoting from within wherever possible and should let the workers know that such a policy exists and that it works. Each company should provide facilities through either the community or its own training program for a worker to obtain the necessary training for any job he has the talent for and aspires to. It should be clearly recognized that a large percentage of workers will never take advantage of these educational opportunities, but the mere fact that they know they are available will make a great difference to all of them.

Clearly, such programs must deal with the question of

economic security. Critics hostile to management will complain that open channels of mobility do little good while widespread economic insecurity exists. Economic security cannot be guaranteed by any single company or any single union. Such security depends upon the health of the economic system generally. As long as the system is strong, anxiety about economic security will always be low, and at such times interest in advancement by workers who wish to succeed will always be very high. If the workers generally believe that opportunity is available for those who really wish to try and for those who have the necessary brains and talent, their faith in the present system will continue strong because it will then be "paying off" for them in the same way that it does for management.

Americans are usually willing to apply new knowledge to new and old situations and from this application develop a better way of life. We have done this in the physical and biological sciences and have re-created our world to make it a better place for men to live their lives. Today, the social sciences are contributing their share of precise and exact knowledge about the private and public worlds which we all inhabit. The social sciences are giving us the knowledge we need to apply to the old and new situations which confront us. I believe it is probable that we will use this knowledge to solve our present problems with the same enterprise and with the same success that we have had in using the knowledge of other scientific disciplines.

The Birth and Mobile Elites

Our own local community studies of social and occupational mobility in various parts of the country revealed little or no mobility from the worker to the managerial levels in this generation, and yet our researches showed that in the previous ones there had been successful mobility in the community and this movement seemed traditionally expected. Therefore, when we combined our own results from community research with those for the nation by Taussig and Joslyn, we developed the hypothesis that the occupational and class hierarchies were closing, that there was less mobility now and a development of fixed status for the individual and a closed class system for the society in general.

If these formulations, partly founded on research facts, were true, then the American dream, with its beliefs and values that cluster around the old fundamental faith that there is equal opportunity for all who possess the necessary abilities and the will to do, was dead or dying. Tomorrow's America would not be a land of democratic equality for the many but of inequality and fixed hierarchies of power and privilege for the well-born few. Obviously this was not a pleasant prospect; yet the insufficient research facts then available seemed to make this the most likely prediction.

To test this hypothesis of reduced mobility and closed hierarchies, nationwide researches were undertaken on the social origins of the present elites, those at the top of the most powerful and prestigeful American hierarchies, the managers and owners of big business and the civilian and military leaders of the American federal government.

The research was so designed that it replicated the earlier study of Taussig-Joslyn in 1928 for the big business leaders of a generation ago. This procedure allowed exact comparisons between then and now and provided a means by which reliable answers could be given to the question about opportunity in America and about trends in the American society that moved toward or away from democratic principles. Over 8,000 big businessmen responded to an elaborate questionnaire, and a substantial number of them and their wives were intensively interviewed and later given personality tests. The leaders came from every variety of occupation and from all over the country. They are executives of only the largest enterprises in each variety of economic undertaking and hold policy-making positions from chairman of the board and president down only as far as secretary and treasurer. They are the elite of big business in America.

Who are these men, where do they come from, were they the sons of the rich and powerful, or did many of them come from more modest origins? Whatever the answers, how did this present generation compare with the previous generation of big business leaders? To learn about these answers, let us look at the occupations of their fathers; in other words, examine their social and economic origins.

They came from all occupational levels but over half were sons of business executives (26 per cent) and owners (26 per cent) and a sizable number (14 per cent) were the sons of the high and time-honored professions—doctors, lawyers, ministers, and similarly well-placed men. Thus, approximately two-thirds of the powerful men, those from business and the professions, seemed to support the pessimistic predictions previously made. Yet, the full evidence needs to be given further analysis. Close scrutiny of Table 1 answers this basic question. Fifteen per cent of the big business leaders had fathers who were manual workers, 8 per cent were the sons of white-color workers, and 9 per cent came from farming backgrounds (see the left-hand column of Table 1). When these more general categories are divided into their components (see column on the right), we learned that these men came from the more highly regarded subcategories of each of the general categories. There were twice as many sons of skilled workers as sons of unskilled workers, twice as many salesmen as less highly ranked clerks, and the fathers who were farmers with paid help outranked all other subcategories of farmers.

Yet we also see that every variety of occupation was represented. We at least know that the system of mobility may be tough and tight, but it is not a closed caste of those

TABLE 1

Occupations of the Fathers of Business Leaders

Occupation of Father (7 Groups)	Percentage	Occupation of Father (22 Groups)	Percentage
Laborer	15	Unskilled or semiskilled worker	4.5
		Skilled worker or mechanic	10.3
White-collar worker	8	Clerk or retail salesman	2.5
		Salesman	5.9
Business executive	26	Foreman	3.1
		Minor business executive	7.4
		Major business executive	14.6
Business owner	26	Owner of small business	17.7
		Owner of medium business	6.4
		Owner of large business	2.3
Professional man	14	Doctor	2.2
		Engineer	2.2
		Lawyer	2.2
		Minister	2.3
		Other professional	4.2
Farmer	9	Farm tenant or farm worker	0.3
		Tenant with paid help	0.4
		Farm owner without paid help	3.7
		Owner or manager with paid help	4.2
Other occupations	2	Military career	0.3
		Government service	1.8
		Other occupations	0.4
Total	100	Total	100.0

who are in and those who are permanently out. While this is good to know, it is not enough. We need to learn how well and in what proportions the different occupational levels in the United States were represented. What occupations in the work force were overrepresented among big business leaders? Which ones had below their "share"? If an occupation has 10 per cent of those employed generally in the United States and 10 per cent of the big business leaders in the present study have fathers of this same occupation, that occupation would have its proportionate share in the big business elite. If it had 20 per cent among the leaders, it would have twice its share, and if 5 per cent but half of what statistical chance would allow us to expect and predict. Figure 5 allows 100 to represent perfect proportional representation between the occupations of the business leaders' fathers (at the time the executives began their careers) and that for the general population for that same period. It shows that present-day leaders come from two occupational levels—business and the professions in far larger proportions than chance would lead us to suppose. The sons of businessmen in 1952 were approximately five times overrepresented and the sons of professionals three and a half times more than their percentages in the working population. On the other hand, three occupations had less than their share: instead of 100, white-collar sons scored but 80, farmers but 33, and laborers but 32.

So today the higher occupations are favored and the lower ones do less well than equality of representation would demand. Yet when we ask how this compares with a generation ago (1928, when the Taussig-Joslyn study was made), two things become very clear: (1) The sons of the favored and highly placed occupations are less likely to be in top positions in big business today than formerly and (2) the sons of less prestigeful positions are more likely to be mobile today than they were in the twenties. In brief, the belief that America is no longer a land of opportunity and that fixed position is on the increase and equal opportunity is decreasing so far as big business is concerned is proved to be not true. The sons of businessmen dropped from 967 for every 100 that would be ex-

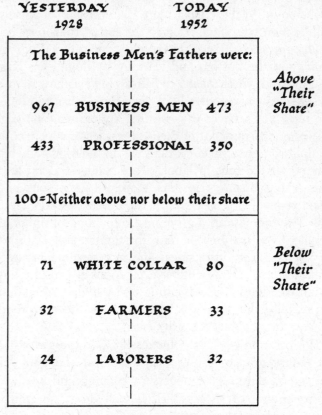

YESTERDAY 1928	TODAY 1952	
The Business Men's Fathers were:		
967 BUSINESS MEN 473		Above "Their Share"
433 PROFESSIONAL 350		
100 = Neither above nor below their share		
71 WHITE COLLAR 80		Below "Their Share"
32 FARMERS 33		
24 LABORERS 32		

Fig. 5.—Equality of opportunity today and yesterday

pected to 473, professionals from 433 to 350 from 1928 to 1952. The mobile white-collar men moved up from 71 to 80, the sons of laborers who had been mobile from 24 to 32. The trend is toward openness in the occupational and status structure. There has been an increase of competition among all ranks for higher position and a reduction of a proportion of those born to high position who stay there. A very similar story is true for civilian and military executives. They, too, come from all levels and from all parts of the country; they, even more than business leaders, are mobile men who have risen to the top of their profession.

The question arises: If mobility by occupation, from starting at the bottom and learning by doing, has largely disappeared, what means did these big business men and the executives in the federal government use to climb to the top? The answer is (as a first approximation) higher education; 57 per cent of the business leaders were college graduates, about twice as many as in 1928. A higher percentage of the sons of laborers are college-trained among today's big business leaders than were the sons of big business leaders who were the top executives a generation ago. The increase in high education among business leaders has been far greater than for the general population. Today's mobility in business and in government—and, for that matter, in all the higher professions and all the highly regarded occupations—is primarily by higher education. It is not only the royal road but perhaps the only road to success for the vast majority.

We must now ask who moves through the primary and secondary grades, passes these hurdles, and goes on to college to acquire the necessary training and symbols of preparation and success? How well do those from the lower levels do?

6

THE FACTORY IN THE EMERGENT SOCIETY AND THE COMMUNITY

The American social system has been drastically changed by the development of industrial institutions; on the other hand, the country's industrial organization has become what it is by virtue of being a part of the larger American social system. The two are interdependent and mutually influence each other; yet we know almost nothing about the nature of the relations that exist between the two. Much is known about the factory as a production and economic unit, but little is known about the influence of the factory on the community and of the community on the factory. We shall attack that problem in the present chapter. To do so, we shall concentrate our attention on one city where the factory and social systems of the community (Yankee City) were carefully studied over a period of years.

The relations of this factory and the community were studied when they were in equilibrium and the various parts of the factory and the city were well integrated and formed a functioning unit. They were also examined when industrial strife and social conflict had disrupted this equilibrium. Social anthropologists study periods of social disruption to gain deeper insight into what normally takes place in a social system, because crisis periods reveal and dramatize the important and significant factors that often lie hidden during times of peace and quiet.

We are going to examine a strike in the shoe industry of an American community to learn what we can about the place of the factory in contemporary American life.

The Strike in Yankee City

In the worst year of the depression, all the workers in all the factories of the principal industry of the community walked out. They struck at management with little or no warning; they struck with such impact that all the factories closed and no worker remained at his bench. Management had said they would never strike, for the workers of Yankee City were sensible, dependable, and, by a long peaceful history, had proved that they would always stay on the job. Union men outside the city agreed that Yankee City could not be organized and held that the local shoe workers were obstinate and "always stupid enough to play management's game." Many of the workers had told us that there would be no strike. Most of the townspeople, from the aristocrats of Hill Street to the people on city welfare in the clam flats, said Yankee City workers would never strike. But they did—the foreigners and the Yankees of ten generations—the men and the women, the very old and the very young, Jews and Gentiles, Catholics and Protestants—the whole heterogeneous mass of workers left their benches and in a few hours wiped out most of the basic productive system from which Yankee City earned its living. Not only did they strike and soundly defeat management, but they organized themselves, joined an industrial union, and became strong union members.

The industrial battle was fought between the owners of seven factories and their workers. Four of the factories, "the larger ones," employed the vast majority of the workers and accounted for most of the "34,000-dollar weekly pay roll." This industrial war lasted a month. It began on a bleak and snowy day in early March and lasted well into April. There were three clearly marked periods, each with different objectives and strategy, and in each the industrial workers and the managers were dominated by different feelings.

In the first period, when management and the union fought desperately to gain control over the workers, the union was successful in organizing the workers, and management was prevented from regaining control over them. The second period began when all the workers requested the union to represent them in the struggle with management; then the union began frontal attacks on management. During this time each continued its intense efforts to influence and dominate public opinion in Yankee City. The union also won this fight, since the public identified the union with the workers and most of Yankee City sided with them. The final phase, that of mediation and peace negotiations, began when a government agency entered and started a series of negotiations that ended the strike.

Other efforts had been made from the beginning, but none of them had been successful.

The ultimate objective of each side, to which each fashioned its strategy, was, of course, to make the other side capitulate and accept its demands. For management this meant that the workers would return to their benches under approximately the same working conditions and wages as they had left; for the workers it meant that management would agree to their demands and increase wages and improve working conditions; and for the union officials it meant that the union would maintain its control over the workers and keep them members of their organization, and management would be forced to deal directly with the union and not with the unorganized workers.

Each side organized itself and developed its strategies of offense and defense. The workers' defense tactics were centered around maintaining their unity and defeating management's offensive strategy of breaking up the workers' group and of destroying their morale. Accordingly, the workers used ritual and ceremonial procedures in which recognized symbols of solidarity, such as the flag, patriotic hymns, and the American Legion band, played prominent parts. They achieved a defensive organization by means of meetings, speeches, entertainments, and the formation of a large number of committees that gave the mass of the workers opportunities to participate and to become and feel a part of a powerful and aggressive group. They took offensive action against management by making a series of demands for better wages and working conditions, by picketing, by making attacks against management in the newspaper, and by using the speaker's platform to influence public opinion. Management's defense was always to take the offensive. The tactics tried included sending foremen to talk to the workers individually, thereby separating them from the group; spreading discouraging rumors; advertising in the paper; insisting on secret balloting by the workers when they voted on the issue of returning to work; and, above all, threatening to move their factories elsewhere, should the workers continue with their demands and join the union. Of course, it must be remembered that each side, throughout the strike, was being deprived of its income—labor of its wages and management of its profits.

The strike occurred almost to the very year of the three hundredth anniversary of the founding of Yankee City and the beginning of the shoe industry. Shoemaking had always been important there, but it was not until near the end of the nineteenth century that it achieved its place of supreme importance in the economy of the town. From the beginning, shipping, shipbuilding, fishing, and the other trades of the sea had dominated Yankee City's economic existence and set their mark on the community. When the New England shipping industries disappeared, Yankee City turned from the sea and sent its many salesmen and manufactured goods westward to make the profits necessary for the establishment and continuance of its factory system. It was then that the textile manufacturers moved into the lead, but throughout the whole period shoemaking contributed significantly to the economic life of the city and, by the end of the nineteenth century, had risen to a commanding place. Yankee City's shoe workers and owners throughout this time were known everywhere in the country for the excellence of their products.

Although the economy of the city went through revolutionary changes, the social superstructure that guided and maintained the lives of its citizens remained very much what it had been at the end of the War of 1812. The physical city stretches in a thin rectangle two miles inland from the harbor along the bank of a large river. Here, when the field study was made, lived 17,000 people. They were distributed from the river bottoms and clam flats to the high ground on which Hill Street is located. The people of high status, some of them the descendants of those who had made their fortunes in the sea trade, lived on this broad, elm-lined avenue. The people of lowest status, many of whom could trace their ancestry through long lines of fishermen to the city's founding, lived in Riverbrook on the clam flats. Between the two were the "Side-streeters," who occupied a middle-class position.

Scattered throughout the status system from the lower-upper class ("new-family" level) to the lower-lower class ("Riverbrookers") were the descendants of the Irish and, at somewhat lower levels, the French Canadians, Jews, Poles, Greeks, and other ethnic groups who began settling in Yankee City in the 1840's and continued until 1924.

All these people were involved in the strike; the bread for most of them was directly or indirectly earned in the shoe factories. Men everywhere in the city asked themselves, when the strike occurred, why such a thing should have happened to the people of Yankee City. Each man had his own answer. The answer of each tended to reveal more about the life and status of the man who talked than about the cause or causes of the strike. More often than not, the explanations were economic. These townspeople forgot that there had been serious depressions before and that there had been no strikes. Each of them forgot that there had been low wages before and that there had been no unions. Each forgot, too, that there had been strikes in this country when wages were high and times were said to be good. Although these economic arguments supplied important and necessary reasons for the strike and the unionization of the workers, they were insufficient explanations.

Reasons for the Strike: Class and Skill and the Emergent Factory Structure

The secrets of industrial strife in Yankee City and elsewhere lie beyond the words and deeds of the strike. They can be found only in the whole life of the community, in which the workers and owners are but a part. The answers of the economic determinists or of the historians, while important, are not sufficient.

If social science is to be of any worth to us, it must be capable of adding significance and meaning to human behavior that will give us deeper insight into human life and explain more fully than common-sense knowledge why human beings act the way they do. Science necessarily solves problems. To solve them, it must know what questions need to be answered. Let us re-examine the questions implied in the statements of the Yankee City townsmen in a more explicit and pointed manner to determine, if we can, what happened in this industrial crisis and to see if such knowledge about the strike can tell us about other similar crises in American life.

The immediate questions are basic to the whole problem, but, of even greater importance, they lead us into more fundamental ones about the nature of our industrial society. We will endeavor to give at least partial answers to some of these larger questions. The first questions we must answer about the strike are:

1. In a community where there had been very few strikes and *no* successful ones, why did the workers in *all* the factories of the largest industry of the community

strike, win all their demands, and, after a severe struggle, soundly defeat management?

2. In a community where unions had tried previously and failed to gain even a foothold and where there had never been a union, why was a union successful in separating the workers from management?

3. Why was the union successful in organizing *all* workers in *all* the shoe factories in the community?

4. Why was the union successful in maintaining the organization, despite the intense and prolonged efforts of management to prevent unionization and break up the shoe union?

5. Why did Yankee City change from a non-union to a union town?

To answer these and other questions, the factories were studied by participant observers, who listened to what the workers and managers had to say while they observed what the men did on the job. Most of the workers and managers were continuously interviewed outside the plant; many were known as personal friends of the field workers. All were particularly questioned about the ranking of the jobs and what had happened to the skill hierarchy. During the strike we attended most of the meetings of the striking men, those of the men with the union organizers, and the gatherings of managers; we were present when all of them met with the government mediators. Meanwhile, we interviewed other citizens of Yankee City, to learn how they felt and thought about what was happening. A large number of excellent documents locally available made it possible for us to trace the history of the development of the shoe industry in Yankee City; others on the shoe industry of the United States were utilized.

Perhaps the best way to gain an understanding of the

strike and of the relations of the contemporary factory and the community is to view the present in the light of the past. The history of Yankee City's shoe factories may be conveniently divided into five periods, ranging from the earliest times, when the family was the productive unit, through the periods of early and late small-city capitalism, to the present stage, when mass production and the machine dominate the industry and control has shifted to New York. Included were revolutionary technological developments, increases in the division of labor, radical modifications of ownership and control, and rearrangements of the relations of producer and consumer and of workers among themselves.

During the technological development of Yankee City's shoe industry, the tools changed from a few basic ones, entirely hand-used, to machines in an assembly line; and their produce changed from a single pair of shoes to tens of thousands in mass production. In the beginning, the family made its own shoes, or a highly skilled artisan, the cobbler, made shoes for the family. In time, several families divided the highly skilled jobs among themselves and their families. Ultimately, a central factory developed, and the jobs were divided into a large number of systematized low-skilled jobs. The history of ownership and control is correlated with the changes in the division of labor. In early days, tools, skills, and materials were supplied by the owner-manager, and soon he also controlled the tools and machines. The sequence of development of producer-consumer relations tells a similar pointed story. The family produced and consumed its shoes, all within the circle of its simple unit. Then the local community was the consumer-producer unit, and ultimately the market became national and even world-wide. Workers' relations changed from those of kinship and family ties to those of occupation, where apprenticeship and craftsmanship relations were superseded and the industrial union became dominant in organizing the affairs of the workers. The structure of economic relations changed from the immediate family into a local hierarchy, and the locally owned factory changed into a vast, complex system owned, managed, and dominated by New York City.

With these several histories in mind, let us ask ourselves what would have happened if the strike had taken place in each of the several periods. In period one, with a family consuming and producing economy, such a conflict would have been impossible. The social system had not become sufficiently complex; the forces had not been born that were to oppose one another in civil strife. In the second phase, several families in a neighborhood might have quarreled, but it is only in one's imagination that one could conceive of civil strife among the shoemakers.

In the third phase, however, there appears a new social personality, and an older one begins to take on a new form and assume a new place in the community. The capitalist is born and during the following periods develops into full maturity. Meanwhile, the worker loses control and management of his time and skills and becomes a subordinate in a hierarchy. There are, thus, distinct and opposing forces set up in the shoemaking system. What is good for one is not necessarily good for the other; but the interdependence of the two opposing groups is still very intimate, powerful, and highly necessary. The tools, the skills, and the places of manufacture belong to the worker, but the materials, the place of assembly, and the market are now possessed by the manager. Striking is possible but extremely difficult and unlikely.

In the fourth period, full capitalism has been achieved; the manufacturer is now the owner of the industrial plant, and he controls the market. The workers have become sufficiently self-conscious and antagonistic to machines to organize into craft unions. Industrial warfare still might prove difficult to start. In a small city where most people know one another, the owner-manager more often than not knows "his help" and they know him. The close relation between the two often implies greater compatibility and understanding that cut down the likelihood of conflict. But, when strikes do occur, the resulting civil strife is likely to be bitter because it is within the confines of the community.

In the last period, the capitalist has become the super-capitalist, and the workers have forgotten their pride in their separate jobs, have dismissed the small differences among them, and have united in one industrial union with tens and hundreds of thousand of workers throughout the country combining their strength to assert their interests against management. In such a social setting strikes are inevitable and certain.

Yankee City and Its Factories in the Emergent Society

An examination of the status of the worker in the factory and in the community reveals another important factor contributing to industrial strife. During the early periods of the factory in Yankee City a skill hierarchy dominated the lives of the workers and helped to establish their place in the community. The introduction of the machine into all parts of the production processes of the factory largely destroyed the skill hierarchy.

Figure 6 illustrates what has happened to craft and skill

in the modern factory. The vertical hierarchy of skilled jobs has become a horizontal layer of low-skilled ones. Each of the skilled jobs has been divided into a number of simple, low-skilled ones, and machines are performing most of the actions necessary for each job. Jobs formerly at the top and bottom of the hierarchy, that were separated by higher and lower prestige and paid accordingly, are now in the same category of prestige and pay.

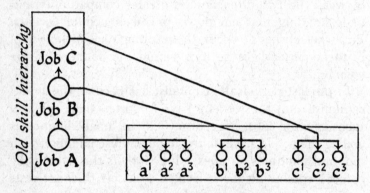

Fig. 6.—Present job arrangement

We believe that the breakup of the skill hierarchy contributed importantly to the outbreak of the strike, to the course it took, and, in particular, to the coming of the union. The hierarchy of crafts that once organized the relations of the workers and provided a way of life for the shoe workers was really an age-grade system. Youngsters served their hard apprenticeship and, as neophytes, learned their task and, even more important, were taught to respect the skills they had learned and those they looked forward to learning. Above all, they acquired respect and admiration for the older men above them who had mastered the skills and who occupied the proud positions of journeymen and master-craftsmen. These youngsters aspired to achieve for themselves a similar high position and to be the objects of a similar respect from their fellow-craftsmen and fellow-townsmen. Each young man, in direct face-to-face interaction with those above, imitated and learned a way of life while being highly motivated by the strong desire to escape the irksome limitations of his present low position. He wanted to attain the higher place, where he would have the satisfaction of making his own decisions and possess the prestige and pay consequent to such great eminence. By the time he had learned how to do the things needed to equip himself for advancement, enough time had passed to mature him sufficiently to act the part of a man.

There can be little doubt that age factors as well as those of skill determined the time for advancement. During this preliminary period the worker learned that he was a craftsman and that he had a particular place in the whole system, with responsibilities and obligations that, once acquired, gave him rights and privileges. Thus, while he internalized this behavior and all its values and their many subtleties and learned what he was as a man, he became an inextricable member of the honorable fraternity of those who made, and who knew how to make, shoes. In this system, workers and managers were indissolubly interwoven into a common enterprise with a common set of values. The internal personal structure of each was made up of very much the same apparatus, and their personalities were reinforced by the social system of shoemaking.

In learning to respect the skill of the master-craftsman, the apprentice learned to respect himself. He had security in his job, but he had even greater personal security because he had learned how to respect it. And, because he was a member of an age-graded male fraternity made up of other men like himself who had the knowledge and necessary skills to make shoes, he possessed that feeling of freedom and independence and of being autonomous that comes from leading a disciplined life. He spent his life acquiring virtue, prestige, and respect, learning as he aged and climbed upward, and at the same time teaching those who were younger than he and who aspired to be like him.

Slowly this way of life degenerated, and the machine took the virtue and respect from the workers and, at the same time, broke the skill hierarchy that dominated their occupation. There was no longer a period for young men to learn to respect those in the age grade above them and, in so doing, to become self-respecting workers. The "ladder to the stars" was gone and with it much of the fabric of the American Dream.

When the age-grade structure that organized the male aborigines of Melanesia and North America into a hierarchy of prestige and achievement was broken under the impact of white civilization in many of these societies, the frustrations suffered by those who had once known self-respect crystallized into aggressive movements or into attempts to abolish the new ways and to retreat into the old and cherished ways of the past. There are, thus, some resemblances to developments in non-European societies.

The parallel between Yankee City's age-grade structure and theirs cannot be pushed too far, but certainly the two share obvious characteristics. In the earlier days of the machine, the Knights of St. Crispin organized themselves and attempted to stop the further introduction of machinery, and most of them longed for the good old days when there were no machines, when a trained hand and eye did the job. These attempts failed, and their organization collapsed, for they could not stop the inevitable advance of our industrial technology.

When the whole age-grade structure of craftsmanship had almost entirely collapsed and the American shoe worker was thereby denied his share of the American Dream, he and his kind were ready for any mass movement that would strike at those whom they charged, in their own minds, with responsibility for their unhappy condition. Much of this behavior was not conscious. Much of it was feeling rather than thought, as, indeed, were the feelings and thoughts that composed the mass movements of the aboriginal Melanesians and North American Indians. It seems certain, however, that American workers, taught from childhood that those who work and apply themselves and practice the ethics of the middle class would be rewarded by achievement and success, would rebel and strike back out of sheer frustration when they found that the American Dream no longer was true and that the hard facts belied the beautiful words they had been taught. It seems even more likely that the effects of the break in the skill hierarchy were potent forces that contributed their full share to the workers' striking and accepting the union as their champion.

The other important causes of the strike must now be dealt with. The first is the expansion of the hierarchy upward, out of Yankee City, through the expansion of individual enterprises and the establishment by them of central offices in distant large cities. The second is the expansion of the structure outward from Yankee City through the growth of manufacturers' associations and labor unions, also with headquarters outside Yankee City and with units in many other shoemaking communities in New England and elsewhere. Both these developments have gone on concurrently, each reacting upon the other. And both decrease Yankee City's control over its shoe factories by subjecting the factories, or segments of them, to more and more control exerted from outside Yankee City.

In the early days of the shoe industry, when the owners and managerial staffs of the factories, as well as the operatives, were residents of Yankee City, there was no extension of the factory social structures outside the local community. The factories were then entirely under the control of the community—not only the formal control of city ordinances and laws but also the more pervasive informal controls of community traditions and attitudes. There were feelings of neighborliness and friendship between manager and worker and of mutual responsibilities to each other and to the community that went beyond the formal employer-employee agreement.

In the days of local capitalism, the shoe manufacturers were accepted by all social strata as leaders of the total community. Shortly after the death of the most powerful of these business leaders, a number of prominent Yankee City men published a memorial volume that contained the usual words of high praise for great men. Since these same words, unlike those of many memorial volumes, were said about him by ordinary men of the street and were used during the strike, it is important to examine them. A member of one of the oldest families of Yankee City wrote:

He [the manufacturer] was one of the most remarkable men ever connected with Yankee City; a businessman of liberal culture, of fine literary taste, gifted as an orator, in music and theatricals. . . . He was an acquisition to any society. He honored any public station, however high. . . . He achieved more in his fifty years of life than most men can point to after marking a very old age. . . .

He was identified with the public health of this city and was a conspicuous figure in all its great social functions as long as his heath permitted it. He was a leading financier and a man who at once took and ever afterwards occupied a prominent position in this community. For years, by common consent, he was the leading man of the city. . . . Forcefulness of character made him the commanding spirit in every undertaking in which he shared and in every circle in which he moved.

Our analysis of the manufacturer's participation in the community provides the crucial evidence to show why he became the powerful collective symbol that was used against the contemporary managers during the strike.

In the business and financial sphere he was:

1. Owner and head of his million-dollar shoe company.
2. President of one of the most powerful banks in the city.
3. Member of the Board of Trustees of the Financial Institute, a firm of the utmost prestige and power in the community.
4. Director of the Security Trust Company, another powerful financial institution.
5. Director of the Yankee City Gas and Electric Company.

He was involved in a large number of civic enterprises and was a member of many civic institutions. He was:

6. Director and one of the founders of the city's most important hospital.
7. Director of the Public Library.
8. Member of the School Committee.
9. Trustee of the Revere Free School.
10. President of the City Improvement Society.

He took an important part in politics. He was:

11. Chairman of the Republican City Committee.
12. Member of the City Council.
13. Delegate to the National Republican Convention.
14. Mayor of the city.

He was also prominent in church and religious affairs. He was:

15. President of the Yankee County Unitarian Club.
16. President of the Yankee County Unitarian Conference.

He was a leader in fraternal affairs and was:

17. Past Master of St. John's Lodge.
18. Member of several important fraternal orders.

He was an active member of some of the most exclusive clubs of the city, including:

19. The Drama Club.
20. The Thursday Night Club.
21. The Friday Evening Club.
22. The February Club.
23. The Revere Club.
24. The Country Club.

The evidence demonstrates that in all these organizations he was active and powerful. This brief survey of some of his participation in the community demonstrates that his activities were ramified throughout the city and that much of the life of the city was centered in him. It also demonstrates that he accepted responsibility for the larger affairs of the community and helped integrate its activities, for he provided responsible leadership for the whole life of the community. "He was a man you could depend on."

Very much the same could be said about his two successors. They, too, were responsible elders of the city. They not only provided jobs and wages through their factories but were citizens of the town and men who felt a duty toward it. Their membership in local institutions compared very favorably with that of their predecessor.

In the days before big-city capitalism took control, local enterprise was financed by Yankee City banks. These banks and other investment houses possessed more autonomy and prestige then than they do now. In the development of the local shoe industry, local financiers played important and necessary roles and, at least part of the time, were silent partners in the business. Much of the wealth they derived from their investments was reinvested in Yankee City. The money was put into new enterprises, their own living, or civic activities. Their white Georgian houses on Hill Street, whose gardens bordered those of the manufacturers, were majestic symbols of their power and prestige and forever reminded and often reassured everyone of the visible presence of these powerful and protecting men in Yankee City.

The Yankee City financiers, too, were men of responsibility, dominated by sentiments of local pride. They did well for themselves, but they also did well for the city. Perhaps the price was high, but the product bought by the rest of her community was substantial and of high quality. Their philanthropies, combined with their power and leadership, contributed enormously to the city's development and provided a firm foundation for the larger civic life of the community. Parks, libraries, hospitals, societies to help the unfortunate and aged, foundations to send young men to college, endowments of schools, churches, and many other worthy civic enterprises were granted and maintained by the money and leadership of the local financiers and manager-owners.

The essential point to remember for these leaders of industry and finance is that they were subject to local control: (1) because they were dominated by local sentiments which motivated them "to take care of their own people" and (2) because they were under the powerful influence of the numerous organizations to which they belonged and of their personal contacts with local citizens, which directly related them to influence from every part of the city.

The advent of big-city capitalism shattered this closely woven network of personal relations, loyalties, and obligations. Yankee City shoe factories are no longer owned exclusively by local citizens. More and more of them have been absorbed by larger enterprises whose executive offices are in New York City. At the time of our study, the largest shoe factory in Yankee City was owned by a company which operated several other factories in New England and which also owned the nation-wide ABC chain of retail shoe stores, all of which were controlled from a central office in New York. Even some of the smaller Yankee City shoe factories, although still locally owned and managed, sold most of their shoes to chain-store organizations.

Yankee City has become but a pinpoint upon the map of industrial empire for these large investment houses. The flow of wealth from Yankee City's banks and factories, once a great local arterial system giving life and strength to the town, now has shrunk to an infinitesimal part of big-city, world-wide capitalism and is of no vital significance in the life of this great system.

The extent of this change may be seen from the following account of the finances of the ABC company, which appeared in a June, 1945, issue of a large New York newspaper:

A group headed by Oppenheimer and Co. and Brandeis and Son, and including the Stultz Co., has concluded an agreement for purchase of the majority of Lion Shoe Corp. stock, it was announced today.

Lion Shoe will be merged into its wholly owned retail subsidiary, the ABC Shoe Corp., with subsequent public issue of securities of the latter company.

Abraham Cohen, associated with the companies in an executive capacity for more than 20 years, will be elected president and general manager. Frederick Stultz, president of the Stultz Co., will be made chairman of the board.

The ABC Shoe Corp. owns a number of factories equipped to manufacture 20,000 pairs of shoes daily and operates a chain of 110 stores in 56 cities.

Decisions on these high levels of national and international finance are being made without regard for the needs and vital interests of Yankee City. The old ties between top management and the community have completely broken down.

As the vertical hierarchy of the factory system extended to executive offices in New York, even the local factory managers came to be, for the most part, "outsiders" and members of ethnic minorities who really lived outside the town, drove down to work in the morning, and left at night. The workers knew or felt that the forces that controlled local men would not control these outsiders. The vast network of relations and memberships that made the former owners local leaders, as well as local manufacturers, had been reduced to a purely economic one of employer and employee. It was that and nothing more. It is small wonder that the workers during this strike "gave the horse laugh to the managers when they talked about being good fellows."

At the time of the strike the few local men who were managers, although born and reared in Yankee City, were little more than the factory managers for big-city capitalists, for they occupied inferior positions in this vastly extended vertical structure. They were not in a position to take leadership. They were not in a position of great power where they were free to make the decisions that always characterized the lives of the owners of the previous period.

Each of these local men felt what had happened very deeply, and some of them were explicit enough about it to say so. We knew some of them well. They were not the weak or unscrupulous men that their opponents made them out to be. Personally, they were men of good reputations in the business world. Some of them had been trained by their own fathers to be community leaders, but their place in the new socioeconomic structure of Yankee City prevented them from playing this role, and each in his own way contributed directly to the defeat of the managerial group. Part of their ineptness was due to their inability to measure up in their own minds to the great men of the past. This was a dead past, glorious and safe, when men knew themselves to be free men and Yankee City was "the hub of the universe." This whole period was symbolized in the memories of the workers and management by the names and reputations of the former owners. The lives of these men epitomized the period for all those who remembered. They symbolized the longing of everyone to return to those days when it was possible for one of them, with all his power and prestige, to stop and gently chide Sam Taylor, the cutter, for not calling him by his first name, and he and Sam could talk about "the trouble in the cutting room." Power was under control, and security was present then; manager and worker were part of a self-contained system in which each knew his part in the total system.

In these days of big-city capitalism, when Yankee City had lost control of its own destinies, few workers would go up to the "big boss" to tell him "what's wrong in the cutting room," and those who did were not considered the respected friends of the workers but "stool pigeons who were getting theirs from management."

During the strike the local men cut poor figures as fighters for management's side. Two of them openly lined up with the strikers. Local sentiment and the feeling against "the foreigners" were too much for them. They materially contributed to the workers' victory.

One of them damaged the cause of management when he tried to fight the head of the union during a peace conference. Everyone said he blustered and acted badly when he used such tactics. He was under the control of higher management and occupied an inferior managerial position, where he had little freedom to assume command and take leadership. Yet he had learned from "one of the grand old men" of the last period, when he worked for him, how his kind of man should act, and he knew that an owner and manager should assume control. It seems a reasonable hypothesis that the conflict between his beliefs about how a manager should act and what he was permitted to do by his status greatly contributed to causing his unfortunate act, an act which materially aided the union. He tried to take command in a situation where it was impossible to do so, and, instead of commanding, he could only "bluster."

His antagonist, on the other hand, was "top manager"

of the union. He did have power, and he could make decisions. His beliefs about what should be done and his status were commensurate, and he used them to the greatest effect for the cause of the union.

All these local men knew somehow they were not the men their "fathers" were, and these dead men, symbolizing the glorious past, overawed and helped to defeat them. While the men of yesterday are dead, "their souls go marching on" in the memories of the living. They have become collective symbols of that lost age when the prestige and power of local financiers and local producers "took care of our own people." These symbols were powerful influences upon the sentiments of workers as well as managers during the strike crisis. Sapping the confidence of the local managers, they gave strength to the strikers, who dramatized their cause in terms of a struggle of Yankee City against big-city capitalism.

From this analysis of today's and yesterday's owners several important propositions can be offered that contribute to our understanding of the strike. The vertical extension of the corporate structure of the shoe-manufacturing enterprises had pushed the top of the hierarchy into the great metropolises and, in so doing, had brought in outsiders who were foreigners in culture, had no local prestige, and were lacking in understanding and feeling for the local workers and the town itself. This extension of the industrial hierarchy reduced the local men to inferior positions in the hierarchy, where they were incapable of making decisions and could not initiate actions that would give them the power of leadership for the workers and for the rest of the town.

The local managers, reduced to inferior statuses in the industrial hierarchy, also occupied lower social-class ranking in the community than their predecessors had. This greatly reduced their strength as leaders who could form community opinion in times of crisis when the position of management was threatened. They could no longer lead the worker or the community. Because of this inferior position of the managers, those men in the community who would once have been their natural allies and who enjoyed top social-class position were now above them and shared none of their interests, were hostile to them, and friendly to the workers.

In "the good old days," the people of Yankee City felt that they all shared in a common way of life, in which business and industry were closely integrated into the community. This way of life had its frictions and conflicts, but it provided all the people with a set of common symbols to guide their behavior, and it also provided effective leadership from the top of the social order. Furthermore, these personal ties made it possible for workers to redress their grievances through going right up to members of management.

When New York financiers assumed control of the industrial hierarchy, the social and civic leaders of Yankee City were no longer directly tied in with the wider life of the community. This split between management and the community made it possible to mobilize the workers into an organization to fight the management.

In the same period, the solidarity of the workers was strengthened by the breakup of the old skill hierarchy. No longer could the workers start at the bottom as apprentices and progress upward step by step as they grew older and acquired the skills and learned the way of life of the skilled craftsman. This age-graded skill hierarchy served to differentiate the workers from one another and to provide increasing security, prestige, and freedom with every step up from the bottom of the ladder. Now the rewards and satisfaction of this way of life are gone forever. Mechanization of the shoe industry has leveled the skills so that there is little room for such differentiation. When workers become interchangeable cogs in a machine, they come to feel that the only security for the individual lies in belonging to an organization of fellow-workers.

What happened in Yankee City appears to have been happening throughout the country. With advances in technology and the development of big-city capitalism, the social distance between workers and management has been increasing, and we seem to be witnessing the emergence of an industrial working class.

The status of the worker has steadily deteriorated, and he has lost his chance to work his way up the craft ladder onto higher rungs of skill or into management. He has also lost the personal ties with management that might enable him to settle his grievances on an individual basis. Since the workers are now sufficiently alike to have had common experiences and anxieties, it is no longer difficult for the industrial union to organize them into a group for collective bargaining. Besides exerting economic pressure, the union gives the workers a new sense of strength and becomes a powerful weapon to force management to recognize their worth as men. To compensate for their loss of status and for their anxieties in a changing industrial civilization, workers have been trying to find status and security in a union organization.

American industry has been undergoing far-reaching changes in technology and human relations. It is only through an understanding of the nature of these changes that it is possible to explain the labor strife that spreads through its cities and towns.

7

AMERICAN ETHNIC AND SECTARIAN GROUPS

Ethnic Persistence and Assimilation

In most cities and large towns of the United States there are a number of groups which are social minorities differing from one another in religious, national, or cultural origin. Through the processes of acculturation and assimilation these groups tend to merge into the general population; during the course of several generations, most of them lose their group identity. Persistence of group identity and resistance to assimilation are often seen among ethnic peoples whose ancestral cultures differ in important respects from the American norms, whose religious systems keep them in a cohesive group, or whose physical characteristics segregate them from the basic American stock.

To make sure we understood the intimate life of the several groups, several research men lived in close association with them. What they did was observed. What they said was recorded. Local histories, diaries, city records, genealogies, and other materials were used to reconstruct the history of the several groups. The family and its generations were traced back to the homeland. Membership lists in churches, associations, and other institutions provided us with good evidence about the composition of each group and helped us determine which of them, many of their members being American-born, continued to participate in the ethnic system.

In popular speech, ethnic groups and color castes are often classed together as "minority groups" or "racial minorities"; at times and under certain conditions their members feel and think of themselves as sharing common problems. Ethnic groups and color castes are alike, insofar as they differ from the dominant group and each is in a subordinate position. But, fundamentally, their positions are quite different. The ethnic position is a cultural difference, something that can be changed even by the adult immigrant. He can and often does become a candidate for social mobility. Very often his children are absorbed by the dominant whites and the American culture. Not so the Negro. He is a born American and has no other culture. His American ancestry may be much older than many or most of those in the white group. But, unlike the ethnic, his status is fixed. He must remain in the subordinate caste. He cannot hope to move up the ladder generally available for all other Americans. He can only hope for social-class advancement for himself within his own color group, and can work to change and improve the relative place of the Negro group.

The ancestral family system of all the Continental European groups who have migrated to America was patriarchal, the mother and children being subordinated to the authority and discipline of the father. With the exception of the Jews, who had been small tradesmen or skilled artisans coming from an urban society, these groups came from a predominantly agrarian economy in which the family had traditionally functioned as a productive unit. All members of a family had particular tasks assigned by the father, whose traditional authority as head of the family was enhanced by the fact that he managed it also as a productive unit.

Because of the attachment to the land, certain sons continued with the family even after marriage, extending the family unit through several generations to become a *grosse Familie*. The father as patriarch of the ever growing family continued in his role of authority until his death; the continuity of generations insured the perpetuation of the family against interruption by death. This system shows strong contrast to that of the American family, which is typically broken up when the children marry and leave the home to establish family units of their own.

In the ancestral Continental European families the father or patriarch was shown great respect, commensurate with his authority. He was the lawgiver to his children, the law-enforcer, the source of all sanctions, and the person around whom all phases of family life revolved. The *grosse Familie* approximated a self-contained unit economically and socially; but this closeness of family life did not imply an easy, affectionate relationship between the father and his offspring. On the contrary, the relationship was formalized to a high degree and was usually lacking in intimacy, affection, or indulgence.

The small immediate American family, on the other hand, psychologically tends to extreme intimacy and great affection or, at times when these are lacking, to hostility. It is an institution in which everyone indulges himself and allows others this same privilege. The role of the parent in the American middle class is usually one of the affection-giver rather than one of authority. The ethnic father must adjust himself to this new situation or face constant criticism or open revolt from his children.

Among the complex factors which contributed to the mass migrations from Europe in the nineteenth century, the economic factor was predominant in almost all cases. For some groups, economic forces of expulsion from the homeland which had resulted in serious dislocations in the society were prime motivators. For other groups, it was the economic forces of attraction of the United States that induced them to migrate. For still others, it was a combination of the two, the attraction of the new country being sufficiently abetted by the difficulties in the homeland to induce seeking new homes.

The Irish were forced to leave Ireland because of the poverty of the economy, which was greatly aggravated by the potato famine of the 1840's. The Jews and Armenians were compelled to leave by economic forces which were greatly aggravated by the antagonism to them on the part of the Russians and Turks. Poverty in Greece and the attraction of possible wealth in the United States combined to lure the Greeks. Similar forces accounted for the migrations of other peoples.

Correlated with the motivation for migration in its effect on the group's adjustment to the American community were the intentions of the individuals in their new life. Some came as single men, intending to make a fortune and return to their native lands. Some came with the expectation of making enough to send remittances back home to support their families. Others came with their families or intending to send for them as soon as possible; they arrived with the intention of establishing a permanent home in their adopted land.

Motives for migration and intention to stay varied from country to country and in different periods of time. Where the forces of expulsion were dominant in the motives, the migrants came in family groups with the intention of establishing a permanent residence. The Armenians and the Jews from particular countries were examples of this mode. Where the forces of attraction of the expanding American economy were dominant, usually only the younger unmarried sons came.

The ethnic group begins its life in the American community at the lowest possible level, sometimes even below a position in which it can be identified in social class, and proceeds at different speeds to make its way up through the social-status system. Although there are sharp differences among the various ethnic groups, in general it can be said that in the beginning they fill the jobs and live in the houses that no one else wants. The Poles, working in the Chicago stockyards and living in back-of-the-yards districts, and the Mexicans and Puerto Ricans in the slums of Chicago, working in the steel mills, are examples of recent ethnic groups who fit this pattern. In time, the ethnic people move into better housing and better jobs.

When the class system of the adopted country, such as America, is permissive and allows the ethnic to come in, the result is highly disruptive to the minority group. Their children respond to the attractions of the class system by breaking their ethnic ties and identifying with the social symbols of the larger community. The ethnic family system is often turned upside down. The younger generation, in learning American ways, speaking English, and identifying with the symbols of the new culture, dominates and often repudiates the ethnic standards and traditional values of the older generation. The parent generation, far from holding the position of traditional superordination which it enjoyed in its ancestral culture—and enjoys in America if the ancestral family system is maintained—is subordinated. For many parents this situation is sufficiently punishing that they suffer a kind of malaise from their inability to understand or solve it. In this period of disruption, the children feel a deep sense of guilt, and the parents feel inadequate and bewildered. When the ethnic family moves upward as a unit toward greater Americanization and all of the members put their efforts into it, the solidarity of the family tends to be increased rather than lessened. Subtle factors are involved, but it follows that, if some members of the family move toward Americanization and others against it, conflict inevitably develops. The acculturation and assimilation changes do not necessarily need to be upward for such conflict to arise, but the process of social mobility is more likely to lead to deep conflict than mere acculturation by itself.

When the institutions of the new community do not permit or encourage mobility, when the social-class system subordinates the ethnic group, its solidarity is increased. All the factors which the community employs to assimilate the ethnic have no influence in disrupting the group if the ethnic individuals are not allowed to move out and up the social ladder.

The ethnic church has been a powerful subsystem of the original society; it is a repository of the sacred values and symbols of the group. It helps to organize the national and cultural attitudes; as such, the ethnic church is an institution of crucial importance in the life of the group and decisive in determining whether assimilation will be slow or rapid. Church structure largely by itself links the ethnic community with the ancestral national community. Associations and parochial and national schools are developed later by the ethnic group to keep the ethnic individual related to the church and the ethnic community and to restrain him from straying too far into the larger American social system. The social structures which appear subsequent to an ethnic people's arrival—for example, associations—usually reflect the changes in the personalities of the ethnic individuals as they become less ethnic and more American.

During the later phases of assimilation and acculturation the ethnic church becomes itself an indigenous American institution; the Lutheran Church is less and less German and Scandinavian and more and more an American denomination. As a matter of fact, this church is taking the lead in developing some of the more indigenous values and beliefs of Americans and church enterprise. The Catholic Church in America increasingly deals with problems that confront all Americans, is less Irish, Italian, or other ethnic group and more an integral part of American life. The same changes are rapidly occurring among the temples and synagogues of the Jews. Many of the Jewish congregations find that the older traditional beliefs while highly honored and respected no longer reflect the same values that they did when previously held by faithful Jews. However, for all of them at many localities, the influence of the ethnic homeland is still vital and important.

Language is an absolute necessity to a social system, not

only as the medium of social relations at a given moment but also as the medium by which the cultural forms of a society are transmitted from one point in time to another. It is indispensable to the persistence of a social system and is inextricably interwoven with the structure of which it is a part. Obviously, those ethnics who speak English will tend to assimilate more rapidly than those who do not. In groups where the mother-tongue is taught in the folk school and spoken entirely at home and in the ethnic community, it is a factor of conflict with the younger generation that learns English in the public school, and it is a factor of cohesion for the rest of the group.

Another factor contributing to or preventing assimilation is the period of time that the group has been in America. Mobility in the larger social system is directly related to the length of residence, if other factors are equal. The size of the population of the group is also important, for a large group is more resistant to assimilation and mobility than a small one which is more easily disrupted.

The Ethnic Family in America

The patriarchal character of the ethnic family begins to alter as soon as the husband and father enters the industrial economy of America. Instead of ruling an almost self-contained economic unit within his own household, he leaves to assume a highly limited and specialized function in the factory and market structures of the larger community. The characteristic division of labor of the new economic system is reflected in the differentiated functions of husband and wife. Most frequently the husband now is the producer, and the wife is completely dependent upon him and subordinate to him. She no longer has a place beside him in his work but functions in the role of homemaker. Small sums which are required for this activity are doled out to her, and larger purchases are made by her husband or under his supervision.

The division between husband and wife is accentuated by the fact that, through his external relations with the larger American life, he learns to speak English, whereas, more often than not, the wife, confined to the home and to very limited social relations within her own family and ethnic group, continues to speak only the ethnic language. Very often this fact subordinates her in the minds of her children after they start to school because they resent having to speak the ethnic language and usually blame the mother for this necessity.

Among some ethnic groups this position of the wife alters as her relationships expand and she begins to move beyond the home, but in others there is a definite effort on the part of the husband to keep the wife in the home.

There are, of course, variations in this theme of the relation of the husband and wife in their new occupational status. Some husbands and wives, after a period of time, enter into small businesses and work together. Other husbands and wives are employed in large industrial enterprises. But in any case the appearance of children usually results in the woman's taking the role of the housewife and being confined to her family and ethnic group.

When the ethnic family comes to America, the father is no longer the head of the family as a productive unit in which the child as he matures is kept in subordination to his parents' will. Moreover, the father is also away from the home during most of the day and the children are at school. Whereas in the old country the schooling was of the rural, primary order which served merely to supplement the teaching and indoctrination given the children in thc home, here the schools function to orient the children to the new American society and away from their traditional group. Play groups around the school, cliques, and gangs further separate the child from the controls of the family.

To the father who has grown up in the old country, who is experiencing all the difficulties of adjusting to the new American environment, his home and family and later his ethnic group often seem to be his only security. His American-born children in their early years are completely integrated with the family and with the ethnic group. But even before they enter school they begin to have play relations with the children outside their own group and to pick up at least a few words of English. When school begins—whether it is public or parochial—the child is taught English, and the ethnic language becomes increasingly unimportant in his daily relations with those around him. The effort of the ethnic or folk schools, which are supplementary to the public schools, to teach the ethnic language is indicative of the symbolic importance of the language to the integrity of the whole group.

The language factor represents a fundamental break between the parent and child, which continually widens as the child grows older. As the schools increase their training of the maturing child in American symbols, his identifications are increasingly with those symbols until more often than not he develops an active antagonism to those of his family's origin.

A Jewish boy, in Yankee City, was heard to remark, "It gets me so mad when I hear some of the Jewish women speaking Jewish out loud on the street. This is America!" And a Russian father complained of his son, "He doesn't understand half of what I say to him in Russian. Sometimes I will be talking for a long time and my son will break in with, 'I can't understand half what you are saying. Why don't we talk English?' This makes me sore."

In school not only does the child learn English and the content of American social symbols, but he learns social attitudes that are opposed to his family's and his ethnic group's traditional ways of life. Self-reliance and independence and freedom of action are highly prized American social virtues which always conflict with the child's compliance to the patriarchal authority of his father. As the child starts up through the grades in the school system, he begins to develop clique relations which draw him further away from his ethnic origins. In Yankee City it was discovered that ethnic children very often do not want to play with children of their own ethnic group but prefer those of other ethnic groups and native Yankees—an indication of their subordination of the ethnic elements in their personalities and unwillingness to be identified with their own group.

The significance of the statement that assimilation of the ethnic children into the American social system turns the ethnic family upside down will now be seen. The forces which the dominant society exerts upon the ethnic groups are exerted primarily upon the child, so that he, rather than the parent, becomes the transmitting agent of social change. Through this new role the maturing child often assumes a superordinate position in the family, and the parents, reversing their usual position, become subordinate. There can be little doubt that this unusual situation has become a factor in the occurrence of juvenile delinquency among first-generation ethnic children. The testimony of social psychologists and of psychoanalysis buttresses the findings of the social anthropologist to support this hypothesis.

Although families traditionally have been the central link between the past and the future, thereby assuring cultural continuity and social stability, in the ethnic families the culture that is to be transmitted to the children is rejected by them; and the changes that are introduced into that cultural system are resisted by the parents and transmitted through the medium of the children. The result is disruptive to the family system, to the ethnic group, and to many personalities that experience it. In the process, the older and younger generations become isolated and estranged from each other.

From this grows the child's challenge to the father's authority. Not only does the child resent the fact that his parents do not act according to American behavioral standards; not only does he resent pressure to act after the ethnic behavioral modes; but, infused with American social logics, he implicitly questions the right of his father to dominate and control his behavior. This conflict between child and parent develops differently in time and degree according to the factors of resistance in the ethnic group, the sex of the children, their ages, and the attitudes of the specific parents.

Conflict within the personality of the child, necessarily engendered by the position he occupies, can be resolved in one of four ways. He may take part in activities which violate both the American and the ethnic standards of behavior. Sometimes this is delinquent behavior. At a more intellectual level he may participate in esoteric religious or political movements that are in conflict with the traditions of both groups. He may become 100 per cent American—more American than the Americans—and reject with hostile feelings his own ethnic society. Or he may reconcile the conflict factors and, as he grows older, take active part either in the Americanization of the ethnic group to which he belongs or in fostering some of the old traditions of the homeland. Very often the first-generation child proceeds through all these stages to resolve his conflicts.

The parent-child conflict is most severe among groups in which the father is oriented completely around ethnic symbols, including the ethnic language and church. For example, the Greek men in Yankee City spend their lives within the Greek community, rarely find it necessary to speak English, attend the Greek church regularly (which is entirely controlled by the men), and have their social life in the Greek coffee houses. The Greek father sees no necessity for his children to be educated or to do anything different from what he has always done. He tries to exert patriarchal authority, and his children chafe under the pressure. Among some of the newer ethnic groups, the Poles, Russians, and Armenians, the reaction of the father to this situation is to exert his authority with increased vigor. One way in which he does this is to appropriate his children's earnings either directly or indirectly as board. These measures result in a great variety of evasions by the children. Their attitudes are that it is not they who are doing wrong but the parents. The parents also try to exert their full authority over courtship and the period before marriage. Here, again, the children have learned how to evade and avoid the consequences of parental control. Sometimes at the other extreme there are parents who exert no authority at all over the children; consciously or unconsciously, they admit their defeat.

One of the consequences of this shift in the authority of the generations is that not only do the children become deviant but very often the father's personality seems to become disorganized, leading to such behavior on his part as assault and battery and drunkenness, which are the predominant offenses among the older generation of the recently arrived ethnic groups. This disruption of the ethnic parent's personality we have called "personality disjunction." Extreme personality disjunction appears only among the Poles, Greeks, and Italians. In these groups, as against the ethnic groups which are their contemporaries, a special factor was their migrational mode—they came singly and, for the most part, as young adults. Few of them came directly to Yankee City; they drifted in from other and larger cities. They had been conditioned, prior to the immigration, to tightly held family controls and had then undergone for varying periods a foot-loose social existence beyond the controls of their families. Some of them, though by no means all, could not weather the sudden release from their parents' restraints, and personality disjunction followed. When they came to marry and establish families, they could not discipline themselves either in their extra-familial relations or in their family functions as disciplinarians. In fact, there are instances in which parent and child were apprehended together in the performance of what the society considered a crime.

Although the husband, in maintaining his superordinate status, can exercise considerable supervision over his wife's participation in the American society, he can no longer exert this same kind of control over his children. While they are in the ethnic and parochial schools usually established by ethnic groups, they are effectively related to the group and its traditions through the teaching of the language, of their national history, and of the ancestral social symbols; but when they leave these schools, the only institution that relates them effectively to the ethnic group is the church. This relation is augmented by the insistence of the parents upon identification with the national church, at least in ritual.

Social Mobility and Ethnic Assimilation

Since there were a number of ethnic groups in Yankee City, eight in all, it was possible, by studying them comparatively, to make certain generalizations about their similarities and differences, particularly their advancement in the larger society and the improvement of their position in the economic and social order. These generalizations have contributed to our understanding of the interrelations of social mobility and assimilation. After identifying all the individuals in Yankee City according to whether they were old American or members of ethnic groups, their place of residence was determined. The residential areas had been drawn in previously on maps and each area rated according to its value in terms of social status (in popular terms, according to whether or not the community considered the neighborhood a desirable or undesirable place in which to live). The lowest area rated 1, the highest 6. The number of households of an ethnic group in an area was multiplied by the rating assigned the area. When the total for all areas for the ethnic group was determined, a figure indicating the social status of the residences of each group was derived by dividing the grand total by the number of households. For example, the 104 Irish households in one year when multiplied by their ratings of the areas in which they lived amounted to 177. This summation (177), when divided by the total of households (104), gives a quotient of 1.7, the residential status index.

By comparing the indexes of the groups, it could be

learned which groups had or had not advanced in residential status. Furthermore, by going back through regular interviews in the past, the rate of advance for each group could be learned and studied comparatively.

The (Catholic) Irish, who arrived first, had an index of 1.7 (see Table 2) in 1850. By 1933 they had advanced to 2.9. The Russians, who arrived in 1920, had an index of 1.3. The indexes of the other ethnic groups, including French Canadians, Jews, Italians, Armenians, Greeks, and

TABLE 2

Residential Indexes of the Ethnic Groups

	1850	1864	1873	1883	1893	1903	1913	1923	1933
Irish	1.7	2.0	2.1	2.1	2.1	2.2	2.4	2.6	2.9
French Canadian					1.7	1.8	1.8	2.1	2.4
Jewish							1.9	2.1	2.8
Italian								2.2	2.4
Armenian								2.4	2.6
Greek								2.4	2.5
Polish								1.3	1.4
Russian									1.3

Poles, who arrived in Yankee City in the order named, were scattered between these two extremes. Ordinarily, the index of advancement for each group corresponds to the length of time the group has been in residence. The Jews and the French Canadians are notable exceptions, the former getting a higher score than might be expected and the French Canadians a lower one. The Jews, higher partly because they are more urban in background than the others and partly because they were practiced in being a minority group before arriving, were better equipped to get what they wanted. The French Canadians, the only group coming from a near-by homeland and more determined to stay what they were and not become English, remained culturally more as they were when they arrived; and, since they were less interested in moving, scored lower in the residential index.

By the same procedure, an index was constructed for occupation. The results showed a distribution of indexes similar to that for dwelling area for each ethnic group. The Jews not only outranked all the ethnic groups for occupational status but were decidedly superior to the old Americans. Obviously, the effects of anti-Semitism are not no-

TABLE 3

Class and Ethnic Group

	Upper-Upper	Lower-Upper	Upper-Middle	Lower-Middle	Upper-Lower	Lower-Lower
Yankee	2.7	2.8	15.9	35.3	23.2	20.2
Irish		0.3	5.9	27.5	53.8	12.5
French			1.0	13.2	40.3	45.6
Jewish			3.0	41.8	47.6	7.6
Italian			0.4	13.7	41.9	44.0
Armenian			1.2	17.9	50.8	30.1
Greek			2.2	5.4	35.9	56.6
Polish				0.7	9.8	89.5
Russian				4.3	25.5	70.2

ticeable in their occupational or residential scores, two characteristics (as the I.S.C. indicates) which clearly reflect the social status of a family.

The distribution of the ethnic groups among the six social classes is also very closely related to the period of time the group has been in the community. In Table 3 we see that the Irish have climbed the highest. They have members in the lower-upper class, a level attained by no other group. It will be noticed that no ethnic people are in the old-family or upper-upper class. This does not mean that all the ancestry of the upper-upper class is Yankee. It means only that the people in that social class whose ancestry is ethnic have been completely assimilated and have ceased being members of ethnic groups. By tracing the lineages of many of the families in the top level, we learned that several had ancestors who had once belonged to ethnic groups.

The ethnic members of the upper-middle class are more likely to marry out of their group or, by simple assimilation, to cease participating in their ethnic social system. Some Catholic Irish marry Yankees and cease being Catholic or Irish. Some Jews give up their religion, and a few become Christians. The higher an ethnic family has climbed in the class system, the more its members are like old Americans socially and individually; those who remain at the bottom tend to retain more of their ethnic characteristics and become stronger members of the ethnic group.

The indexes for residence and class position of the older and more recent groups, present observations in Yankee City indicate, have changed, but the same processes of geographical movement correlated with social class mobility continue. There are no complete statistics such as the earlier ones, but the social class position of all ethnic groups has greatly improved. From recent field observations and interviews we find that the twenty-odd-year interval has seen a few Irish Catholics move into the highly ranked social clubs and their status generally has been heightened. All ethnic groups have upper-class members and others have advanced to lower-upper ratings. Smaller proportions are now present in the two lower classes. The combined influences of assimilation, acculturation and social mobility, for those ethnic members here in America and the great reduction of the number of immigrants have produced a people whose present generations are very like those of all American stocks. In fact, many have ceased being members of ethnic groups and disappeared into the total society. Increasingly the values of their "own" institutions are less ethnic and more committed to the beliefs and values characteristic of larger populations of this country.

Family, Church, and School

Of the ethnic families studied in Yankee City, the ~~Greeks~~ Greeks showed the least deviation from the ancestral family system. The women were highly subordinated and confined to domestic interests in their activities, except for visiting among themselves. In the Greek Orthodox church structure the woman has no status except through her husband, since only the men are recognized as members. The women are segregated from the men in the seating arrangements and are subordinated in the church ritual, having only a passive role, while the men chant the responses and act as altar assistants. The sacred ritual in the home is performed by the woman. She performs such family rituals as burning incense on Saturday night and carrying it ceremonially through the house.

Control of the Greek church lay with the local community rather than with the national hierarchy, as in the case of the Roman Catholic church. Selection of the church leaders was based on more or less complete identification with the Greek community and on closeness to the ancestral tradition.

The Armenians in Yankee City were members of both the Apostolic and the Congregational churches. The latter group met with the established Congregationalists but later separated to form a church of their own. The fact that the Armenians had no strong national church and that many of them were, in fact, Congregationalists, a church with a solid New England identification and tradition, may account for the fact that the Armenian women, unlike the Greek, participated in the larger Yankee City community. It certainly facilitated the rise of the Armenians in the Yankee City class system, although this factor affected the wife the least of all.

The mobility of the Irish ethnics in the community of Yankee City has been greatly aided by their common use of the English language. But, in spite of the advance of the Irish group in the community and of the length of their residence, Irish wives are more retarded, as compared with Jewish wives, in their status within the family and in the local Irish community. The reason for this is to be found in the relation of the Catholic church to the family structure. The Catholic church transcends the community in its power and maintains control over the family, despite the impact of the American social system. This explanation of the effect of the church upon the role of the Irish wife is reinforced by the fact that French-Canadian wives, being Catholic, are also subordinated in the ethnic community.

Although the Roman Catholic church system transcends national lines in terms of content, within each country the church system is a subsystem of the national culture. In Yankee City the two Catholic churches are national churches, focuses for the nationalistic sentiments of their most important parishioners. The community system of the Irish in Yankee City and of the French Canadians, too, is the church parish, its school, and the many associations which are part of the church structure. The priest represents the extended church system. For many years, more often than not, throughout America, the Catholic church provided an over-all social structure which organized, regulated, and helped to maintain the culture of a particular ethnic group. The priest became the leader and focal center of a particular national culture. Although the church is recognized as universal, having a hierarchy that interrelates all the various nationalistic groups, the religion of the local parish in the big cities and towns of America was usually organized on an ethnic basis.

The Jews are an example of a group who came from a social and economic, but not a religious, system similar to America's. They were an urban people in Europe in possession of urban social and technical skills who, consequently, did not have the difficulty of adjusting from an agrarian economy to our urban civilization. They easily took their places in American trade centers. Furthermore, because they were a minority group in the urban centers of Europe from which they came, they had acquired the skills necessary to participate where it seemed wise and to evade and avoid participating where it did not fit their basic traditions.

In the folk school connected with the synagogue, Hebrew, the formal language, is taught. The children hear Yiddish only at home. The parents are eager for their children to have as much education as possible. This attitude fits their traditional great emphasis on education and, at the same time, fits the practical importance of education in their new culture. This new education is secured in the public schools, where the children learn to speak English and where they are rapidly oriented to American national and social symbols.

The synagogue is a very strong factor in maintaining the identification of the Jewish group; but even here adjustments are made in religious observances to adapt the group to its new community.

In Yankee City the older generations of Jews are orthodox, but the younger ones have developed a modified system of religious observances that is better adapted to the economic and social system of the larger community. This so-called "Reformed" system is but a modification of Orthodox Judaism. There is little indication that the Jews are being affected by, or attracted to, Christianity as a sacred ideology. However, there is considerable evidence to show that, within their own social system, they are influenced by Christianity through the culture in which they now live.

The nature of the husband-wife relation gives a measure of the degree of adaptation achieved by the Jewish group in the new society. Jewish wives, especially of the generations of Jews who arrived in America when they were very young and socially unformed, are given more autonomy than those of any other ethnic group that has been studied. This, of course, is very different from the role allowed them in the ghettos of Poland, Russia, and Germany.

During the course of the research in Yankee City, an episode occurred in the planning of the new synagogue which is symbolic of the shift in attitude toward the women of this group. Traditionally, the women have always been seated in the rear of the congregation, but, when plans were made for the new synagogue, the women, especially the younger ones, protested against this segregation. Supported by their husbands, they succeeded in having a compromise worked out by which the traditionalist husbands and wives were seated at opposite sides of the congregation and the families who wished to sit together were given a space down the center. The new arrangement made it possible for the husbands and wives who believed in equal status, but who still felt some of the force of the traditions which separated the sexes in the church, to sit as it were side-by-side in co-ordinate positions rather than putting the wives in a subordinate place at the rear of the church; and it was also possible for the others who felt even more strongly about this change in the traditional relations to sit together, thereby violating one of the oldest traditions of Judaism.

In their desire to see their children advance in the new society, the Jewish generation who arrived in America as children attempts to support its own children in the new ways; but the generation of people who arrived as adults, finding its security in the traditional orthodox way of life, in its life around the synagogue, is in great conflict. Parents in this latter group feel that their children lack respect and reject authority; the children complain that their parents are old-fashioned and without understanding.

In Yankee City a father who was traditional and had come from the old country after he was grown was extremely bitter:

Children are not worthwhile. What do you get out of them? Once you used to get respect and honor at least. Here they throw you away. You become a back number. My daughter had a birthday party last Sunday and she had some friends up. You know where we stayed? In the kitchen until I got disgusted and said to my wife, "Let's go to bed." That was about eleven o'clock. What time they went to bed, I don't know. But do you think in Europe you would leave a girl alone with a boy? Never on your life.

In Russia the Jewish children would give their lives for their parents, so devoted were they. But here the children may respect their parents but they don't have the reverence of the old country.

The older generation has given up in the conflict except to conform to traditional patterns of behavior at home and in prohibiting relations of their marriageable daughters with Gentile boys. But even in the home many traditions have given way. The radio is played on the Sabbath, for example, because the children threaten to go somewhere else if this is not allowed. The reaction of the children to any enforcement of the old standards is expressed by a Yankee City girl, who said (in speaking of her father, a person who would be treated not only with respect but with fear and reverence in the old country):

Oh, he gets me sick. Every time I have some friends to the house he wants to sit up with my mother in the parlor. You know what that does to a crowd of young people. What have we in common with them? Nothing. So then they sit in the kitchen with the door open so they can hear everything that goes on, peeking on us! As if we can't be trusted. Besides, at every little thing I do he preaches to me. Not that he forbids me to do it. He has more sense than that. He simply is always telling me how they used to do things in Russia. Well, that's all very interesting, but this happens to be the United States of America, not Russia, and the twentieth century, not the nineteenth. His body may be here but his mind is still in Russia and in the nineteenth century. And it will never be any other place. He thinks I don't respect him. Well, he's right and you can see my reasons.

American Sectarian Groups

The role of the church in maintaining the identity of an ethnic group is best seen in the extreme example of a religious sect—a type of grouping of which there are numerous examples in American life. Sects can be ethnic, that is, divergent in social background, or American (for example, Jehovah's Witnesses). The essential point about a sect is that its ideology is in conflict with the prevailing one of the larger community. Usually the members of the sect place such a high value on its ideology that they are willing to do anything to maintain it.

American sects can be classified into two kinds. Some are interested in maintaining a brotherhood where all men are equal. They are willing to take in new members but are not much interested in increasing their number. The other type of sect, the Mormons, for example, permits status differences among the members of the group. They proselytize heavily and are willing to create another self-contained society which will comprise only their own way of life. The first kind, usually a small religious group, gets into difficulties with the larger society because it fights the class system and holds its members tightly within the sect. Such groups as the Brethren of Christ, the Church of the Brethren, the Amish, the Hutterites, the Mennonites, and others are often characterized by prescribed variations of dress from the American norm, by strict rules governing social behavior, prohibition against out-marriages, and common love of equality and of brotherhood and a belief that, while all others are lost, they are saved souls.

Because the home is so fundamental in the life of the sect, the church has exercised very rigid control over domestic life. Conflicts that arise between parents and children over the enforcement of the strict sectarian restrictions often lead to the children's taking part secretly in activities outside the sect and, later, leaving home as soon as they are old enough to get jobs. To make this choice is exceedingly difficult, for within the sect are the unity and security seldom found in the larger world. However, if the individual succeeds in finding a group beyond his own which provides satisfactory status for him, the power of the sect to discipline him ceases to exist. To meet the challenge of the younger generation, many sects have established colleges to continue indoctrination of the young. Others have modified their creed to the extent that they are losing the characteristics of the sect and assuming the aspects of a religious denomination.

In the small middle-western city which we have called Jonesville there is a Norwegian-Lutheran group which has many of the characteristics of a sect. It, too, is in conflict with the standards of behavior of the larger community because it has a set of moral values organized by its church which are not acceptable to the rest of the community and, in turn, the members of the sect reject many of the values of the larger community. This group is regarded by the rest of the community as peculiar, isolated, and non-cooperative, for they will not, or cannot, participate in some of its most highly valued civic activities. Whereas most ethnic sects have migrated to this country as fully developed social units, units already at warfare with their larger society, the Norwegian-Lutheran group of Jonesville developed as a sect after their arrival in America. The community has responded to their insistence on isolation by refusing to admit some of the more assimilated Norse into associations of very high prestige. This helps to maintain their subordination and, at the same time, helps to strengthen the solidarity of the Norwegian-Lutheran group.

As the first and second generations of American-born children of the Norse have grown up, there is increasing replacement of ethnic symbols by religious symbols. In their desire to lose the stigma of foreignness, they have replaced Norwegian with English in the church services and have given up other aspects of their ethnic origins, until now the only formal bonds which maintain the group are the moral ones given structural form by their church. The pressure for Americanization comes only from those who have risen in the class structure of Jonesville. Those who have remained in the lower class cling to the traditional behavior of the ethnic group, as well as the religious symbols, in order to increase their feeling of security.

It is not always easy to distinguish between ethnic groups and sects. Each has ways of living which differ from those of the whole society. In varying degrees, each is in conflict with the majority group, but, to survive, each has partly accommodated itself to the larger community. However, despite the many similarities between the sect and the ethnic group, a careful investigator can soon identify the group he is studying as being one or the other.

Primarily, the difference between them lies in the intensity of the group's feelings about retaining the characteristics of its mother-culture and its refusal to alter its original status and original ideology. The sect more often strives to hold each generation within the fixed confines of its rigidly limited structure. The ethnic group more easily compromises and permits its individuals—grudgingly, yet half-willingly—the right to seek their fortunes and advance their interests in the larger American community.

The number, size, and importance of ethnic groups and sects in American life decrease almost yearly. Many of them are disappearing, and others yield much of their cultural substance to the influences of the outer American world. All increasingly adjust to the major outlines of American society. There are too many factors involved, including those in the ethnic group, America generally, and the larger world society, to predict accurately whether all these groups will continue to exist or will surrender to the forces of assimilation and acculturation, but it seems likely that most, if not all of them, will ultimately disappear from American life.

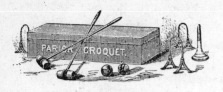

8

SOCIAL PERSISTENCE AND PERSONALITY DEVELOPMENT

The Relation of Species Behavior to Social Persistence

Contemporary social theory and method have been occupied largely with problems of social change. The problems set, more often than not, are concerned with why a particular institution or society exists; the answers are frequently sought in the immediate or distant past. Social data tend to be examined as events in a changing series rather than as evidence to prove or disprove a proposition about the nature of man in society. The questions tend to be: How did a particular (social) artifact become what it is? What is the nature of social change? What are its processes? And what are its basic causes?

Many students of anthropology and sociology have actually gone so far as to define the nature of the two sciences as bodies of knowledge having to do only with history; and history seems to be viewed by them as no more than social change. Important contributions have been made by some of these students; but social inquiry limited only to this viewpoint has often impeded the progress of social science by excluding all possibility of achieving the more important task of working out an integrated social science, a science which could encompass the theories, methods, and evidence of the several social and psychological disciplines.

I want to ask different questions in this chapter from those asked by most historical anthropologists. For present purposes, I shall not be interested in social change as such but in why societies and institutions *persist* through changing generations. If it is important to know how and why social forms change through time, it is even more important to know how and why they persist. The processes involved are complex and difficult to understand. I can do no more than deal with part of this problem. The answers will be sought in the development of personality in society, for it seems to me that social persistence is inextricably interwoven with the formation of personality. I am sure that, if we can learn the interrelations between social persistence and personality formation, we shall have a better understanding of each.

When we ask the two kinds of questions as if they were distinct and separate—What is personality and how is it formed? and What are the processes and principles of cultural persistence?—we do not learn very much.

The first question, narrowly conceived, can tell us only what the psychologists put into its meanings; the second says no more than what the social or group scientists put into the meanings of their questions. I do not believe that either is sufficient. We need better answers, and, to get better answers, we need better questions. When we put the two kinds of questions together by adding them, we achieve no more than two poorly harnessed separate answers that will not pull together. Something more is needed. For our purposes, there should be not two questions but one, and but one answer.

The basic question is: How do adult personalities, who are interconnected and in varying degrees influenced and controlled by the social relations of a society, become socially interrelated with the newly born and growing members of their group so that the social relations which comprise a society persist through changing generations of new personalities? The component parts of this question indicate that some of the answers lie beyond the conventional confines of the study of either group or individual psychology. They must come from a common core of fact in which both sciences are represented.

Although human individuals must learn their own core of species behavior through their experiences with other members of their group, they must also make part of themselves the skills, rules, and symbols of their outer cultural world. During their physical growth, they develop semi-autonomous selves, organized into coherent systems or private worlds, and, by use of the prevailing social system, they interrelate themselves with other persons in the group. While developing their own private selves, human individuals connect and relate themselves with their social system by learning the appropriate use of symbols, skills, and rules and the several relations in which they interact with others. The self thus established (as George Mead, Jean Piaget, and others have pointed out) is largely a private replica of the outer social world (or some part of it) of which the individual is a part; its social relations are mere continuations of those already existing within the group.

To survive, the organism must become a person capable of interacting in a persistent and acceptable manner within his group. The society, aided and sustained by a continuous flow of species behavior, teaches its young the skills, rules, and symbols necessary for social persistence. To say this somewhat differently, and to paraphrase and amplify Freud by placing his concepts in a social framework: the introjected parents and the society of the older generation survive and continue living in the personalities and the contemporary social world of the young. In each succeeding generation the dead generations persist, and their members maintain themselves in the private worlds and social relations of those who live.

During the remainder of this chapter I shall describe how the persisting processes of social class and social mobility operate on the learning and development of human organisms in the United States. I shall do this to illustrate how personality development and the persistence of social systems are interconnected and, from my point of view, comprise one process.

The Learning Maze of the Class System

It will be necessary to describe how the class system operates on the immature. The family is of first importance in this process; since I have previously explained how it functions in the American class system, I shall do no more than review some of the principal points that we should remember at this time.

The training of most immature, preschool children in

middle-class families is different from that in the lower class or in the upper class. It is more severe; it punishes physical aggression but encourages the discharge of such energies in social achievement. Ideally, it trains for individual responsibility and autonomy. It frowns on the free expression of impulses and rewards restraint, foresight, and the acceptance of superior, but more remote, goals. When such training is successful, persons are produced who are often active candidates for social mobility.

Let us now follow up on this introductory period of the individual in American society and examine the social structure which organizes the life of the children after they enter school. We shall attempt to learn from our analysis how the social structure forms and controls the development of the personality according to the values of social class in American democracy.

I shall begin by showing the relation of the school board, which sets policy and is the ultimate authority for the schools of each community, to the social-class system. We shall see that there is a definite relation between the two.

The overwhelming majority of the members of the school boards which administer, control, and set educational policy for the communities we studied were people from the upper-middle and upper classes. Approximately 95 per cent were in the Level above the Common Man and only 5 per cent from the Common Man Level. Ordinarily, in the smaller cities the school boards are elected, and any citizen of the town has the right to run for the office, but closer inspection demonstrates that those in office tend to select those who will succeed them. They choose people in the town who they believe will be appropriate and suitable for such a respectable position. With the best of intentions, they tend to select men and women like themselves. This means that the grammar school and the high school—public institutions supported by local taxation—are largely controlled by the values and ideas of people from the superior classes. Although most of the members tend to be upper-middle class, their decisions very often are dominated by their deference to the opinions of the upper class. In Jonesville the members of old families who had been on the school board, by force of their social position, often dictated decisions about such matters as building new schools or increasing taxation for their support. This was not done in an autocratic manner but rather by the weight of their opinion.

The overwhelming proportion of teachers in the grammar schools and high schools are middle class, often lower-middle class. Many, if not most of them, have been mobile from the upper-lower class. Teaching is one of the most accessible and socially visible professions for ambitious women to enter. In the town of Midwest, 98 per cent of the teachers were middle class; in Yankee City, 97 per cent; and in Deep South, 92 per cent. None of the teachers in Midwest was upper class; only about 3 per cent in Yankee City; and 5 per cent in Deep South. There were no teachers from the lowest class in any of these communities. Only 2 per cent of Midwest's teachers were upper lower and 3 per cent of Deep South's. All of Yankee City's teachers were middle class or better. The teachers tend to be a step or two below the school board in status, but, on the average, they occupy a superior position to that of most of their students. Approximately 60 per cent of the students are lower class, 30 per cent lower middle, and about 10 per cent upper and upper middle (see Fig. 7). This means that well over half the children are in direct relations with teachers whose values and ideas differ from their own.

Since the teachers' judgments of the children and of standards of performance · are inevitably based on their own personal standards, buttressed by those set up by the school as an institution, the lower-class child is at a disadvantage when competing with children from the middle classes. Furthermore, the formal learning problems set by the school, which the child must solve to advance to higher

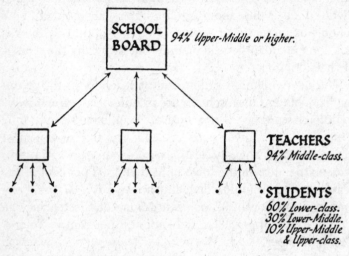

FIG. 7.—Status and social structure of the school

grades, and the subject matter taught tend to be expressions of middle-class beliefs, values, and experience which place the lower-class child at a very serious disadvantage. In addition, it must be remembered that the majority of the lower-class children who enter school come from families where they did not acquire strong motivations to succeed in school, as did most middle-class children. The early formative period in which the personality acquires a rudimentary system of values and beliefs prepares the children differentially for competition in the local schools. The later period in the school, reinforced by the continuing influences of the home, completes what the family begins. The formal academic learning maze strengthens, supports, and continues what the family has started.

The schools in many communities of the United States divide their children into sections which represent the teachers' estimates of the children's ability. Deep South had such a system, in which the children were divided into good, average, and poor sections. The Gardners and Davises, who did the research there, compared the teachers' ratings of their students with the social class of the children's parents and followed up this procedure by interviewing the teachers. They found that upper-middle and upper-class children were considered by the teachers to be overwhelmingly above average in their scholastic aptitudes, while only a small proportion of the lower class were rated as "good scholars." To be more precise, over four-fifths (85 per cent) of the upper and upper-middle children were given top rating, whereas only 11 per cent of the children from the lower class achieved this rating. On the other hand, only 6 per cent of the children from the higher statuses were given a poor rating, as compared with 36 per cent of the lower-class children.

What is the meaning of these great differences between the teachers' ratings of the aptitudes of the children from the two classes? The interviews with the teachers themselves were very revealing and demonstrated how status values operate in the democratically conceived "public" school. Some teachers felt in all sincerity that, even though a child from a higher class did not show high ability, it would not be right to place him scholastically in a section that was below his social station, because "he would not be with his own kind and would be forced to go around with children that were not of his cultural level." Other factors were involved. Some of the lower-class children did not do as well because they were inadequately equipped; others, because they had little or no interest; still others, because the teachers misjudged their lower-class manners, behavior, and speech for lack of ability.

Later studies in Jonesville and elsewhere have verified much of what we only suspected from the Yankee City and Deep South studies. Further research by Allison Davis and Robert Havighurst on the cultural (social-class) bias of the standard I.Q. tests demonstrated that the "lower intelligence" scores of the average lower-class child are due to the fact thaht the tests are built on middle-class culture. Such words as "orchestra" and many of the experiences which the tests imply are less likely to be in the world of the lower than that of the middle classes. Since middle-class children are trained in such a culture, learn at home how to solve such problems, and are motivated to do so, they perform well, whereas the lower-class child often has little experience with such cultural situations and cares even less about the problems presented by such tests. He drops out of school, not so much because he is inherently stupid as because he has learned from his social maze not to want to be anything more than what he is. Although most lower-class children remain in their own class, a few do use the school to rise. Some of them come from homes which teach them to rise, some appeal to teachers who take a special interest in them, and others form friendships which carry them beyond their own levels to higher ones and provide them with the desire to do well in school and advance themselves in life.

Since the school is one of the principal mobility routes

and higher education almost a necessary prerequisite for advancement in social status, we examined the curriculums of all the high-school children in Yankee City and in Midwest. We learned that all children of the upper classes took courses that prepared them for college, that 9 out of 10 of the upper-middle did, whereas 4 out of 5 of the lower-middle took such courses, and less than 3 out of 10 of the lower classes did. These statistics are for college expectations and are not the same as the figures for those who go to college. The Midwest figures and others show that a very small fraction of the lower classes get to college and fewer stay after they enter.

When we began these investigations in Yankee City, it was not believed by us that class values deeply influenced the way children rated one another. We believed in the "democracy of childhood" and felt that class values were learned and applied at adolescence. Our subsequent researches proved this assumption false. In the Jonesville study Bernice Neugarten designed a test to show how children rated one another. She used the so-called "Best Friend" and "Guess Who" tests. The children in one school were asked to say whom they would like for a friend and whom they did not want for friends. The social class of each child's family had been previously determined and was examined in the light of all the positive and negative votes he received in the test. Figure 8 (corrected for the size of each class) shows that there is a mirror-like reflection of the social-class position of the children in their selection and rejection of friends. The long bar at the top of the left-hand side shows that the top group was heavily favored as "someone I'd like for my best friend," and the steps downward show that each succeeding class is favored less and less. The bars on the right-hand side show that the lower-lower group was overwhelmingly rejected and that very few of the lower-middle and upper-middle children were.

In the world of the eleven- and twelve-year-old child, the same general status values are operating as in adult life. Most of the lower-class children feel, and in fact are, rejected, whereas most of the higher-placed ones feel, and in fact are, approved of and accepted.

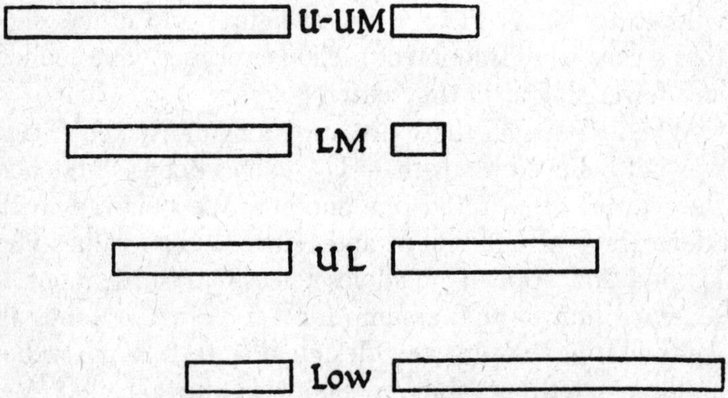

FIG. 8.—Best friend   Don't want for a friend

The "Guess Who" test further documented the conclusions about children's evaluations of one another. The children were first interviewed to determine what criteria they generally use when judging one another. Such social characteristics as whether a child is considered good or bad looking, popular or unpopular, plays fair or does not play fair, were typical items mentioned. These characteristics were then put on a list, and the children were asked to place opposite each positive and negative characteristic the names that occurred to them for each. Later interviewing helped make sure the results. The numbers in Table 4 are index numbers (for the number of children in each class) which provide an accurate measurement of the way children judged one another. (It gives only the positive results.)

The children in the top group were considered 39 times more popular than those in the bottom, over 2½ times more than those in the lower-middle class, and about 5 times more than those in the upper-lower. Members of the top

TABLE 4

How Children Rate One Another
(Eleven and Twelve Years of Age)

	Upper and Upper-Middle	Lower-Middle	Upper-Lower	Lower-Lower
Popular	39	15	8	1
Leader	41	12	5	1
Good manners	41	15	5	3
Plays fair	28	11	6	4
Likes school	45	15	9	3
Good time	27	14	5	5
Well-dressed	93	33	14	3
Good-looking	43	27	11	1
Clean	44	16	8	2

group were said to be leaders 41 times more than those in the bottom (see Table 4), 3½ times more than lower-middle, and 8 times more than upper-lower. Similar ratings were made for the social characteristics that were shown by interviews with the children to be important to them.

All the ratings strongly reflect social-class values—some of them more than others, but all were sufficiently clear to indicate that something more is operating than the objective judgments of the children about the qualities of their peers. The children from the top classes were rated 22 times cleaner than those from the bottom. It is possible for the adult investigator to examine the objective facts to see if these ratings are really warranted. This could be done easily by selecting the children who were rated as clean and not clean and inspecting them by the ordinary standards of our culture. When this was done, it soon became evident that many of the lower-class children came to school with their faces and bodies well washed and their clothes neat as well as clean. It was also clear that some of the children from the higher classes, by any objective standards, would rate lower than many of those from the bottom levels. When this rating of cleanliness is interrelated with all the others, it is quite clear that the youngsters are grading their peers by a set of stereotypes based on their class, rather than on the basis of their objective individual characteristics.

The high-school children followed a similar pattern but did not make such categorical and rigid judgments by class values as did those from the elementary school. Since the older children are presumably more the product of their culture than the younger ones, there appears to be a contradiction here about the influence of class values on the judgments of individuals. Actually, the reasons for the differences in judgment help verify our hypothesis. The children in the high school, being products of American society, have learned to be less open and more careful about what they say and how they feel on the tabooed subject of status. Furthermore, they have learned to use American values of individualism and are able to make clearer discriminations about the worth of an individual than are the younger children. Moreover, fewer children in the lower classes are at the high-school level, and these who are there have usually been mobile and have lost the marks of their class origins. As long as they remain dependent on their family, they are rated by us as being at the level of their origin. But many of them have already made the climb to a level which in all probability they will succeed in retaining when they become independent adults.

It might be supposed that I am saying that the younger children are consciously applying class values. Such is not the case. It is doubtful whether more than a few would know the meaning of social class. Our interviews with the parents, teachers, and people generally in the community lead us to believe that the children are uncritically and somewhat innocently applying stereotypes that they have learned at home—stereotypes, by the way, that their own parents would be very careful to disguise and use oblique- ly when making evaluations of their own peers.

Although at first sight the figures for class discrimina- tion are devastating, it must be remembered that a con- siderable number of the children at the lower levels are rated favorably and, furthermore, that a minority have learned what they need to know to become mobile and to advance themselves to the higher levels of American so- ciety. However, an inspection of the evidence so far indi- cates that a larger number of mobile children come from the lower-middle class than from the levels beneath it.

In the next section we shall learn what the personality type of upward-mobile persons is like when it is studied by social and psychological methods.

The Persistence of Business Enterprise and the Personalities of Business Executives

The school and the larger social world of the child dur- ing his period in school complete what the family begins. The social differentiation represented by the several classes is maintained and continued by a number of institutions training American children to become different kinds of persons, who develop social relations in which the established order persists. All persons are informally taught certain class and democratic values, and some are taught to be mobile, while others are not.

We have seen what the training is; let us now inspect some of its results. For our purposes here, we might examine the personalities of the apathetic, non-mobile, lower-class worker or some of the mobile ones. It would be instructive to describe the personality type of the non-mobile, lower-middle-class woman (who is described in Chap. 10) or the mobile career girl. It would also be worth while to examine the personality formation of some of the upper-class "traditionalists." But I shall here describe only one personality type and demonstrate how it fits into and maintains one of the important subsystems of contemporary American life, thereby showing the processes of personality formation.

One of the most important and well-recognized personality types in America is the successful, hard-working, hard-driving businessman. He has appeared in literally hundreds of novels and thousands of short stories and is one of the dominant figures in some of the more important activities of his country.

During the last several years, my colleagues and I have been engaged in a number of studies designed to understand what the businessman is as a person and what his status and functions are in the larger life of America. Professor William Henry, of the Committee on Human Development at the University of Chicago, in collaboration with several others, has examined the personalities and social worlds of several hundred successful and unsuccessful American businessmen. From this combined study of the personalities in the social situations in which they were active, Henry provides us with a valuable understanding of the upward-mobile American businessman. Since his studies the work of Warner and Abegglen on big business leaders has added to and verified Henry's conclusions.

The procedures used in the research were certain projective techniques and systematic interviewing about the social structure of a business organization. The projective technique allows the respondent to tell a story about a picture and thereby helps him to "project" his private world in a way which can be interpreted by the scientist.

All the successful men have a common personality pattern, largely formed in childhood and adolescence, functioning in such a way that, when they join a corporation, they help re-create and continue the structure and values of this business organization. At the same time, as the years go by, they help select and train younger men of the same personality type as their own. The persistence of the business organization is maintained by their ability to continue sets of relations which are necessary for its existence when competing with other organizations like it.

The *social role* of the upward-mobile businessman, striving to succeed and to achieve a higher position than the one he has, is very similar to his (private) personality structure. Although each successful businessman has certain unique characteristics of his own, he fits into the common personality pattern of his type. Let us briefly characterize this upward-mobile, successful, upper-middle-class American businessman.

As would be expected, his achievement desires are very high. He conceives of himself as a hard-working man who can be happy only when he is accomplishing something.

We must precisely understand his conception of achievement, for this kind of upward-mobile, successful executive "looks more to the sheer accomplishment of the work itself" than he does to the glory which may accrue when he achieves his end. The man who stresses the latter kind of achievement more often than not is unsuccessful. The satisfaction of the successful man is in immediate accomplishment—immediate accomplishment that leads on to the next immediate accomplishment in a never ending series.

Such a personality has very high mobility drives. He feels the deep need of continuous upward movement, but he strives less for the upward movement than for the increased responsibility that comes with it, accompanied by the feeling of satisfaction he gains from completing a task and being prepared for the next one. This kind of motivation is quite different from that of another group that looks rather similar when first put under examination. In this latter group there is the struggle for the social prestige gained by increased status. For its members, the first objective is the higher status rather than what it is that they do to get it. They tend to be less successful; the general class goal must follow the more specific and immediate ones of the job.

The upward-mobile executive's idea of authority is also of crucial importance in understanding him. He looks to his superiors for help and feels happier when involved in the controlling relationship that is established with them, for he believes he can consult with them on special problems and get special aid that he cannot receive from others. Above all, he does not see a figure of authority as one that is destructive or likely to be harmful to himself. Those men who do view authority figures as destructive are likely to have difficulties in adjusting themselves to their superiors, and very often they are the ones who fail on the job.

The view which such men have of their own organizations and the world in which they live is exceedingly instructive and tells us much about the relation of social persistence and personality. All such upward-mobile men who are successful in their business enterprises have a high ability to organize situations and understand the meaning and significance of what it is they have organized. They never see events as isolated and unconnected but as interrelated, and they draw significance from the interrelationships. In other words, they are constantly making decisions and judgments based on their organizing ability in a social structure which is ever changing and where new adaptations are forever necessary for the success of the person and the success of the enterprise. They have personalities capable of holding together the parts of a changing society —persistence and type of personality are intertwined and parts of the same process.

It comes as no surprise that decisiveness is another personality trait of this type of man. It is not so much that he is the popular idea of the quick-thinking, fast-talking American businessman who makes a dozen decisions every second, but rather that he has the ability to form the necessary judgments and arrive at the necessary decisions among a variety of alternatives and not be harassed by making them. The changing social structure (business enterprise) ordering the flow of a changing technology must have men with this characteristic to survive. The less successful businessmen find decisions difficult, and some of them become neurotically ill when, with a variety of alternatives, they are forced to make the decisions that constantly face those who occupy the higher levels of business enterprise. .

Another characteristic of successful businessmen is the great fear of failure; most of them, Professor Henry discloses, harbor a rather pervasive feeling that they may not really succeed and be able to do the things they want to do. With the fear of failure acting as a kind of whip, combined with their strong sense of self and the ability to initiate action, such men must always keep moving and must always see the immediate goal ahead.

For our immediate purposes, one of the most significant characteristics of this type of personality that is produced by American social class and social structure is that such men look to their superiors for identification—they tend to feel akin to them and to pattern their behavior after them, and to do it more or less on a personal basis, whereas, with their inferiors, they tend to be more impersonal and more detached.

Perhaps their most important personal characteristic, and one that carries obvious meaning for our present problem, is that they have developed their lives in such a way that they feel they are on their own and that their emotional identifications with their parents have been dissolved. Literally and spiritually, they have left home. It must be stressed that the emotional severance of their relations with their parents does not mean that they do not carry on happy relations with them, nor does it mean that there is any resentment of them. Rather, they are emotionally autonomous and capable of making their own decisions and do not consciously or unconsciously refer their decisions back to their parents.

The unsuccessful man is not able to release himself from his ties to his parents, and, accordingly, he is overly dependent upon his superiors or resentful of them in the work situation. The successful, upward-mobile man tends to have a positive relation with his father; he does not feel a strong emotional tie with his mother. Men who have made these adjustments with their families of orientation can relate themselves loyally to the authority of their own corporation and identify their own careers with the over-all goals of the organization. Essentially, the principal things they value—accumulation and achievement, self-initiation of action, individual autonomy, their never ceasing activity, and the kinds of rewards they consider significant—as well as their constant fear of losing ground, are all basic characteristics of the upward-mobile, upper-middle-class American.

The American social-class system persists partly because, through the activities of its members, it is capable of attaching new members to its group and forming them into a variety of personalities which fit the system. In such a complex society, the newly born individuals, if they are to fit the society and if the form of the group is to persist, must be differentially trained. Consequently, some organisms learn to be persons who are in many respects the exact opposites of others. Some are trained for upward mobility, others for fixed status. Although other important factors are involved too, so long as the group is successful in attaching new organisms to the social system and provides them with adequate personalities which relate themselves to the several parts of the group, the present form of the society is likely to persist.

9

ASSOCIATIONS IN AMERICA

The Place of the Association in American Life

Secret societies, fraternities, and civic organizations have been prominent and important features of American life from the very beginnings of the Republic. These voluntary associations permeate every aspect of the society. Whether for trivial and ludicrous or serious and important purposes, Americans use associations for almost every conceivable activity. Sinclair Lewis' middle-class Babbitt joins and is active in associations with the same zest and faith as John Marquand's "Boston Brahmins." When "something needs to be done" or "a serious problem must be solved'" in the United States, private citizens usually band together in a new association or use one already available. They do this with the same ease and lack of thought as primitive peoples might when acting within the traditions of an ancient folkway. The association is the perfect social instrument for those Americans who wish to be private citizens and free individuals and yet, at the same time, public men who are socially bound in their daily lives.

This chapter examines the structure and functions of voluntary associations in the United States and tells something of the significance of their symbolic activities. We shall begin this discussion by describing the structure and place of associations in community life; later we shall devote considerable time to an analysis of their activities and the meaning of what they do for contemporary America.

Voluntary associations, wherever found, in the simple societies of Melanesia, in the more complex ones of Africa, or in contemporary America, are institutions which, unlike age grades or social classes, do not cross-cut or encompass the whole society. They include certain people and exclude others. They usually divide their membership into official and ordinary members. Formal associations have definite rules of entrance, membership, and exit. The basic difference between formal and informal associations lies in the nature of their rules. Informal associations, such as cliques, have implicit rules which govern their members' conduct; formal associations have explicit rules, sometimes augmented by implicit ones, which control the actions of their members and relate them to the larger society.

As we have said, associations perform a great variety of functions in contemporary America. Some of the more important of these are the integration of the larger and more basic institutions, such as the church, schools, and ethnic groups, into the larger society and the organization of the interests of special groups, such as ethnic peoples. They also separate special groups from the rest of the community, while regulating and integrating the relations of these groups to the larger society.

Associations perform special and important functions for the social classes in excluding the many and including the few; they are excellent institutions to maintain social distance between the higher- and lower-class levels. But they often act as escalators by which people of lower levels are brought into the more intimate society of higher people; consequently, they function to help the mobility of some, while hindering or preventing the upward rise of others.

We found slightly over 800 associations in Yankee City, a community of only 17,000. Not all of these existed simultaneously: some were formed during the period of our investigation, and others disappeared. Many associations have a very ephemeral life, some of them being designed for a specific purpose and a very short existence.

We were able to study, learn the membership, and observe the activities of 357 associations. With few exceptions, they were those which were more or less permanent. Most of them were small, over half having less than twenty members. When we studied membership, we learned that, according to the combination of members belonging to the several classes, associations were divided into 19 class types running from one that had only upper-upper women to a few that had only lower-class people. About two-thirds of the associations had members from 3 or 4 classes; only 6 per cent had members from 2 classes; and only one-tenth from as many as 5 classes.

Because of the popularity of such novels as *Babbitt* and the many other publications on the American middle class by the novelists of the 1920's, many believe that middle-class Americans are the ones who are more often the members of formal associations. In fact, upper-class Americans are likely to be supercilious about the joining habits of the middle classes. The percentage of individuals in each class who belong to one or more associations tells a different story.

Approximately 72 per cent of the people in the upper classes belong to associations, 64 per cent of the upper-middle class, and only 49 per cent of the lower-middle class. The percentages continue to drop as one moves down the class levels, for only 39 per cent of the upper-lower and 22 per cent of the lower-lower class are members of associations. The percentages for the two lower classes are somewhat misleading, since they are heavily weighted with members of ethnic groups who belong to ethnic associations. The lower-class old American is not a joiner. More often it is the members of the classes Above the Common Man Level, particularly the upper-upper old families, who are members of associations. They are the joiners. Associations aid them to control the social life of the community.

The associations which the three highest groups join are the Garden Club, the Woman's Club, civic associations, the historical societies, the societies for aged men and women or for children, country clubs, and various dining and discussion groups. The lower-middle class and the lower classes are more likely to belong to fraternal orders, insurance societies, patriotic groups, religious associations, and those with ethnic affiliations.

Churches in contemporary society are very similar in form to associations. In the United States their relation to the class system parallels the way associations are connected with it. Although churches accent and believe in Christian brotherhood under the Fatherhood of God and are open to everyone, their membership clearly reflects class values. For example, in Jonesville, whereas only 15 per cent of the population were in the upper and upper-middle classes, 43 per cent of the Federated Church (Presbyterian and Congregational) belonged to these classes. On the other hand, none of the Baptists was upper-class and only 9 per cent upper-middle. A dissenting Protestant group called the Gospel Tabernacle had no one from the upper or upper-middle class. The lower-lower class, with the exception of a small percentage, do not join churches or associations. Generally, the lower-middle and upper-lower classes are the ones who not only join but go to church.

Activities and Symbolic Behavior

The activities of associations provide rich material for symbolic and functional analysis. Much, if not all, of their behavior is directly or indirectly, consciously or unconsciously, symbolic, since what they say and do in a given activity usually stands for something else and conforms to our definition of symbolic activity (see pp. 30–31). The full meaning of an associational activity is found not only by treating it for what the members of the association say it is, but by studying the activity, its implications and meanings, in terms of the structure itself and the satisfactions which the members receive from what they do. Associational activities are valuable for symbolic analysis because they enter into every part of the American social structure and reflect the variety of sentiments, attitudes, and values of every part of American society.

Before continuing, let us define what an activity is to the observer. An activity is a recognized and socially defined public use of symbols in a set of formal or informal social relations. An activity is recognized as such by those who participate in it and by those who study it at the explicit and open level of social behavior. Each activity occurs in an interactive situation which involves the relations of the members alone, or the members of the association in relation to the rest of the community. Each activity includes a symbolic situation in which the members exchange symbols among themselves or with other members of the society, according to the nature of the relationship. For example, the members might belong to a secret society such as the Masons, where they perform rituals which are known to and participated in only by members of their own group. On the other hand, these same members might participate in an interfraternity activity, where all are involved in a ritual whose successful performance demands that they exchange symbolic objects among themselves or co-operate in some community activity, such as fundraising.

To gather representative data from the complex variety and large number of associations of Yankee City, we attended meetings, collected records on activities, and carefully followed the detailed reports in the local newspaper. Since most of the news stories were provided by the members themselves and since we were able to check them by our own observations, we learned to accept what was said as reliable evidence.

We systematically studied the activities of associations for a period of two years. Five thousand eight hundred events (activities) were recorded. They covered everything from the most sacred to the most profane and secular, from extreme forms of competition and opposition to the most intense co-operative activities, from the polar extremes of utility and Yankee hardheadedness to the ultimate in philanthropy and good will. They also ranged from the most reasonable and sensible behavior to the ultimate in triviality and nonsense.

We observed these 5,800 events or activities that occurred during the two-year period and were able to classify them into 284 forms (subtypes) and then into 19 types. (Table 5 lists the 19 types.) For example, a boys' club might play a baseball game with another team. The particular game was counted as an event and listed under type of activity as an athletic game, while the form (subtype) of activity was listed under the heading "Baseball." (There were 22 other "forms" of athletic games observed.)

We shall be concerned here only with the public mean-

TABLE 5

Events, Forms, and Types of Activities

Rank Order of Events	Type of Activity	Number of Events	Per Cent	Number of Forms (Subtypes)
1	Drama and talent exhibitions	828	14.28	41
2	Speeches	744	12.83	1
3	Organization	567	9.78	13
4–5	Eating	499	8.60	24
4–5	Fund-raising	499	8.60	22
6	Ritual, secular-external	335	5.78	30
7	Ritual, sacred	333	5.74	23
8	Ritual, secular-internal	306	5.28	21
9	Gifts	291	5.02	14
10	Sedentary games	214	3.69	15
11	Hospitality	198	3.41	8
12	Contests	158	2.72	8
13	Athletic games	157	2.71	23
14	Crafts and skills	126	2.17	8
15	Ritual, secular-sacred	123	2.12	8
16	Socials	119	2.05	2
17	Outings	118	2.03	10
18	Teaching and learning	99	1.71	7
19	Social dancing	86	1.48	6
Total		5,800	100.0	284

ings of the activities of associations. We are going to be concerned less with the interpretation of the meaning of an activity than with pointing out the multitude and variety of activities of American associations and drawing certain conclusions by using our knowledge about the functional significance of these activities. Let us examine the activities themselves.

The social scientist can recognize four types of public ritual among the activities of the associations. The four include only those forms which are purposely and consciously used by the association for ritualistic purposes. As such, they are pure forms of symbolic behavior. All the other types of activity have varying degrees of ritual in them, but they are not designed primarily for ritual ends; that is, their ritual significance, when present, is secondary and often not recognized by the participants as ritual. The four forms of ritual are sacred ritual; ritual which combines sacred and secular elements; secular ritual concerned largely with the community beyond the association; and secular ritual wholly or almost completely concerned with the inner world of the association. As used here, the term "ritual" means that the members of the association express in overt symbolic acts the meanings which socially evaluated objects have for them and that, at the same time, they also state in symbols what their relations are with such objects. The devout Christian, for example, does this in the rite of Communion, as does the patriotic American in some of the exercises customary on Lincoln's Birthday.

Sacred ritual symbolically relates the participants to sacred things—the Deity, the spiritual dead, and such things as emblems which represent the gods and the sacred dead. Secular ritual expresses the value and attitudes of the daily round of life in the community and symbolizes the importance of the ordinary things which compose the lives of most of the people. Some of these secular rituals, such as adopting and maintaining a European war orphan, symbolize the American alliance with certain European countries and the present feeling of unity with these countries. At the same time, they serve to relate the members of the association to the larger community beyond the association itself. Others, such as celebrating Lincoln's birthday, flag ceremonies, and similar patriotic rituals, relate the association to the whole community. Still others tie the association symbolically to the families, schools, and the local community. There are thirty forms of these secular rituals.

Twenty-one forms of ritual activity concerned with internal relations are largely composed of symbolic elements which have been created by the members of the associations. Their function is to tie the participants more closely together, emphasize their unity, and indirectly maintain in the feelings of the members their separateness from the larger society.

The several types of ritual, when combined, compose about one-fifth of all the activities of the associations of Yankee City, the other four-fifths being divided among fifteen other categories (see Table 5).

When the types of ritual are not combined, drama and talent exhibitions are the most popular type of activity. Dramatic exhibitions include everything from classical and contemporary plays to tap-dancing and jazz-band concerts. Usually they are expressions of the talent of the local people; but what is said and done on the stage is usually pure symbolic communication. Many people in the community, particularly those in the lower classes, use talent to help improve their stations in life and gain social recognition. If they are successful, two developments may follow. They may be recognized economically and advance themselves accordingly, or, and what is more likely, they may be recognized socially by more highly placed people and participate at a higher level in the social system. Very often, to the observer, the efforts are pathetic, since they accomplish nothing for the participant and even evoke ridicule—the ever present risk which mobile people must take. The plays vary from modern and classical, which present rigorous and almost scientific representations of modern life and employ the skill and dexterity of first-rate artists, to those which are little more than an opportunity for the participant to exhibit himself in a public place. There were 41 subcategories and 828 events of this sort, composing over one-seventh of the total.

The members of associations of Yankee City and, in fact, those throughout America seem never to tire of listening to speeches. The unfriendly critic, particularly the field worker who must attend many of these functions, might well say that many of the speeches are dreary, uninformative, and filled with wind. But speeches, even when not listened to by the members, are felt to be necessary and are appreciated as part of what should happen when members meet. Analysis of speeches indicates that a considerable proportion of them, when stated in propositional form, are often composed of ritual rather than reason. Some of the "best speakers" freely avail themselves of well-tried symbolic and ritual materials and resort to reason only when it is necessary to disguise what they are saying. One-eighth of the many thousands of activities we observed were speeches. Speeches, unlike talent presentations, are usually given by outsiders; the association members merely listen. Like the social situation for dramatic activities, the amount of participation of most people tends to be minimal. We were unable to classify the speeches into types of subject matter, but our list of subjects indicates clearly that they ranged over every variety of topic.

An activity of associations to which a great amount of time is devoted, ranking third in importance, is organizational work. These activities, including "reading the minutes," "new business," "making new rules," and "voting," are largely concerned with maintaining the formal organization of the association by expressing the rules in group action and emphasizing the social autonomy of associations, as well as that of the members, by making new rules or rescinding old ones. Usually to the observer, and often to some of us who participate in such organizational forms, what is done seems dull and unimportant; but the prosaic outward forms themselves must be given further examination, for their meaning is of great importance. For example, long boring discussions take place over the rules of order which give opportunities to define the status of the members and their officers and, above all, permit the organizational activities of the members to symbolize and state the democratic character of the association and of the society generally. Criticism of an association's chairman or president, heated reference to "railroading," and declarations about one man's vote being as good as another's are all recognitions of how organizational activity very often expresses something more than "the business of the day" or the rules of conduct which govern the actions of the members. The uncritical, hostile observer, however, leaves with a feeling of futility, for he sees "more time wasted in the discussion of the rules than in action." No doubt this is sometimes true, but, more often than not, what is being observed and defined as not important is of the utmost significance because of its meaning to those who participate and the emotions which these activities arouse. Ten per cent of the activities were concerned with rules and organization.

Eating, although a biological act, in its social form consists in the sharing of food at a common meal. As Robertson Smith and Ernest Crawley pointed out long ago, it is one of the strongest ways to engender sentiments of oneness among participants while they share group attitudes. Eating is an activity which is used in the greatest variety of ways to promote solidarity or to separate the members of a particular association from all others. Sometimes the participants themselves recognize the unity that the function of "breaking bread together" implies. Their behavior always expresses this significance. A great variety of ways of eating were collected. They range all the way from the utmost formality, etiquette, and prestige, through varying shades of formality, to informal basket lunches and suppers. The various forms of eating communal meals comprise about 9 per cent of the activities.

Fund-raising ranks with eating in importance. Twenty-two ways of collecting funds were observed. They include everything from benefit shows and suppers to tag days, auction sales, rummage sales, campaigning, and bazaars. An activity was identified as belonging to this general category if one of its immediate explicit purposes was to increase the amount of money in the association's treasury. If another element, such as eating, as in the case of a supper, was present, this element was also counted under its appropriate category.

Fund-raising includes getting money from within and without the membership of the organization. The women's organizations show much more ingenuity and diversity in their fund-raising enterprises than do the men's groups, often disguising or de-emphasizing the purpose. Members and outsiders are invited to play at benefit card parties, eat a benefit lunch, or buy a piece of bric-a-brac at a bazaar and, accordingly, are doubly rewarded by getting an object of utility and having the moral satisfaction of making a contribution to a worthy cause.

Furthermore, patterns of mutual obligation are often established among the associations, for the members of one organization feel obligated to attend a fund-raising card party or supper of another because their own has just had a similar event. The exchange of services and money, usually in the pleasant context of entertainment, constitutes one of the great contributions of the associations to the social unity of the community, for it knits diverse groups tightly together. Fund-raising may not be easily viewed as of symbolic significance. There can be no question that part of its ultimate use is purely utilitarian and technical. However, the giving and taking of money in such a context and in the set of relations usually established for such an activity symbolically define what the set of relations is or what it should be. Very frequently, fund-raising is little more than a gift exchange, sometimes with overtones of competition in it, that looks very much like some of the competitive and co-operative elements of the potlatch of the Northwest Coast Indians. It will be recalled that these Indians made elaborate and very expensive gifts to each other at public ceremonies; the unfortunate recipient, to save face and protect his status, was forced to return an even more elaborate gift, or conspicuously to destroy a highly valued object. In passing, let me remind you that Thorstein Veblen did not find it difficult to transfer Franz Boas' account of the potlatch among the

Indians of the Canadian Pacific Coast to his own theory of conspicuous expenditure in contemporary America.

The following episode taken from *Social Class in America* demonstrates how fund-raising functions and how money conspicuously spent for worthy causes can advance the social aspirations of those who spend it. It illustrates how individual social mobility is related to joining a club and how money as such must be translated into behavior in an association which meets the approval of the class above in order to advance a mobile man.

This . . . is supposed to be a true story of what happened to a Mr. John Smith, a newly rich man in a far western community. He wanted to get into a particular social club of some distinction and significance in the city. By indirection he let it be known, and was told by his friends in the club they had submitted his name to the membership committee.

Mr. Abner Grey, one of the leading members of the club and active on its membership committee, was a warm supporter of an important philanthropy in this city. It was brought to his attention that Mr. Smith, rather than contributing the large donation that had been expected of him, had given only a nominal sum to the charity.

When Mr. Smith heard nothing more about his application, he again approached one of the board members. After much evasion he was told that Mr. Grey was the most influential man on the board and he would be wise to see that gentleman. After trying several times to make an appointment with Mr. Grey, he finally burst into Grey's offices unannounced.

"Why the hell, Abner, am I being kept out of the X club?"

Mr. Grey politely evaded the question. He asked Mr. Smith to be seated. He inquired after Mr. Smith's health, about the health of his wife, and inquired about other matters of simple convention.

Finally, Mr. Smith said, "Ab, why the hell am I being kept out of your club?"

"But, John, you're not. Everyone in the X club thinks you're a fine fellow."

"Well, what's wrong?"

"Well, John, we don't think you've got the *kind* of money necessary for being a good member of the X club. We don't think you'd be happy in the X club."

"Like hell I haven't. I could buy and sell a half-dozen of some of your board members."

"I know that, John, but that isn't what I said. I did not say the amount of money, I said the kind of money."

"What do you mean?"

"Well, John, my co-workers on the charity drive tell me you only gave a few dollars to our campaign, and we had you down for a few thousand."

For a moment Mr. Smith was silent. Then he grinned. So did Mr. Grey. Smith took out his fountain pen and checkbook. "How much?"

At the next meeting of the X club Mr. Smith was unanimously elected to its membership.

Mr. Smith translated his money into philanthropy acceptable to the dominant group, he received their sponsorship, and finally became a participant in the club. The "right" kind of house, the "right" neighborhood, the "right" furniture, the proper behavior —all are symbols that can ultimately be translated into social acceptance by those who have sufficient money to aspire to higher levels than they presently enjoy.

Gift-making and taking, explicitly recognized, occupy an important part in the life of the associations. The gifts are made between members or given to, and accepted from, other associations. Examples are ceremonial presents to a retiring officer, gifts to churches or to worthy philanthropies. There were some fourteen ways listed as proper for giving and receiving gifts. The presents which are supposedly given voluntarily and graciously from one association without thought of compensation, like all gifts, set up obligations for a return of goods and services in the future or imply repayment for something done in the past. This exchange pattern organizes most of the associations into a system of interaction which emphasizes reciprocity. The goods and services are given as free-will offerings and are returned as such, with no hint of a commercial transaction; yet informal judgments are constantly being made which determine the sequence of gift-making and the quality of the objects exchanged.

When it is realized that gift-making is one of the many ways of symbolically stating the relations among people and establishing an equilibrium among organizations, the importance of this activity to the associations and to the stability of the community can be understood. Such types of activity as fund-raising, various forms of secular and sacred rituals, games, contests, hospitality, outings, dancing, as well as most of the other nineteen types, contribute their share to the interactive co-operation and help to organize the competition and subordinate the hostilities that exist between the various social levels, ethnic groups, economic interests, and religious faiths. Although rather obvious, it cannot be too strongly stressed that most of the activities, particularly gift-making, are ways which increase, by act and symbol, the basic integration of the community and help to maintain its present form.

The gifts between two associations may have little value; yet they are visible emblems of social solidarity, and the act of giving evokes latent feelings of solidarity, unity, and interdependence. This cohesiveness is further related to the interconnections established by the interlocking memberships of related associations. This intricate web, when first viewed, is almost overwhelming.

Structural and membership interconnections, our interviews and observations tell us, organize and express some of the feelings, attitudes, and values of the people who belong to the different associations. The activities among these associations express both the structural connections and membership interconnections. When two or more associations possess a common core of membership, the members often bring them together for common enterprises which are frequently joint actions or symbolic statements of the common membership structure and social values. For example, members of the exclusive dining clubs belong to the less exclusive Rotary Club; their wives, who are members of the Garden Club and other exclusive associations, also belong to the more lenient Woman's Club. The core of the more highly placed men in Rotary and high-status women in the Woman's Club carry the influence of their other associations into the life of these two clubs. To a lesser extent they take back the effect of some of their experience in Rotary and the Woman's Club to their more highly valued associations. Thus the web of associations functions to draw status distinctions while, at the same time, drawing the several social levels together.

The Activities of the Social Classes

Although class differences among all types of activities are quite marked and reveal themselves immediately to the observer, they are difficult to demonstrate in number terms. For example, a comparison of lower- and upper-class associations shows that there is only a small difference in the percentage of total activities devoted to eating (8 per cent for the upper class and 7 for the lower); yet scrutiny of the forms of eating and, of course, actual observation of the style tell quite another story. It was impossible to develop a method which would permit recording of stylistic differences which could be easily counted, but the ordinary procedure previously described of classifying events under their *forms* and *types* did reveal decided differences. Although a comparison of the 284 forms would bring out all the significant differences, I shall content myself with only an example: a comparison of some of the types of activities of associations which are composed of members from the three upper (upper-upper to upper-middle) and three lower levels (lower-middle to lower-lower). Certain tendencies, often masked as types by the more general classification, are sufficiently revealed to bring out some of the significant similarities and differences.

Well over a third (38 per cent) of all the activities of the lower group were involved in purely symbolic behavior—in drama (16 per cent) and ritual (22 per cent) —where symbols are used as symbols of symbols and are designed to evoke emotions rather than refer the attention to objects and things. Less than a sixth of the activities of upper-level associations were devoted to symbolic behavior (drama, 6 per cent; ritual, 10 per cent). Closer inspection of the two categories tells a significant story. It will be recalled that there were four types of ritual, ranging from sacred to secular and from the secret and private to rituals which directly functioned to relate the members to the community. The lower associations were eleven times more active in sacred rituals than the upper, and five times more in those that combined the sacred with the secular (see Fig. 9). Furthermore, whereas there were two and a half times more occurrences of secular rituals concerned exclusively with the private world of the lower-class associations, the secular rituals which related the associations to the general community showed no differences in their percentages between the two levels.

The statistics made it seem probable, and interviewing and field observations verified these conclusions, that organized public activities of the lower classes are concerned far more with religious observance and with use of sacred collective representations which give the feeling of belonging and being related "to the things of the World that matter." Moreover, the use of rituals which relate the associations only to their own members, paradoxically enough, seem to have a similar function; for they, too, encourage

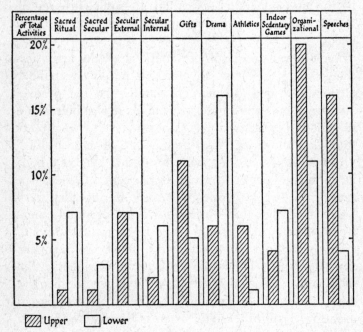

Fig. 9.—The activities of the lower- and upper-class associations

the exchange of symbols only among those who belong and thereby encourage the twin feelings of exclusiveness and belongingness, the mutual regard and respect for the symbols used giving them importance and significance for each participant.

It must not be overlooked that symbols which evoke emotion, rather than refer to specific objects and ideas, are more easily used by the participants and retain their attention through longer periods. This preference of the lower levels for evocative symbols becomes more sharply significant when the preferences of the higher levels are known. Over a third (37 per cent) of the activities at the higher social level were concerned with speeches and organization and business, compared with slightly more than a seventh (15 per cent) at the lower level. Both these activities demand quite different kinds of participation from ritual and drama. Granted that many of the speeches were designed to arouse the emotions and that some of the business had elements of ritual in it, each of these activities tends to be more directly concerned with reality than the other two. The words of speeches have to be placed in propositional and logical form; their meanings more often make reference to ideas and things than do those of drama and ritual. Since members of upper associations have had enough training in school and have acquired a higher education than members of the lower associations, it is not surprising that this high preference is shown. Business activities demand similar interests and in general, the more precise relating of people to one another. Furthermore, authority and superordination are more easily maintained by their proper exercise.

Twelve of the nineteen types of activity showed considerable difference. Some of the differences between the upper and lower classes are graphically displayed in Figure 9. Those favored by the lower levels are drama, the rituals mentioned above, sedentary games, "social hours," crafts, and teaching and learning. The preferences of the higher levels were for speeches, business and organization, gift-making, and athletics. There were only minor differences in the occurrence of the other types of activities.

Although there are many changes occurring in the associational life of America, in preference for certain types, rejection of others, and the relinquishment of older activities to accept new ones, fundamentally the basic structure and function of these institutions in the society have changed very little. It seems likely that they will continue important in the lives of Americans, for they serve their members well and conform to the way Americans do things. George Babbitt, busy with his real estate, Martin Arrowsmith in his scientific laboratory, and Pulham, Esquire, in Brahmin Boston, will always pay their dues and remain "members in good standing."

10

MASS MEDIA: A SOCIAL AND PSYCHOLOGICAL ANALYSIS

Mass Communication

Effective communication is necessary for the proper functioning and maintenance of simple societies, but it is even more crucial for the survival of complex ones. Such societies must have a common core of basic understanding known and used by everyone, or their complex and diverse symbolic superstructures will not stand. They need general symbol systems that eveyrone not only knows but feels. The increasing structural diversity and social complexity of contemporary society, the greater development of individual autonomy, the growth of specialized symbol systems referred to in the previous chapter—these and many other factors raise serious difficulties for people trying to work and communicate with one another. If more and more problems are to be solved and greater and greater areas of reality grasped and conquered, the social labor of a society must be increasingly divided, and symbolic advancement must maintain pace with technical and social achievement. Symbolic advancement requires not only the invention of new symbol systems but the development of new forms of discourse containing the old core of general meanings common to the whole group.

The problems of general communication, crucial for survival in complex societies, are partly solved by the use of certain of the traditional institutions to train all the children from every background in the rudiments and core meanings of symbols that must be used feelingly as well as knowingly by everyone. Common social conditioning creates common ways of response. The learning experiences of the several social levels and of the numerous ethnic and other groups take place in a social maze so constructed that all groups have certain experiences in common and some groups have other experiences as special groups. Institutions such as the family and the school function in both capacities. The evidence derived by the psychoanalysts from the inner words of their patients demonstrates that even their most neurotic patients have common experiences and use symbols common to the whole society. Most (one is sometimes tempted to follow the lead of certain analysts and say all) of these symbols, acquired in early childhood and forming the solid inner structure of the personality, are products of the individual's experience in the family. The family of orientation provides everyone with feelings, beliefs, and ways of seeing the world and themselves that have common meanings. The social logics of the group, that set of rational or irrational assumptions on which common action and common feelings are often based, are greatly dependent on the family for their persistence.

The school also teaches people to think and feel by using general symbols from the common heritage, such symbols conforming closely to the canons of rationality and individual logic, thereby teaching everyone how to think and arrive at common solutions when they work with symbols on whose meanings the society has previously found conventional agreement.

When a society has only one church, very frequently it functions to interrelate the non-rational and rational worlds into one coherent system; but, in those societies which share a world civilization, the churches contribute increasingly to diversity and the difficulties of sharing common symbols.

We shall see how American society has developed new general public symbol systems, often sacred in character, such as Memorial Day and Thanksgiving, and created heroic myths, such as Lincoln's and Washington's, which have common core meanings that are similar for the diverse subcultures. We shall examine how these symbolic devices are used by a complex society to achieve communication with common meanings permitting thoughtful and emotional collaboration for common ends. The more such public symbol systems tend to be sacred in character and based on assumptions that pay little regard to the logic of science and rationality and the more feelings and emotions and the social fit of things become the criteria of what and how people should think, the less such symbols will be useful tools for communication in the ordinary daily life of this secular society. The invention of new technologies for communication, including the so-called "mass media," has been of primary and crucial importance for the integration of the diverse secular worlds of modern men into coherence and unity.

The mass media of which I am speaking include such well-known phenomena as newspapers, mass magazines, the so-called "comics," movies, advertising, best-sellers, the popular fiction and advertising of book clubs that appeal to hundreds of thousands, if not millions, of people, greeting cards for holidays, birthdays, and other occasions which are sent by literally millions of people, popular music records, radio, and television. There are, as well, many others that are not often thought of as mass communications, such as the newspaper picture supplements and other forms of pictures used by the masses. They all function as distributors of symbols with common meanings to mass audiences.

We must remember that mass media are the products of the new machine technology—a machine technology that feeds 180 million people and supports a diverse and complex social group which spreads across the continent and includes every variety of subculture in American life. Technically, they are new forms of communication, dependent on inventions which supplement the older forms. They allow tens of millions of people to be one audience and, at given moments in time, one group—because of a core of common response to the same symbols.

Methods of Research

There is a variety of methods used by sociologists, psychologists, and other social scientists for the study of mass media. The principal interest of the research group with which I work has been to understand the meaning and function of symbol systems in contemporary life. Although each mass medium is a set of special techniques and symbol forms designed to fit special audiences, our studies of them all demonstrate that the same scientific method can be used for understanding their meaning and significance to their various audiences, indicating that the principles of all must be basically the same.

Whether one studies radio, motion pictures, popular music records, or television, the following fundamental questions must be asked and answered:

What is the symbolic content of the radio program, the motion-picture story, the advertisement, or other mass medium being studied?

What are the social characteristics of the audience which accepts or rejects the radio program and other mass media?

What are the psychological characteristics, conscious or unconscious, of the individuals who compose the audience?

How does the symbolic system under analysis stimulate the public and private worlds of the individuals in the audience, who are, of course, members of the general American society? (I might say, parenthetically, that the answer to the last question gives the investigator the symbolic meaning of the program, story, and advertisement being studied.) The research man must also ask how the radio program or motion picture functions in the lives of the people and what effect it has on them as private individuals and public members of the society.

Some will want to ask two other questions:

Is the effect of a particular mass symbol system good or bad on those who are stimulated by it? And is the effect of a particular medium good or bad for the society?

The answers to these questions can be learned only by the collaboration of the social and psychological sciences. The necessary apparatus to find the answers includes both psychological and social instruments. It cannot be a combination of them, by which one is merely added to the other, but the skills and knowledge of the group and individual disciplines must be integrated into one research design that modifies and changes them. They must each function as a synchronized part of a larger instrument, an instrument designed to answer a problem about human behavior.

We have learned by sad experience in our work that the predictive value of research on mass media is greatly limited if it is reduced to no more than a social study, or to a separate psychological investigation, or to the cumbersome and more usual device of adding two research projects together after the field work of each has been completed. The research design, I repeat, must be so fashioned that the skills it uses are organized to take advantage of all the social and psychological sciences when they are needed to answer the several basic questions.

To answer questions about the symbolic content of a radio or movie program or any other mass medium, a preliminary analysis must be made of the symbols involved in the system. Here one uses what previous research has taught us about American symbolic life. This part of the preliminary period is followed by a brief field investigation which pretests the accuracy of the first analysis. From this preliminary period, tentative hypotheses about the meaning of the program, magazine story, or other mass product are developed. They provide a flexible guide for investigating what the meaning of the symbol system is likely to be for its potential audience.

Sufficient answers about the social characteristics and the social life of the audience are provided by the field methods of social anthropology. One can learn from their use about such social categories as social class, age, sex, ethnic, and other similarities and differences spoken of in earlier chapters.

The study of the psychological characteristics of the private worlds of the individuals who make up the audience raises more difficult problems. A technique is needed that will get beneath the surface and immediately lay open the intimate and private world of the individual with all his beliefs and values about his social world and the people in it and about himself. Obviously, it is impossible to use economically the detailed analysis developed by psychiatrists and psychoanalysts and other depth psychologists. Consequently, it has been necessary to use other methods which will permit the researcher to study a large number of people, learn about who and what they are, and, at the same time, manage time and expense in such a way that the methods of the investigation are not too costly. We have used several of the so-called "projective techniques." When integrated with other tests and with interviewing, they provide a satisfactory method for understanding how the symbols of mass media stimulate or do not stimulate their audiences and what their meanings are to different kinds of people who read, look at, or listen to a particular medium. I shall refer to how this is done in a later section of this chapter. Once research has yielded these answers, the other answers follow, since with this evidence we can ascertain the medium's effect on the lives of various kinds of individuals and learn how it functions in contemporary society.

Although media are different, the symbolic themes, the audiences, and the relations between themes and audiences often are the same or very similar. For example, under the same research conditions or at the same time, we have studied radio programs, magazine stories, motion pictures, popular novels, and music records in a number of communities and found that their audiences were often the same people; that their symbolic themes, although superficially different, were basically similar; and that the way the symbols stimulated the private and public worlds of the individuals and their effect upon them as members of society were fundamentally the same.

Since it is impossible to present the results of all these studies and because they are so similar regarding effect on the audience, I shall choose one specific mass medium and describe what we learned from its investigation.

"Soap Opera" on the American Radio

From the great variety of programs offered by the several radio networks which cover the United States, we selected a type that is one of the most popular and has a large number of habitual listeners. In formal language it is called the "daytime serial" but is popularly known as the "soap opera." Less elegant but more expressive, this sardonic term implies in American slang that the advertising carried by the program sells soap and that the clichés of the plot and stereotyped characters remind one of traditional opera.

The soap operas' continued stories are performed at the same time each weekday for a grown-up audience. These serials once numbered over thirty; each is fifteen minutes long. The audience, which is mostly female, numbers about twenty-odd million. On the average, about six programs are heard daily by the habitual listener. Five days in the week and fifty-two weeks in the year, the heavily stereotyped characters of each serial usually spend their fifteen minutes getting in and out of trouble.

On the surface, these programs are little more than flat, insignificant, modern-day folk tales. But even casual analysis soon indicates that the characters and the actions of the plot represent something more than their superficial aspects reveal. The soap operas are symbol systems which are closely related to the private and public worlds of the women who listen. For our purposes, we chose the most popular program on one of the larger radio networks. After studying the scripts and listening to the programs, it soon became clear that this so-called "daytime serial" is a verbal symbol system, a small drama which is "an idealized representation of human life" that has deep meaning and functions significantly in the lives of certain types of American women.

To study it, Dr. William Henry, of the University of Chicago, and I used a number of research instruments. They were: two "projective" techniques, interviews taken during and after the radio program, and a schedule which included the Index of Status Characteristics to provide us with the necessary social information about the audience.

To permit an intensive investigation of the soap opera and its meaning to the audience, we selected only one example of one type of soap opera and further reduced the number of variables by selecting only women who were the most nearly typical listeners. By use of the I.S.C. we chose those who were young or middle-aged wives of men who belonged to the Common Man Level. The great majority listened to several programs daily.

The research plan included information which identified the women in social place. The private world and personality structure of each woman were learned by interview and the use of the Thematic Apperception Test. The latter is a series of standardized pictures to which the subject responds. He tells what he "sees in each picture." He is asked to tell a story about what has happened, what is happening, and what will happen, the theory and fact being that he "projects" his own inner world on the picture and thereby reveals what he is as a person. The combination of the several techniques yields evidence which allows the investigator to know the socio-psychological world of the subject. Comparison of the results of the T.A.T. on all the women studied showed that, although each had her unique characteristics, she shared a common personality type with the others. By knowing this and understanding the way of life of the wives of the Common Man, we could move to the next part of the research plan—the relationship of the symbols of the program to the private worlds of the women who listened. Before describing and interpreting this relationship we must briefly summarize the content of the soap opera studied. The serial appeared over the Columbia Broadcasting System and was called "Big Sister."

"Big Sister" was the story of Ruth and John Wayne. They were a happily married couple who lived in a charming two-story house in one of the better residential areas of a small middle-western city. The story revolved around their lives and around Ruth's patient efforts to run her family well, to protect her relatives and friends from their own mistakes, and to keep herself and John out of difficulties. John, a successful doctor with a large practice, was a good and faithful husband to Ruth. They both lived contentedly in their home but were always entangled in the troubles of their relatives and friends, among whom were Christine, Billy, and Tom, whose indiscreet behavior put them all into compromising situations. Ruth, the Big Sister to them all, saved herself and John from the dangerous situations which the other got them into and helped to solve the problems of all of them. Christine was the daughter of an old and dear friend of the family. Although she appeared very pleasant, Christine was a scheming woman. She always had an interest in John and in John's favorite nephew, Billy, who was a young and inexperienced fellow living with Ruth and John. Tom was the rather nervous and undependable stepbrother of Ruth, who had recently arrived in town. His questionable behavior exerted a bad influence upon some of the other people in the story and was a constant source of trouble to everyone. Throughout their troubles, they all depended upon Ruth, and she helped them.

Several stories were fashioned by us from this simple plot and its characters and submitted to the subjects. They were informed that the stories were possible leads for new programs and they were asked to respond to them. The stories operated to focus the daydreams of the women around the symbols and principal themes of the "Big Sister" program. There is space for only one of the "verbal projectives." (It is designed to bring out the common responses to "good and bad women" in their relations with the principal male character.) Here is the "suggestion":

"One afternoon when Ruth is visiting John in his office, the office doorbell rings. It is Christine all dressed up in her very best. She seems somewhat surprised to see Ruth—as though she hoped to see John alone. As she takes off her coat, Christine seems to be thinking out some plan of action. She finally turns to Ruth and says that she really came just to talk to her—that she has a problem which she has to discuss with Ruth.

"While John is still there in the room, Christine goes on and tells Ruth that she feels John is really in love with her,

Christine. This is a distinct shock to Ruth, and she asks Christine how she knows. John has never told her, she says, but she can really tell from the way John has been acting toward her. John is strangely quiet through all this and seems somewhat embarrassed—not really sure how much of it all is true and how much Christine's maliciousness; Ruth is very upset and doesn't quite know what to do.

"What will happen next? What will Ruth do? How will John act? What will Christine do?"

From the answers to this and the other stories we learned how the fantasies of the listeners were related to the characters and plot of the story.

Each woman was also asked to tell what each character looked like and to describe his personality. Since she was entirely dependent on hearing and could not see the actors, this proved an excellent "projective" and was very revealing of what the women made out of characters in the story and how they identified with them. The following is a good example.

Mrs. Black is the wife of a skilled worker. In response to the question of what the characters looked like, she said:

"Ruth—about five feet tall, dark, home-type girl—not a bit flashy. Very plain—likes suits—not flashy colors. About twenty-eight years old. [This is also a description of Mrs. Black.]

"John—tall, dark, very distinguished looking—the home and business type. Dresses very plain, no sports clothes. About thirty-one. He may have some gray hairs, though.

"Christine—I see her as being taller than Ruth and thin. She's flashy. Wears a lot of makeup and is out to get the men. She dresses very flashy." [Query: I'm a mere man, what does a woman do when she wants to look flashy?] "Now, you're kidding me." [Since you have used the word "flashy" several times, I thought it would be helpful if you told me what it means.] "Well, she wears dresses to attract men's attention. She could be a sweater girl. Wears flesh-colored sweaters for sports. She wears real low-cut dresses, something that fits right and really shows her figure. You know what I mean—real high heels and lots of cheap jewelry. That kind of woman.

"I picture her as a girl who dyes her hair blond. She's about twenty-four. [Laugh.] Of course, I see Christine as quite a bit like the girl Harris [Mrs. Black's husband] is running with now. I guess that's natural. She dyes her hair blond and pretty soon it starts to turn black around the scalp. Her husband told me, 'Harris thinks he's got something pretty good now, but wait until he wakes up some night and sees what's there beside him, why he'll think a truck must have run over her with all that stuff she wears nights.' That's one thing about brunettes, they look the same day and night. There doesn't have to be any of this sleeping in different rooms because hubby might catch you with your face off. Men go for blonds, though. I guess they're nicer to play around with. I saw this woman of his just once. It was in the good weather, and I ran into them. They didn't see me, though. I would have died if they had. I didn't even know she was in that part of town. They would have thought I was spying on them. [Pause.] Shall we go to the next one? I keep getting off the subject—it must be annoying to you." [Assured her it was not annoying.]

It will be noticed that the degree of identification of Mrs. Black with the story is considerable and that she easily interrelates her private life with the characters and plot.

After we had interviewed the women, used the social

schedule and the other tests, several women were selected for observation during the program and interviewed afterward to check on the reliability of our research design. Finally, for purposes of contrast, we selected several mobile upper-middle career women to test the results from the research group.

Let us now examine the results of the study.

The Women Who Listen to Soap Opera

The personalities of the listener group appear typical of the women who belong to the Common Man Level of American culture. They have been trained in the traditional and basic values of that social system. As females in American society they have learned by rewards and punishment, from birth to sexual maturity, to conform to the rigid conventions of "middle-class" culture. They have been trained by their families to be wives and mothers and, unconsciously, to carry out and maintain the rules, moral beliefs, and values of their social level. This they do most effectively. Should they fail in this behavior, American society, as we now know it, would not continue.

They now operate within the narrow but extremely powerful codes that constitute middle-class family organization. Here they play the statuses and roles which constitute all the most important activities of their existence; they express their most important functions as adult human beings within the confines of this family pattern. While playing these roles, they interact within the rigid limits of the relations they have with other conventional roles (their husbands, children, etc.) who compose the conventional American family.

It will be shown below that our research demonstrates that their training is highly effective and that the private

worlds of these women are family-centered, highly routin-
ized, and rigidly controlled by intellectual and moral out-
looks; their responses are psychologically stereotyped and
repetitive and sociologically traditional and conventional.

The women tended to be non-mobile in fact as well as in
their imagination. All of them, it will be recalled, were
wives; none had jobs; and all of them were primarily concerned with their duties within the household. Most of
their experiences had been exceedingly limited and fitted
into a narrow routine. Their backgrounds were of a similar
sort. All of them had very rigid moral and social codes by
which they judged themselves and other people. These
codes were exceedingly conventional and were the ones
expected of wives and mothers at their class level. They
were hesitant about attempting anything new and with-
drew from any proposals that seemed to be departures
from the conventional way of doing things. Part of the
reason for feeling this way was their fear of the criticism of
their friends and family. It must be noted, however, that
they themselves found it not too difficult to accept this
criticism because they, too, believed in the standards held
by their intimates. Possibly it is unnecessary to say that
their way of life demanded little originality and imagination and that creativeness was comparatively low among
them. From the point of view of the outsider, their world
seems monotonous, dull, and rather drab. Despite this
fact, these women have a strong determination to do their
tasks well, and they derive deep satisfaction from dis-
charging their responsibilities to their families and to their
friends.

Their hopes are basically centered around carrying on;
most of them take the form of not wanting their present
routine disturbed—they want to continue as they are, but,

while so doing, better their circumstances and gain more freedom. Their fears are of the same kind. Fundamentally, they are afraid of anything that may threaten the family unit and their status as wives and mothers. They are definitely insecure when they have to deal as autonomous beings with the larger world outside their own family and its immediate circle. Despite the routinization of their lives, all these women need to feel that they are "going somewhere," that what they do is valued as important, and that maintaining a family is recognized as of fundamental importance.

The use of the Thematic Apperception Test yielded quite specific results about the private worlds of the women who listened, as well as knowledge about the inner life of the upper-middle-class career women who served as a contrasting group. The principal psychological character-istics of the women who listen to soap operas are that in their imaginations they cling tightly to the past and to their parental families and do not give their psychic ener-gies to the present and the future. They severely repress their deep emotional life, often related to their sexuality, and are fearful of giving it free expression because they believe it threatens their safety. They find it impossible to initiate action and feel that they have no real control over their own fates except within the narrow confines of their immediate family.

They fear that they will be unable to control their per-sonal lives and that this will bring disaster upon them. They are in need of constant reassurance that these fears are unjustified. They conceive of their interpersonal rela-tions in stereotypical fashion, rarely thinking of people as concrete individuals but as social types. Furthermore, their interpersonal relations, particularly heterosexual relations, are felt to be difficult and filled with tension. They see the world outside themselves as monotonous, highly repetitive, and in terms of the past rather than of today and tomorrow. Moreover, this world is unrewarding and likely to punish them for any moral deviations that do not fit their rigid conception of moral correctness. They do not view a new situation as challenging but as filled with decisions that arouse dread rather than anticipation. Consequently, there is deep apprehension of the unknown.

These non-mobile, lower-middle-class housewives, who rigidly define their world in terms of the past and cling to it, clearly are the exact opposite of the upper-middle-class, mobile men that I described in an earlier chapter.

The Response to Soap Opera

The verbal projective technique that we used on these same women to determine how the characters and the action of the plot of the "Big Sister" program were related to their private worlds yielded results that helped verify and strengthen some of our conclusions about their personalities; but, above all, it demonstrated how the symbol systems of a mass medium are related to the lives of some of the people who use them. In the first place, there was strong identification with Ruth, the Big Sister in the lives of the other characters in the plot. Through this symbol they gained a feeling of security and consolation for their renunciation of the larger life provided by other types of careers for women in America. Almost without exception, these women looked upon the action of the program as real and as giving a true conception of life, whereas the career woman group readily rejected the characters and their actions as not real and not true to life. Moreover, they gained a satisfaction from the program verging on enthusiasm for the characters and for the solutions which the plot worked out for them. The characters of the story were people they wished to emulate.

On the other hand, the group of career women refused to identify with the characters or the action. There was a general negative feeling among them about the solutions, the action of the plot, and the characters. As mass symbols, they were unacceptable to this type of woman. They felt a strong sense of unreality about the whole program. They thoroughly disliked the character of Ruth, as was well expressed in this statement: "I dislike Ruth heartily. I do not like people who put themselves up as God. I think I am prejudiced against Ruth. If her husband is so wishy-washy that he gets in trouble with another woman [aggression], it's only what he deserves. He no doubt [said she scornfully] is one of those men who is immaculate and with a passion for cleanliness and sanitation." Throughout the interviews with this group, there was a great element of sophistication, wider interest, and more appreciation of what the scientist would call "the social realities" than among the group of lower-middle-class women who listen.

The social and psychological functions of the "Big Sister" program for the mass of non-mobile women who belong to the Common Man Level of American life are not difficult to determine. Some of the principal ones are: These women, being a class level below the characters of the "Big Sister" program (who are upper-middle), can emulate these women in their fantasies without having to make any effort to do so in their daily lives.

The principal symbolic theme of such a program is deeply satisfying to these women. This primary theme declares that good and noble women who are wives and mothers are invincible within their own arena of life, the American family. Men, who are superordinate eleswhere, are sub-ordinate and dependent on the wisdom of the wife. This primary theme always triumphs over the secondary one, which runs counter to it, that family ties can be broken and a woman's security threatened chiefly by the loss of the husband to other women and, quite secondarily and obliquely, by death. From the point of view of the women who listen, these two things are the basic expressions of their own reality.

The basic theme of "Big Sister" also expressed the vir-tues of American middle-class morality. In it, the good, carefully disciplined, largely sexless woman in the role of a mother was praised and rewarded. This program aroused normal anxiety in the women and provided symbolic solu-tions to reduce the anxiety that had been aroused. The private worries and distractions of the women were often solved in their fantasies by this modern morality play, and thereby the women's sense of security was increased.

Because the program dramatized the importance of the family and of women in it, those who identified with Ruth, the Big Sister of the program, felt themselves to be im-portant, and this feeling decreased their sense of futility. Characters like Christine, the woman who often threatened the security of Ruth but who always lost to Ruth, were punished for their "bad behavior." They confirmed the lis-teners' feelings about suppressing their own impulses and emotions. The program functioned socially to stabilize and strengthen the structure of the family and, thereby, the general structure of American life, particularly of the wife and mother. Although artistically the program was dull and unexciting, it did perform social and psychological functions for the mass of women who are a large and important segment of the social life of America.

With perhaps very little exaggeration, it can be said that the "Big Sister" program was a contemporary morality play which expressed for our time the moral feelings and beliefs of one segment of the masses of the people. The symbols of the play were basically roles and actions that personified good and evil. The good characters always triumphed over the machinations of the evil ones, and good deeds over bad ones.

Interpretation of the Meaning and Function of the Program

The outside world for the women of the Level of the Common Man is not highly rewarding or an easy place for them to be. They must constantly try to maintain peaceful and well-ordered relations within their families, or they endanger their security. They must continue to do this while they struggle to live within the means provided by their husbands' modest salaries and wages. They feel the pressure of the surrounding environment and know the need of restraining their actions within the limits of what their economy permits and within the moral confines of the traditional roles of women and mothers as they are defined by the conventions of the Level of the Common Man.

The comparatively free courting period, when love and sex are dominant, is past. Adaptation then meant the prudent use of sex symbols and sex sentiments to achieve the goal of winning a mate. At this earlier period in their lives, society positively affirmed and approved of such behavior. Now—married and often mothers—their social and economic tasks become the dominant pattern of their existence; and impulse behavior, while present, is treated as of secondary importance and, if allowed to take a dominant place in their activities, as wicked or absurd.

The marriage relation permits sex expression within its limits; but the obligations and duties assigned to women by American society in their roles of wives and mothers, as well as the realities of being a housewife, reduce this once dominant theme in the life of the young woman to a secondary and restricted one in the activities of the mature married woman. To make such an adjustment from a period of freedom to a period of constraint is not easy. To these women, Ruth is a symbol of a socially superior woman who has done this successfully, who is still attractive, and still a "nice person to know." Christine, on the other hand, is a mature woman who continues long after youth to make egoistic demands and is roundly condemned by those who listened. It is interesting to speculate on the intensity of listener hostility that would have developed had the Christines of the "Big Sister" story been rewarded for their demands and to wonder how long the radio listeners would have continued to be loyal to the program. The Ruths of American culture—symbols of sublimated impulse life and figures of social and economic reality—must be rewarded and triumph; and the Christines—symbols of uncontrolled emotion and ego satisfaction—must always fail; for therein lie hope and confidence for those who listen to daytime serials and, it is not too much to say, for American society. The women of the Level of the Common Man carry the heavy load of tradition and convention wherein are stored the most treasured beliefs and valued sentiments. It is no accident that these women are rigidly trained and under constant constraint, for American cultural stability and the continuance of that way of life are greatly dependent upon them.

The listeners' anxieties, shown in their responses to our tests, express their own difficulties in adjusting to their way of life. Their responses to what happened to the characters in the "Big Sister" program show their awareness of the difficulties of normal adjustment to life's realities; but the effect of this program was to direct their hopes into more confident and optimistic channels. Eighty-five per cent of the responses of the women to the question, "What do you think will happen to them in the future?" were positive and optimistic ("Ruth and John will succeed," and other good outcomes); whereas only 15 per cent were pessimistic ("Ruth and John will fail to solve their problems," or "Nothing good will happen"). The outcomes of the stories had a similar tone. A confident theme ran throughout the predictions for the future. In all of them there is an underlying assumption that this is a moral universe, where evil is punished and virtue is rewarded.

The evidence on all these symbolic points and on the social and psychological functions of the program is vivid and clear. The women respected and admired Ruth, identified with her, and therefore, in varying degrees, imitated her. It was important for us to know what their conception of her was. Ruth to them was the perfect wife. She was a person who kept control over herself, whose impulse life was sublimated, whose moral code was strict, and whose outlook on life was highly regulated. Her outward appearance, her clothes, her physical traits, were symbols of what they considered her reality to be. The answers to the question of her appearance almost unanimously agreed on these points. Christine's outward appearance symbolized what her personality was to her listeners. She was a symbol of explicitly condemned, but implicitly accepted, impulse life. Her dress expressed her sexuality; Ruth's, her character and moral worth.

Christine was always viewed in all respects as the antagonist of Ruth, thereby pitting impulse against character and moral restraint. According to the attitudes of the listeners, Christine—instead of being a "normal" woman—made strong and uncontrolled sex and emotional demands, and she used them as a weapon for her own egoistic purposes and, accordingly, was forever being punished. Uncontrolled impulse life was thereby condemned, but at the same time there was an implicit approval of it. The attitude toward this character was always ambivalent. She always lost to Ruth and was condemned for what she did; yet there was sufficient identification with her emotional experiences to give the women vicarious satisfaction in what Christine did.

The "Big Sister" serial was a drama which functioned to express the hopes and fears of its audience. Its basic themes portrayed these anxieties and hopes. The themes were symbolically expressed in the plot and action through the personalities of the characters. The audience, identifying with the plot and characters of "Big Sister," related their own personal problems to those of the play.

The program was a drama of the middle-class family. "Everything in the world" was centered within the focus of an upper-middle-class family (Big Sister's). Consequently, social realities outside the family were secondary and entered only as reflected in the structure and action of the family. As conceived by the listeners, the program expressed the psychological realities of their place in life, for it stated the traditional symbolic themes of family life which they have learned from American culture. This statement means that, for most listeners, the characters motivated the plot and their motives were usually plausible; new themes could be added (to this serial and others like it) only if they conformed to the basic one of the drama; social and economic situations (the realism of social science) could be developed only in a very secondary way, never as basic to the story.

The characters in "Big Sister" were men and women of the upper-middle class; for the great majority of the audience, this was essentially a device whereby the behavior and morals of the heroine were copied by the listeners because she was of higher status and because she expressed the moral ideals of the listeners.

The women who listened were distributed through the several socioeconomic levels of our society but belonged in most cases to the Common Man social level. At this level ordinarily the woman is economically dependent upon the moderate salary or wage of her husband, and her security, as well as that of her children, depends on her husband. The world beyond the family is largely outside her sphere of action, but it threatens her security. The moral code is more rigid and strict, particularly for women, than at the top and bottom social levels. Adaptation to changing conditions and real anxiety about it are phrased in moral terms; for the behavior of the woman must be highly prescribed and closely regulated, or she will lose her position as wife and mother and, thereby, her security. Because her economic position and her larger social situation are dependent upon others (particularly a male) and beyond her control, anxiety develops. Also, with the decreasing role of the housewife in this society, she often questions her utility and, consequently, worries about being a good wife and mother.

The "Big Sister" program had specific psychological functions that were expressed in the responses of the women studied. It aroused normal anxiety about the realities of life in the women who listened and directly and indirectly condemned neurotic anxiety about unreal contingencies. The program provided moral beliefs, values, and techniques for solving emotional and interpersonal problems for its audience and made them feel they were learning while they listened. (Thus: "I find the program is educational.")

It directed the private reveries and fantasies of the listeners into socially approved channels of action and increased the women's sense of security in a world they feel is often threatening, by reaffirming the basic security of the marriage ties (John's and Ruth's); accentuating the basic security of the position of the husband (John Wayne is a successful physician); "demonstrating" that those who behave properly and stay away from wrongdoing exercise moral control over those who do not; and showing that wrong behavior is punished.

"Big Sister," in dramatizing the significance of the wife's role in basic human affairs, increased the women's feeling of importance by showing that the family is of the highest importance and that the wife has control over the vicissitudes of family life. It thereby decreased their feeling of futility and made them feel essential and wanted. The women aspired to, and measured themselves by, identification with Ruth, the heroine; however, the identification was not with Ruth alone but with the whole program and the other characters in the plot. This permitted sublimated impulse satisfaction by the listeners', first, unconsciously identifying with the "emotional life" of the bad woman and, later, consciously punishing her through the action of the plot. Unregulated impulse life was condemned, since it was always connected with characters who were condemned and never related to those who were approved.

The primary social function of the program (how it worked) was to strengthen and stabilize the basic social structure of American society, the family. It so functioned by dramatizing family crises and the ideals and values involved, as they are understood and felt by the women who listened, and by making the good wife (Ruth) the center of action and power. American society, by offering a choice to women between being housewives or career women, frequently creates a dilemma for them. The career woman's role is attractive because it is usually of higher status than the occupation of the Common Man Level and offers more moral and emotional freedom. On the other hand, such a role is often frightening, demands hard work, ability to resist the system, and the capacity for self-initiated action. Most of the life of such women is outside the family. The "Big Sister" program played up the importance of the role of the wife and, therefore, obliquely depreciated the role (career women) which the ordinary listener has avoided or not been able to take. It helped to resolve any conflict she may have within her for not choosing the other role (that once might have been open to her) and reinforced her present position.

Essentially, the "Big Sister" drama was a contemporary minor morality which expressed, as did the morality plays of ancient times, the feelings and beliefs of its audience by use of idealized symbols of good and evil and of things feared and hoped for (the characters and their actions). It differed from the morality play of earlier times primarily because modern culture is secularized, whereas earlier society was dominated by sacred beliefs and values.

Mass media are products of technical invention and the increasing efforts of modern society to develop better methods for interrelating the peoples of the nations and the world into a closer community. Increasingly they are being influenced by the attitudes and needs of the Common Man. The rise of the masses is not purely a political and economic process, but more and more it means the use of symbol systems formerly confined to the top levels of society. The latter people, trained in what they consider to be canons of good taste, ridicule the popular arts or denounce their "debasing" effect on the older arts and the newer forms of communication. Very often they forget that the popular, lowly folk arts of yesterday became the prized possessions of today's sophisticates. The despised "primitive paintings," "the crude peasant woodcarvings," or, more recently, the mystical adoration of certain Continental music critics for "the superb art of jazz" are eloquent testimony to the fact that not all popular art forms are "debased and degraded" and that some which may now be despised may be the beginnings of new cultural forms. Whatever the ultimate verdict on the media of the masses may be, it is far better for the scholar and scientist to restrain his condemnation of them and devote his efforts to understanding their significance and meaning in contemporary life.

READER'S GUIDE

This part of the book is not so much a bibliography as a guide to help the reader increase his understanding of the several topics discussed in the text of each chapter. Below, under the heading "Books and Articles," there is a numbered list of authors with their selected works alphabetically arranged. After each there is at least one numeral which refers to the chapter where the selection might be used; pages of the book or article that are most useful with the chapter are given, too, in some cases.

Following the bibliographical list, the chapter headings are arranged sequentially; there the appropriate items from the bibliography are listed numerically.

Books and Articles

1. Arensberg, Conrad M., *et al.* (eds.). *Research in Industrial Human Relations: A Critical Appraisal.* New York: Harper & Bros., 1957. (VI.)
2. Bailey, Wilfrid C. "The Sacred and Profane Worlds of Jonesville," in W. Lloyd Warner and Associates, *Democracy in Jonesville.* New York: Harper & Bros., 1949. (IX, 149–67.)
3. Barnard, Chester I. "Functions and Pathology of Status Systems in Formal Organizations," in William Foote Whyte

(ed.), *Industry and Society.* New York: McGraw-Hill Book Co., Inc., 1946. (VI, 46–83.)

4. BARRON, MILTON L. (ed.). *American Minorities.* New York: Alfred A. Knopf, 1957. (VII.)

5. BURGESS, E. W., and LOCKE, HARVEY J. *The Family: From Institution to Companionship.* New York: American Book Co., 1945. (IV, 333–59.)

6. DAVIS, ALLISON, and DOLLARD, JOHN. *Children of Bondage.* Washington, D.C.: American Council on Education, 1940. (IV, 263–78.)

7. DAVIS, ALLISON; GARDNER, BURLEIGH; and GARDNER, MARY R. *Deep South: A Social Anthropological Study of Caste and Class.* Chicago: University of Chicago Press, 1941. (IV, 59–136.)

8. DAVIS, ALLISON, and HAVIGHURST, ROBERT J. "Social Class and Color Differences in Child-rearing," *American Sociological Review,* XI (December, 1946), 698–710. (IV.)

9. ———. "The Measurement of Mental Systems," *Scientific Monthly,* LXVI (April, 1948), 301–16. (V.)

10. ———. *Father of the Man.* Boston: Houghton Mifflin Co., 1947. (IV, 8–16; 215–19.)

11. DOLLARD, JOHN. *Caste and Class in a Southern Town.* New York: Harper & Bros., 1949. (III, 134–72.)

12. DOLLARD, JOHN, and MILLER, NEAL E. *Personality and Psychotherapy: An Analysis in Terms of Learning, Thinking, and Culture.* New York: McGraw-Hill Book Co., Inc., 1950. (I, 25–47.)

13. DRAKE, ST. CLAIR, and CAYTON, HORACE R. *Black Metropolis.* New York: Harcourt, Brace & Co., 1945. (IX, 531–36, 687–710.)

14. DRUCKER, PETER F., "Business Objectives and Survival Needs: Notes on a Discipline of Business Enterprise," *Journal of Business,* Vol. XXXI, No. 2 (April, 1958). (VI.)

15. DUBIN, ROBERT. *The World of Work: Industrial Society and Human Relations.* New York: Prentice-Hall, Inc., 1958. (VI.)

16. DURKHEIM, ÉMILE. *Elementary Forms of the Religious Life.* Translated by J. W. SWAIN. New York: Macmillan Co., 1926. (I, 23–47.)

17. ———. *The Rules of Sociological Method.* Translated by SARAH SOLOVAY and JOHN H. MUELLER. Chicago: University of Chicago Press, 1938. (II, 1–14.)

18. ELKIN, FRED. "The Psychological Appeal of the Hollywood Western," *Journal of Educational Sociology,* XXIV (October, 1950), 72–86. (X.)

19. ELKIN, FRED. "God, Radio, and the Movies," *Hollywood Quarterly,* V (Winter, 1950), 105–14. (X.)

20. FITZGERALD, F. SCOTT. *The Great Gatsby.* New York: Charles Scribner's Sons, 1925. (V.)

21. FRANK, L. K. "Projective Methods for the Study of Personality," *Journal of Psychology,* VIII (1939), 389–413. (X.)

22. FREUD, SIGMUND. *New Introductory Lectures on Psycho-analysis.* New York: W. W. Norton & Co., Inc., 1933. (X.)

23. GARDNER, BURLEIGH B., and MOORE, DAVID G. *Human Relations in Industry.* Homewood: Richard D. Irwin, Inc., 1955. (VI, 40–95.)

24. GINZBERG, ELI. *The Negro Potential.* New York: Columbia University Press, 1956. (III, 3–60.)

25. GORDON, MILTON M. *Social Class in American Sociology.* Durham, N.C.: Duke University Press, 1958. (III, 85–165.)

26. HAVIGHURST, ROBERT J. and NEUGARTEN, BERNICE. *Education and Society.* Boston: Allyn & Bacon, 1957. (V, 1–78; VIII, 181–354.)

27. HENRY, WILLIAM E. "The Thematic Apperception Technique in the Study of Culture-Personality Relations," *Genetic Psychology Monographs,* XXXV (1947), 3–135. (VIII; X.)

28. ———. "The Business Executive: Psychodynamics of a Social Role," *American Journal of Sociology,* LIV (January, 1949), 286–91. (VIII.)

29. HESS, R., and HANDEL, G. *Family Worlds: A Psychosocial Approach to Family Life.* Chicago: University of Chicago Press, 1959. (IV, 1–19.)

30. HILL, MOZELL C., and ACKISS, THELMA. "The 'Insight Interview' Approach to Race Relations," *Journal of Social Psychology,* Vol. XXI (1945). (II.)

31. HOLLINGSHEAD, A. B. *Elmtown's Youth.* New York: John Wylie & Sons, Inc., 1949. (VIII, 148–62, 204–43.)

32. HOMANS, GEORGE. *The Human Group.* New York: Harcourt, Brace & Co., 1950. (VI, 48–80.)

33. HOWELLS, WILLIAM DEAN. *The Rise of Silas Lapham.* Boston and New York: Houghton Mifflin Co., 1910. (V.)

34. HUGHES, EVERETT C. *French Canada in Transition.* Chicago: University of Chicago Press, 1943. (VII, 46–83.)

35. HUGHES, EVERETT C., and HUGHES, HELEN M. *Where Peoples Meet.* Glencoe, Ill.: Free Press, 1952 (VII, 116–29.)

36. HUNTER, FLOYD. *Community Power Structure.* 1953. (III, 8–26.)

37. JOURNAL OF EDUCATIONAL SOCIOLOGY FOR APRIL, 1952 (Vol. XXV, No. 8), (VIII).
   a) BECKER, HOWARD. "Social-Class Variations in the Teacher-Pupil Relationship."
   b) MULLIGAN, RAYMOND A. "Social Mobility and Higher Education."
   c) SMITH, BENJAMIN F. "Wishes of Negro High School Seniors and Social Class Status."
   d) ABRAHAMSON, STEPHEN. "Our Status and Scholastic Rewards."

38. JUNKER, BUFORD H. *Field Work: An Introduction to the Social Sciences.* Chicago: University of Chicago Press, 1960. (II.)

39. KAHL, JOSEPH A. *The American Class Structure.* New York: Rinehart & Co., Inc., 1957. (III, 19–53.)

40. KERR, CLARK. *Unions and Union Leaders of Their Own Choosing.* New York: Fund for the Republic, 1957. (VI.)

41. KIMBALL, SOLON T., and PEARSALL, MARION. *The Talladega Story.* University: University of Alabama Press, 1954. (II, 1–53; 186–202.)

42. KINSEY, ALFRED C.; POMEROY, WARDELL B.; and MARTIN, CLYDE E. *Sexual Behavior in the Human Male.* Philadelphia: W. B. Saunders Co., 1948. (IV.)

43. KLAPP, ORRIN E. "The Creation of Popular Heroes," *American Journal of Sociology,* LIV (September, 1948), 135–41. (X.)

44. LA FARGE, CHRISTOPHER. *The Wilsons.* New York: Coward-McCann, 1941. (V.)

45. LOOMIS, CHARLES P. *Social Systems.* Princeton, N.J.: D. Van Nostrand Co., Inc., 1960. (II, 1–47.)

46. LYND, ROBERT S., and LYND, HELEN M. *Middletown: A Study of Contemporary American Culture,* and *Middletown in Transition: A Study in Cultural Conflicts.* New York: Harcourt, Brace & Co., 1937. (II.)

47. MALINOWSKI, BRONISLAW. "Supplement I," in C. K. OGDEN and

I. A. RICHARDS, *The Meaning of Meaning*. New York: Harcourt, Brace & Co., 1936. (I, 296–336.)

48. MARQUAND, JOHN P. *Point of No Return*. New York: Grosset & Dunlap, Inc., 1951. (V.)

49. MARTIN, NORMAN H., and STRAUSS, ANSELM L. "Patterns of Mobility within Industrial Organizations," *Journal of Business*, Vol. XXIX, No. 2 (April, 1956). (V.)

50. MASON, EDWARD S. *The Corporation in Modern Society*. Cambridge, Mass.: Harvard University Press, 1959. (VI, 25–45.)

51. MAY, ROLLO (ed.). *Symbolism in Religion and Literature*. New York: George Braziller, 1960. (I, 11–50.)

52. McGUIRE, CARSON. "Social Mobility: The Rise and Fall of Families," in W. LLOYD WARNER and ASSOCIATES, *Democracy in Jonesville*. New York: Harper & Bros., 1949. (V, 55–76.)

53. ———. "Family Life in Lower- and Middle-Class Homes," *Marriage and Family Living*, XIV (February, 1952), 1–6. (III.)

54. ———. "Age-Mate Acceptance and Indices of Peer Status," *Child Development*, Vol. XXIII (June, 1952). (VIII.)

55. MEAD, GEORGE. *Mind, Self, and Society*. Chicago: University of Chicago Press, 1946. (I, 61–75, 135–208.)

56. MEEKER, MARCHIA. "The Joiners—Male and Female," and "Status Aspirations and the Social Club," in W. LLOYD WARNER and ASSOCIATES, *Democracy in Jonesville*. New York: Harper & Bros., 1949. (IX, 115–48.)

57. MERTON, ROBERT K., and KENDALL, PATRICIA L., "The Focused Interview," *American Journal of Sociology*, Vol. LI (May, 1940). (II.)

58. MORRIS, CHARLES. *Signs, Language, and Behavior*. New York: Prentice-Hall Book Co., 1946. (I, 1–60.)

59. MURRAY, H. A. *Explorations in Personality*. New York: Oxford University Press, 1938. (X.)

60. NEUGARTEN, BERNICE. "The Democracy of Childhood," in W. LLOYD WARNER and ASSOCIATES, *Democracy in Jonesville*. New York: Harper & Bros., 1949. (VII, 77–88.)

61. NICHOLS, JAMES HASTINGS. *Primer for Protestants*. New York: Association Press, 1951. (I.)

62. OGDEN, C. K., and RICHARDS, I. A. *The Meaning of Meaning: A Study of the Influence of Language upon Thought and of the*

Science of Symbolism. New York: Harcourt, Brace & Co., 1936. (I, 1–23.)

63. PIAGET, JEAN. *The Moral Judgment of the Child*. New York: Harcourt, Brace & Co., 1926. (VIII.)

64. ———. *The Language and Thought of the Child*. New York: Harcourt, Brace & Co., 1932. (I, 5–49.)

65. RADCLIFFE-BROWN, A. R. *A Natural Science of Society*. Glencoe, Ill.: Free Press, 1957. (II.)

66. ———. *Method in Social Anthropology; Selected Essays*. Edited by M. N. SRINIVAS. Chicago: University of Chicago Press, 1958. (II.)

67. RAINWATER, LEE; COLEMAN, RICHARD P.; and HANDEL, GERALD. *Workingman's Wife*. New York: Oceana Publications, Inc., 1959. (IV, 15–144.)

68. RAINWATER, LEE. *And the Poor Get Children*. Chicago: Quadrangle Books, Inc., 1960. (IV, 1–166.)

69. RIESMAN, DAVID. *The Lonely Crowd*. New Haven: Yale University Press, 1950. (VIII, 3–35.)

70. RIESMAN, DAVID, and BENNEY, MARK. "The Sociology of the Interview," *Midwest Sociologist*, XVIII (1956), 3–15. (II.)

71. RUESCH, JURGEN, *et al. Chronic Disease and Psychological Invalidism: A Psychosomatic Study*. Berkeley and Los Angeles: University of California Press, 1941. (V, 1–7, 301–41.)

72. SCHULBERG, BUDD. *What Makes Sammy Run?* New York: Random House, 1941. (V.)

73. SEELEY, JOHN R.; SIM, R. ALEXANDER; and LOOSLEY, ELIZABETH W. *Crestwood Heights; A Study of the Culture of Suburban Life*. New York: Basic Books, 1956. (II, VII.)

74. SEELEY, JOHN R., *et al. Community Chest; A Case Study in Philanthropy*. Community Surveys, Inc., Indianapolis. Toronto: University of Toronto Press, 1957. (IX, 3–106.)

75. SIMPSON, GEORGE E. and YINGER, J. MILTON. *Racial and Cultural Minorities: An Analysis of Prejudice and Discrimination*. New York: Harper & Bros., 1953. (II.)

76. SMITH, WILLIAM ROBERTSON. *Lectures on the Religion of the Semites*. New York: D. Appleton & Co., 1889. (I, 29–81, 251–78.)

77. STEIN, MAURICE R. *The Eclipse of Community; An Interpreta-*

tion of American Studies. Princeton, N.J.: Princeton University Press, 1960. (VII, 13–116, 229–50.)

78. TARKINGTON, BOOTH. *The Magnificent Ambersons.* Garden City, N.Y.: Doubleday, Doran & Co., 1919. (V.)

79. TAUSSIG, F. W., and JOSLYN, C. S. *American Business Leaders.* New York: Macmillan Co., 1932. (V, 233–70.)

80. THOMAS, JOHN L., S.J. *The American Catholic Family.* Englewood Cliffs, N.J.: Prentice-Hall Inc., 1956. (IV, 99–172.)

81. THOMAS, W. I., and ZNANIECKI, F. *The Polish Peasant in Europe and America: Monograph on an Immigrant Group.* Chicago: University of Chicago Press, 1918–20. (VII, 87–156.)

82. TROELTSCH, ERNST. *The Social Teaching of the Christian Churches.* New York: Harper Torchbook, 1960. (I, 461–514.)

83. VEBLEN, THORSTEIN. *Theory of the Leisure Class.* New York: Modern Library, 1931. (IV, 68–102.)

84. WARNER, W. LLOYD. "A Methodology for the Study of the Development of Family Attitudes," *Social Science Research Council Bulletin,* No. 18 (1933). (IV.)

85. ———. "The Society, the Individual, and His Mental Disorders," *American Journal of Psychiatry,* XCIV (September, 1937), 275–84. (II.)

86. WARNER, W. LLOYD, and LUNT, PAUL S. *The Social Life of a Modern Community.* ("Yankee City Series," Vol. I.) New Haven: Yale University Press, 1941 (II, 8–75; III, 81–126, 127–201; IX, 301–55.)

87. WARNER, W. LLOYD; JUNKER, BUFORD H.; and ADAMS, WALTER. *Color and Human Nature.* Washington, D.C.: American Council on Education, 1941. (III, 1–30, 192–264.)

88. WARNER, W. LLOYD; HAVIGHURST, ROBERT J.; and LOEB, MARTIN B. *Who Shall Be Educated?* New York and London: Harper & Bros., 1944. (V, 33–72, 98–109.)

89. WARNER, W. LLOYD, and SROLE, LEO. *The Social Systems of American Ethnic Groups.* ("Yankee City Series," Vol. III.) New Haven: Yale University Press, 1945. (VII, 1–30, 67–155; IX, 254–82.)

90. WARNER, W. LLOYD, and LOW, J. O. *The Social System of the Modern Factory.* ("Yankee City Series," Vol. IV.) New Haven: Yale University Press, 1947. (VI, 1–7, 54–65, 134–58.)

91. WARNER, W. LLOYD, and HENRY, WILLIAM E. "Radio Day Time Serial: A Symbolic Analysis," *Genetic Psychology Monographs*, Vol. XXXVII (1948). (X, 3–71.)

92. WARNER, W. LLOYD, and ASSOCIATES. *Democracy in Jonesville*. New York: Harper & Bros., 1949. (VI, 101–14.)

93. WARNER, W. LLOYD, and ABEGGLEN, JAMES C. *Big Business Leaders in America*. New York: Harper & Bros., 1955. (VIII, 59–107.)

94. ———. *Occupational Mobility in American Business and Industry*. Minneapolis: University of Minnesota Press, 1955.

95. WARNER, W. LLOYD. *A Black Civilization*. New York: Harper & Bros., 1958. (I, 193–450.)

96. ———. *The Living and the Dead*. ("Yankee City Series," Vol. V.) New Haven: Yale University Press, 1959. (I, 101–226, 426–506.)

97. WARNER, W. LLOYD, and MARTIN, NORMAN H. *Industrial Man*. New York: Harper & Bros., 1959. (IV, 1–22.)

98. WARNER, W. LLOYD; MEEKER, MARCHIA; and EELLS, KENNETH. *Social Class in America: A Manual of Procedure for the Measurement of Social Status*. New York: Harper Torchbook, 1960. (III, 3–46, 251–75.)

99. WARNER, W. LLOYD. *The Family of God*. New Haven: Yale University Press, 1961. (I, 3–44.)

100. ———. *The Community, the Corporation, and the Emergent Society*. ("Ford Distinguished Lectures," Vol. IV.) New York: Harper & Bros., 1961. (VI.)

101. WEBER, MAX. *The Protestant Ethic and the Spirit of Capitalism*. Translated by T. PARSONS. London: George Allen & Unwin, Ltd., 1948. (I, 35–78.)

102. WEDGWOOD, CAMILLA H. "The Nature and Functions of Secret Societies," *Oceania*, No. 2 (1930), pp. 128–45. (IX.)

103. WEST, JAMES. *Plainsville, U.S.A.* New York: Columbia University Press, 1947. (II.)

104. WHITE, R. CLYDE. *These Will Go to College*. Cleveland: Western Reserve University Press, 1952. (V, 3–84.)

105. WHORF, B. L. *Language, Thought, and Reality; Selected Writings*. Cambridge: Technology Press of Massachusetts Institute of Technology, 1956. (I, 246–70.)

106. WHYTE, WILLIAM FOOTE. *Street Corner Society*. Chicago: University of Chicago Press, 1943. (IV, 3–51; IX, 3–51.)

107. ———. *Man and Organization*. Homewood, Ill.: Richard D. Irwin, Inc., 1959. (VI.)

108. WILLIAMS, ROBIN M. *American Society: A Sociological Interpretation*. New York: Alfred A. Knopf, 1951. (IX, 443–82.)

109. WIRTH, LOUIS. *The Ghetto*. Chicago: University of Chicago Press, 1928. (VII, 195–240; 282–91.)

110. WRAY, DONALD. "The Norwegians: Sect and Ethnic Group," in W. LLOYD WARNER and ASSOCIATES, *Democracy in Jonesville*. New York: Harper & Bros., 1949. (VII, 168–92.)

111. YOUNG, PAULINE. *Scientific Social Surveys and Research*. New York: Prentice-Hall Book Co., 1946. (II, 243–64.)

Readings for Each Chapter

I. *AN AMERICAN SACRED CEREMONY*
   12, 16, 47, 51, 55, 58, 61, 62, 64, 76, 82, 95, 96, 99, 101, 105.

II. *THE STUDY OF CONTEMPORARY SOCIETY*
   17, 30, 38, 41, 45, 46, 57, 65, 66, 70, 73, 85, 86, 103, 111.

III. *SOCIAL CLASS AND COLOR CASTE IN AMERICA*
   11, 24, 25, 36, 39, 53, 86, 87, 98.

IV. *THE FAMILY IN A CLASS SYSTEM*
   5, 6, 7, 8, 9, 29, 42, 67, 68, 80, 83, 84, 106.

V. *INDIVIDUAL OPPORTUNITY AND SOCIAL MOBILITY IN AMERICA*
   10, 20, 26, 33, 44, 48, 49, 52, 71, 72, 78, 79, 88, 104.

VI. *THE FACTORY IN THE EMERGENT SOCIETY AND THE COMMUNITY*
   1, 3, 14, 15, 23, 32, 40, 50, 90, 92, 94, 97, 100, 107.

VII. *AMERICAN ETHNIC AND SECTARIAN GROUPS*
   4, 34, 35, 60, 73, 75, 77, 81, 89, 109, 110.

VIII. *SOCIAL PERSISTENCE AND PERSONALITY DEVELOPMENT*
   26, 27, 28, 31, 37, 54, 63, 69, 93.

IX. *ASSOCIATIONS IN AMERICA*
   2, 13, 56, 74, 86, 89, 102, 106, 108.

X. *MASS MEDIA: A SOCIAL AND PSYCHOLOGICAL ANALYSIS*
   18, 19, 21, 22, 27, 43, 59, 91.

INDEX

bility, 144–45; social persistence of, 219–25; social structure of, 223

Businessmen: characteristics of, 224; executive, 222–23; leadership of, 127; as personality types, 220; in relations with parents, 224; social roles, 221; upper-middle, 221–25; upward-mobile, 221, 222

Calendar, ceremonial, 7

Capitalism (or Capitalistic system), 145, 162, 171, 172, 175, 178

Catholics: in associations, 30; and gods, 32; hierarchy, 185–98; in social ritual, 16

Cemetery: and ceremonies, 15–16; and sacred symbols, 8, 9–10, 32–34

Ceremony: function of, 30–34; of Memorial Day, 8–16; sacred, 5–34, 233

Changes, in communities, 24–26

Chicago, caste and class system in, 93–98

Children: and class system, 210; and class values, 219; ethnic, 182, 187, 189–92, 201–2; family orientation and training of, 73, 102–25, 209–10; lower-class, 107–10, 112–13; middle-class, 110–11, 113; of mixed marriages, 88; Negro, schooling of, 97; Negro-white, 88, 97; in school, 119, 210, 212–13; in social class, 73, 211; and social structure, 210; upper-class, 110–12; *see also* Families

Church: and associations, 227, 229–30; and ethnics, 184–85, 193, 197–201; and faith, 30; Negro, 98; and sacred symbol systems, 6, 11–13, 32; sectarian, 202–5; and social symbols, 249; *see also* Catholics; Jewish group

Civic leaders: among Negroes, 98–99; in upper-middle class, 75; *see also* Leadership

Civil War, 6, 20

Cliques: among ethnics, 188; and social mobility, 74

Clubs: and color caste, 71, 95; and social mobility, 74

Collective representation: in association activities, 244; of ceremonies, 30–31; of Lincoln, 19–23

Color caste, 86–101; and associations, 71, 95; and education, 97; and marriage, 88; and parallelism, 92, 98–99; in politics, 95–96; and segregation, 97; and social class, 87–88, 98–99, 116, 180; and social and economic opportunity, 99–100; subordination, 87, 89–90, 97, 100; and Supreme Court, 95

Committee on Human Development, University of Chicago, 136, 220

Common man, elements of, in Lincoln Image, 22

Communication: mass, 247–50; newspapers, 62; public, 62; in social symbols, 249; *see also* Language; Mass media

Community: and associations, 227–28; and ceremonies, 30–34; in conflict situations, 159–60, 161–62; and ethnics, 184; and the factory, 154, 159–60; and leadership, 170–71, 177; and management, 173, 177; as research laboratory, 39–50; solidarity of, 26–29; study of, 41 ff.; and symbol systems, 30–34; unification through Memorial Day ceremonies, 8; values in class ranking, 72

Controls of the environment, 56, 59–60

Cult, 31–32, 34

Government: and Negroes in office, 96; as segmental hierarchy, 68–69

Greek Orthodox Church: in associations, 30; in social ritual, 16; *see also* Church; Ethnic groups

Havighurst, Robert, 105, 214

Henry, William, 220–24

Hierarchies (social), 116; segmental, 68–69; and social status, 68, 129; *see also* Economic hierarchies

Holidays, sacred and secular, 5–8, 8–19; *see also* Memorial Day

House type: of ethnics, 183; in rating techniques, 84–85; and social status, 119–20

Immigrants, 181; *see also* Ethnic groups

Income: in rating techniques, 84–85; in social class, 80

Index of Status Characteristics (research method): in mass media, 255; in social class, 80, 83–85, 193–95

Individual: autonomous, 53, 62, 138, 208, 247; and mobility, 132; opportunity, 126–52; sense of worth, 27–29; in society, 37, 52, 208–9; and species behavior, 208; and status, 65, 66–67, 138

Individualism, 138–39, 218; and child training, 108, 122

Industrial institutions, 153; *see also* Factories

Interviewing, as research technique, 81, 82–83, 255, 257–60

I.Q., and social class, 135–37, 214

Jewish group, 199–202; and child training, 123; and God, 32; in social ritual, 16; *see also* Ethnic group

"Jim Crow," 97–98; *see also* Segregation

Jonesville: churches, 230; class distribution, 78; class system, 82–85; as research laboratory, 41; schools, 211, 215–17; sectarian group, 204–5

Kinsey, Alfred, 114–16

Language: common, 61; of ethnics, 184, 187, 188–89, 199; and learned behavior, 53; as research problem, 49; scientific, 61; and social relations, 186, 187

Leadership: of businessmen, 127, 168–72, 173–74, 177; of union, 127, 167

Learning: animal, 53, 54; the class system of, 209–10; and ethnics, 248; and family, 102–3, 105; human, 53–54; and language, 53; and punishment and reward, 54; and social class, 213–14

Level above the Common Man: in associations, 229; composition of, 75; and schools, 210–11

Level of the Common Man, 75–76; and mass media, 256, 266; and schools, 210–11, 266

Life, of social systems, 36–37

Lincoln, Abraham, 128; birthday of, 233; as collective representation, 19–23; as symbol of American success story, 22; as symbol system, 249; as symbol of unity, 14, 22, 30; and war, 20

Lodges, and sacred symbols, 7, 15

Lower class: association activities of, 244; families and child training, 209–10; I.Q., 214; students, 212–13, 214; and talent mobility, 234–35

Lower-lower class: in associations, 229; characteristics, 76–79; child training, 106–9, 112–14, 124; and ethnics, 76, 194–95; I.Q., 136–37; in Jonesville, 82; ratings, 84; sexual behavior, 113–14

Lower-middle class: in associations,

229, 230; characteristics, 75–76, 78–79; child training, 105, 122–24; and ethnics, 195; in Jonesville, 82; in radio audiences, 263; ratings, 84–85; sexual behavior, 112–13; students, 212, 216–17; teachers, 211

Lower-upper class, 117; and ethnics, 195; size of, 77; and social mobility, 76; *see also* Upper class

Magazines, as mass medium, 44, 250

Magic, and religion, 55

Managers and management: and the community, 173, 177; and social and economic status, 64; and unions, 175–76; and worker relations, 127, 143, 145–46, 155, 160, 163, 168, 173, 176, 177

Marriage: and class considerations, 92; and color caste, 88, 92, 94; and sex relations, 267; and social class, 73, 88, 117; and social mobility, 132; and status, 63

Mass media, 44, 49, 247–73; research in, 250–60; and social class, 263; and symbolic themes, 253–54, 263

Memorial Day: and Christian church's sacred sacrifice, 34; cult of the dead, 34; function as unifier of community, 8; organization of ceremonies, 13–16; as sacred ceremony, 5–19, 20, 23–24, 30–31, 33–34; as symbolic behavior, 5–19, 23–24, 30–31, 249; themes of, 8

Middle class, 228; family and child training, 209–10; I.Q., 214; in radio themes, 260, 264; teachers and child training, 211; *see also* Lower-middle class; Upper-middle class

Middle West: and social class, 74, 78–79; as symbolized by Lincoln, 20, 23

Midwest: community research, 48; schools, 211, 215

Minority groups, 180, 183; *see also* Ethnic groups; Negroes; Sectarian groups

Money: in social class, 74–75, 80, 117; and social mobility, 133

Monkeys, social life of, 52–53

Moral order, 58–59

Moral organization, 56

Motion pictures: as mass medium, 44, 250; as symbol system, 62, 251

Myths, of Lincoln's life, 21

Negro, 180; child training, 107–8, 123; civic leaders, 98; in government, 96; marriage, 88; as a political force, 96; segregation, 95–98; in social class, 79, 89–92, 98; and Supreme Court decision, 95; voting, 96; and white children, 95; *see also* Color caste

New England: social class, 74; worker relations with management, 154–78; *see also* Yankee City

"New families": in Jonesville, 82; and ritual, 120; and social status, 74–75

Newspapers, 10–11; as mass medium, 44, 250; as symbol system, 62

Numbers, as problem in research, 46, 47, 49

Occupation: of ethnics, 183, 195; in rating techniques, 84, 85; and skill hierarchies, 160, 163–64, 166–67; and social mobility, 132, 133, 134, 136–37, 144–45; in status criteria, 115

"Old family": aristocracy of, 74–75; child training of, 11; in Jonesville, 82; ritual, 119; and schools, 211

Organizations, civic, 226

Parallelism, in caste relations, 92, 99

Parents, 181–82; of American businessmen, 224; and child training, 103, 106, 111–12, 121–25; ethnic, 181, 186–87, 189–92, 210–12; *see also* Families

Patriotic organizations: and social class, 29–30, 76; as symbols, 30

Personality: of businessmen, 220–25; formation or development of, 104, 108, 190, 207, 209–10, 220, 226; of radio audiences, 263–64; and social persistence, 216–25; structure of, 103, 106

Politics: hierarchies of, 42, 43; ideologies, 142; and Negroes, 96

Power and prestige factors: in civic affairs, 171; in Lincoln's life, 128; in social mobility, 132, 133; among workers, 164–66

Protestant Ethic: and child training, 110–11; of lower-middle class, 76

Protestant group: in associations, 30; and God, 32; in social ritual, 16

Psychology: projective techniques, 221, 253, 256, 267–68; in research, 45, 106, 250, 251

Race relations, 93–95, 99; *see also* Color caste

Radio: as mass medium, 44, 250; "soap opera" or daytime serials, 254–73; as symbol system, 62, 251

Rank, 127; in color caste, 87–88; function of, 127–31; order, 73, 131

Research methods: of business executives, 221; in child development, 106; in contemporary society, 35–50; and criteria, 41–43; in ethnic groups, 180; and ethnocentrism, 49; in interviewing, 80–82, 83; in mass media, 250–

60; in social change, 206–7; in social class, 193–94; and symbolic analysis, 48; *see also* Evaluated Participation; Index of Status Characteristics; Interviewing

Rituals or rites, 5, 9–10, 11–12, 13–15, 56, 59, 233–34; in associations, 233, 244–45; of lower-upper class, 120; and myths, 55; of upper-upper class, 119

Role, 66–67; of businessmen, 221; of the church on Memorial Day, 11–13; social evaluation of, 67; in social organization, 63

Rules: of culture, 37; family training in, 104; of social structure, 52

Sacred symbols, 60–61

Sacred symbol systems: in associations, 7; in ceremonial calendar, 6; in churches, 8, 30–31; in collective representations, 30–34; of Memorial Day, 8–9

Sacrifice: in democracy, 10, 11, 23; equality of sacrifice, 10, 27–28; of individual purpose for the good of the group, 8; of Lincoln, 8; as sacred symbol, 8; of the soldier dead, 8; in war, 33

Sanctions, social, 54; of color caste, 93–94; concerning marriage, 88, 116; concerning social mobility, 131

Schools: and associations, 227; boards, 210–11; and class backing, 75; and ethnics, 185, 187–89, 192, 199; and Negroes, 97, 99; in patriotic programs, 9, 10; and segregation, 97; and social class, 110, 116, 209–19; and social mobility, 119, 136, 138, 214–15; social structure of, 209–19; and social symbols, 219; teachers in, 211; in wartime, 28; *see also* Education

Sectarian groups, 202–5

Secular symbols: in ceremonies, 6; in rituals, 233

Segregation, of Negroes: in dwelling areas, 97–98; in schools, 97

Sex mores: of lower class, 109–10, 112–13; of middle class, 109–10, 112–13

Sex relations, between whites and Negroes, 92, 94–95

Skills: and economic hierarchies, 143, 145; family training in social, 104; hierarchy of, 160, 165, 166, 177–78; and social mobility, 132

Social anthropology, 35–36, 37, 206; concepts of, 50–61; methods in study of contemporary man in, 35–50, 154, 252

Social change, 45–46, 89, 127, 141, 153–78; in caste relations, 99; in research, 251, 253; and social theory, 206–7

Social characteristics: of businessmen, 222–25; of color caste, 87–88, 93–101; of middle-class goals, 110; rating techniques, 83–87, 217

Social class, 68–101; and associations, 29–30, 75–76, 228–29, 242–46; and behavior, 80, 104; of business executives, 221, 225; and child training, 73, 102–25, 209–19; and children, 105–6, 110–11, 219; and color caste, 86–101; and dwelling area, 84–85; and economic factors, 80; and education, 75, 135–38, 209–10; of ethnic groups, 76, 180, 183, 194–95; and families, 102–25; in Far West, 78–79; and fixed status, 140; and house types, 84, 119–20; learning, 209–10; and learning problems, 212, 248; levels, 74; and marriage, 72–73, 92; and mass media, 255, 260–73; in Midwest, 78–79; and money, 117; of Negroes, 90–92, 180; in New

England, 74–76; of "new families," 74–75; and occupations, 84; of "old families," 74–75, 111–12; and parents, 106, 111; and personality development, 108–12, 209–19; prestige factors, 80; as rank order, 73, 131; ratings, 80–81, 83–85; research methods in, 80, 83–85, 193; and schools, 110, 116; and sexual behavior, 106, 109–16; and social mobility, 132–33; and social participation, 105; and source of income, 84; in South, 78; values, 210, 215; and wartime, 28

Social Class in America, 239

Social conflict, 153, 154, 175; and blocked mobility, 142; within ethnic families, 184, 190, 191, 201; within personality, 190–91; in sectarian groups, 203

Social control, 37; through associations, 227

Social distance: between parents and children, 11, 119; in upper-class behavior, 116, 117

Social identification, and integration in wartime, 24, 26, 28

Social interaction, and religious symbols, 30–31

Social institutions, status of members, 63–64

Social labor, division of, in complex societies, 62, 64

Social life: and learned behavior, 53; of monkeys and apes, 52–53

Social logics, 24, 89, 138, 190, 248

Social mobility, 79, 116; and associations, 228, 239; blocked, 135, 139–46; of business executives, 220, 222–23, 224–25; and child training, 11, 209–10, 220; and color caste, 88–89; and democracy, 129–30; downward, 131, 134, 136–37, 144; of ethnics, 180, 184, 193–97; and family, 118–19, 132; and individual opportunity,

125–52; and marriage, 132; and money, 133; motivations for, 133; of Negroes and whites, 180; through occupations, 132, 133, 134, 136–37, 144–45; in radio audiences, 261; routes of, 131–39, 140, 144; sanctions of, 131; and social learning, 133; through social skills, 132; stages of, 133; through talent, 132; of upper-lower class, 76; of upper-middle class, 75; vertical, 73, 129, 132

Social opportunity: equal, 99–100; Negro and white, 99–100

Social organization: and human adjustment, 55–61; and social relations, 63; and species behavior, 52–53; and status and role, 63–64

Social participation: in association activities, 244; and child training, 105; and leadership, 168–72

Social persistence, 186, 209; of business enterprise, 219–25; of ethnic groups, 179–86; and personality development, 206–25; and species behavior, 206–9

Social position, 65–66, 210–11; see also Social status

Social relations, 54; in community, 51; and language, 186; and personality, 207, 219–20

Social science, 104, 159, 206–8, 233, 269–70; in research, 146, 251

Social solidarity, 62; of ethnic family, 184; in wartime, 24–29

Social status: anxiety about, 144, 178; characteristics of, 84–85; and child training, 110; economic, 63–64; and equality, 129; of ethnics, 193; and family members, 63, 79; fixed, 140; form of, 65–67; function of, 64–65; and hierarchies, 69; and mobility, 131, 133; of Negroes, 93–94, 98–99, 180; systems of, 129, 136,

137; unequal, 127–28; values of, 216; of workers in the factory, 163–64

Social structure, 52, 185, 271–72; of business enterprise, 223; and child training, 105, 209–10; complex, 61–62, 64–65; of factory, 167; rules and symbols of, 52; of schools, 210–11; and social status, 64–65, 79, 139–40, 211

Social symbols, 208; in associations, 230, 233, 243–45; in calendar, 7; ceremonial, 7, 31; and church, 249; in color caste, 88; and ethnic groups, 184–85, 188, 192, 199; and family training, 104; group sharing in, 61; in Lincoln, 14, 19–23, 30, 249; mass, 44, 249, 251, 253, 264; national, 199; sacred, 7, 30–31; and schools, 249; secular, 7, 30–31; and social class, 82; in social mobility, 133; and social structure, 52, 61, 62, 176, 177; and species life, 36–37; and status, 85–86; system of, 248, 249, 250, 252, 255, 263, 273; of the technology, 54; of unity, 14; in war, 23–30; Washington, 14, 30, 249; written, 44; see also Sacred symbol systems

Social system, 126; and industry, 153–54; and mobility, 73, 193; persistence of, 209; research in, 36; segmental hierarchies, 69; status in, 66, 79; in wartime, 24–25

Society (human), 54–55, 186; as adaptive order, 52; communication in, 247–48; contemporary, 36–37, 250–51, 253; and hierarchies, 68–69; individual in, 36, 52; industrial, 159; persistence of, 37, 207; and personality, 208; and social symbols, 248–49; and status function, 64

Socioeconomic levels, 136, 270

Socioeconomic structure, 42–43, 174
Sociology, 206–7; in research, 39–41, 45, 49–50, 250–51
Soldier dead, 6, 8 9; as sacrifice, 11; Unknown Soldier, 12–13, 14
South, the: and color caste, 89–100; and social class, 74, 79, 90–93; *see also* Color caste
Species behavior, 52, 103, 208; life of, 36–37; social persistence of, 206–9; and status functions, 65
Strikes, 143; and social change, 154–78; in wartime, 28; *see also* Management; Workers
Subordinates: ethnic elements of, 189; ethnic parents of, 184, 186–87; ethnic wives of, 197–98; lower-upper parents of, 119; Negro caste, 87, 89–90, 100; ranks of, 69; status of workers, 64, 163, 173–74, 178
Superordinates: ethnic children as, 184; ethnic husbands as, 181, 192; generation of, 118; Negro class, 90; ranks of, 69; status of managers, 64; white caste, 87–88
Symbols, 6–7, 31; systems of, 30; *see also* Social symbols

Talent: in social class, 80; in social mobility, 132, 234–35
Taussig, F. W., 135
Technology, 56, 124; as control, 54–55
Television: as mass medium, 250; as symbol system, 62, 251

Unions, 143; leadership of, 127, 166, 178; and management, 175; and strikes, 154–56, 158–59, 160, 163
Unity: in sectarian groups, 203; in social ritual, 15–16; in wartime, 28–29
Upper class: aristocracy, 74–75; in associations, 228, 229; and child training, 110, 209–10; and ethnics, 195; in Jonesville, 82; and marriage, 117; Negroes, 90–92; rated, 84; and schools, 110, 210–11; size of, 77–78; and social distance, 116–17; students, 212, 213, 215–18
Upper-lower class: in associations, 229; characteristics of, 76, 78; and child training, 107–10, 112–14, 123–24; and ethnics, 195, 196; in Jonesville, 83; ratings of, 84; and social mobility, 141; students, 216–17; teachers, 211
Upper-middle class: in associations, 229; businessmen, 221; characteristics, 75, 76, 78; child training in, 107, 123–24; in Jonesville, 82; Negroes in, 90, 92, 98–99; ratings of, 84; and schools, 210–11; and social mobility, 141; students, 212, 213, 215–18
Urban centers, and Negroes, 93–100

Values: of the American system, 218; in child training, 121; of the middle class, 123–34; of the moral order, 36, 271; sacred ethnic, 184–84; in social class, 72, 83, 210, 215, 219; in species life, 36–37; status, 216
Veblen, Thorstein, 238
Veterans: organizations of, 15–16; in social rituals, 13

War: and community organization, 24–26; positive value of, 27; sacrifice in, 33; and social interaction and solidarity, 24–31; and symbols, 23–24
Washington, George: as symbol system, 249; as symbol of unity, 14, 23–24, 30
West, the, and class systems, 78–79
White group: and child training,